To MayBelle and Bill,

　How very much my Father loved you too. He commented about it often.

　Blessings to you.

　　　Kongoi mising!

　　　　Sarah

" The Darkest Time is

Just Before the Dawn"

A glimpse of the human side of mission work

By
Sarah S. Werner
Anna Verne Lee

with
David R. Smith & John M. Smith

The Smith Children

Printed in the United States of America

Cover photography by Leslie G. Werner

ISBN: 1-59571-066-3 hardback
ISBN: 1-59571-067-1 softback

Library of Congress Control Number: 2005922285

Word Association Publishers
205 Fifth Avenue
Tarentum, Pennsylvania 15084
800-827-7903
www.wordassociation.com

CONTENTS

ACKNOWLEDGEMENTS
PROLOGUE

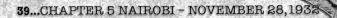
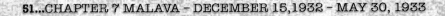
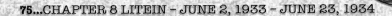

Robert and Catharine Smith

ACKNOWLEDGEMENTS

Our father's and mother's endlessly vivid, animated, and oft-repeated accounts of their experience in Africa formed the basis for this story. Others have contributed greatly to our understanding of the events that took place. Most importantly, we would like to thank our matriarch, Grandmother Biesecker, who faithfully saved so many of Mother's letters all those years, bringing authenticity to this account. Another resource was her scrapbook that contained memorabilia from the ships, as well as photos and all of the "Call to Prayer" articles written during those early years. There are missing letters, most notably those written after our Grandfather Smith became ill. Since our grandmothers lived in the same town, they often shared letters. Perhaps Mother Smith, during Grandfather's illness, was unable to return the letters.

We also owe a huge debt of gratitude to Bunny and Jerry Fish who interviewed Mother and Dad on nine different occasions as they did research for their book *The Place of Songs,* a history of the mission in Kenya under which our parents worked. Those three-hour taped interviews were shared with us in addition to the book itself and other materials they had researched.

We have drawn from other accounts of Kenya experiences, including those of our "nearly brother," Richard Adkins. Edna Boroff, a veteran missionary nurse of forty-four years, shared firsthand experience of medical consequences of female circumcision. The life story of Jefferson Ford, *Footsteps of a Good Man,* by Esther Ford; Johana Arap Ng'etich's story, *Call to Battle,* by Gerald and Burnette Fish; *Then and Now in Kenya Colony* and *Sketches from a Dark Continent,* by Willis Hotchkiss; *We Were Pioneers,* by Alta Hoyt; *Missy Fundi,* by Mary Honer; *African Game Trails,* by Theodore Roosevelt, Kipsigis tribal customs compiled by Earl Andersen; Elsbeth Huxley's many books on Kenya; and game books by Peter Capstick have all been sources of inspiration.

We also want to thank readers who aided us with suggestions: Les Werner, Richard Adkins, Pat Smith, David Lee, David and June Strickland, Lori Cameron, Dixie Ehrenreich, and Annice Edmundson.

Pictures are, in large part, the originals from Grandma's scrapbook or from our own collections. The sayings appearing in long hand were from a collection written by our father. Those in typed form are ones known to be favorites of our mother.

The letters are transcribed as they are written. The dots represent deleted portions of the letters that refer to information that is of doubtful general interest.

The book is based on fact and written as closely as we can come to the way it was, based on our parents' own recorded stories, their usual mannerisms, ways of speaking, and our collective memory of their stories. In the shaded inserts of the book, we have also added our perspective as our parents' lives interfaced with ours and they shared with us their life journey.

PROLOGUE

Honor thy father and mother: that thy days may be long upon the land which the Lord thy God giveth thee." Exodus 20: 12

The motive for writing this account is primarily to honor our parents Robert and Catharine Smith—not necessarily to presume on the promise of long life! Because we four children have been so captivated with the authenticity of our parents' lives through the stories we have heard from their lips and the events we have witnessed, we felt their saga must be told for the sheer joy and blessing of sharing it. Many things we didn't know were safely concealed in letters from the faithful pen of our mother to her family.

There are four of us Smith children, and while each of us has had completely different experiences and each holds a somewhat different perspective, we share a delight in our parents' experience. So when we found the treasure of our mother's letters to her mother and read them, we all wanted their story to be known.

John, the eldest, received his PhD in microbiology and taught in the United States but revisited Kenya and followed the work closely, as his wife's sister married a pediatrician who worked at Tenwek Hospital, while she carved out a ministry with the African women. Of the four of us, Anna Verne's life journey most reflected her parents' vision as she, having obtained her master's degree in nursing, returned with her husband to Kenya and served in the same mission organization. David expanded his African experience by living with his family in Nairobi, Kenya while working for the Firestone Company. Sarah and her husband, both physicians, with their children visited and worked at Tenwek Hospital on repeated trips. And through the years, as we observed our parents in their final years, listened to their stories and relived with them the adventure, we came to realize that the first term, which this story covers, was a defining time in their lives that shaped their attitudes and changed them in inexplicable ways. Therefore, we have chosen to tell that part of the story. It was the authenticity of their search for truth and meaning up to the very day of their deaths, and their willingness to acknowledge failure, as well as the joy and delight with which they viewed the Christian adventure that continues to make their story most real and compelling to us. We want it known that their propelling vision was realized through toil and tears, love and sacrifice, determination and courage. Dad, with the confidence and support of Mother, set about to lay foundations for a permanent, far-reaching, God-honoring enterprise. By gathering the support and assistance of nationals and fellow missionaries, Dad sculpted a thriving mission/church center from a brush-covered hillside. While he built houses, roads, and bridges, Mother taught primary education to child and adult alike. Until a nurse came to pilot the formation of medical services, ailing nationals were treated at the door from our medicine cabinet. As converts increased, local congregations met where preaching points were established. The need for national workers was evident; so was need for Bible training of potential pastors. The first "seminary" classroom was the shade of a thorn tree. As new missionaries joined, great care was given to the organization of a responsible mission unit, reporting regularly to the U. S. mission headquarters. We have been told that the organization and management of the Kenya field was, and is, exemplary—a model for other fields. From the initial mission site, three other stations were established within the local tribe. In years to follow, the church and mission would extend to other tribes as well as reach from rural to urban areas. What began at the primary level of education matured to college level; what was a dispensary in its infancy is now a state of the art (for Kenya) hospital, staffed with doctors and registered nurses, together with a nursing school and a laboratory technician school; what was once a single preaching point has blossomed into an established indigenous church led by college/seminary graduates and composed of more than 1,500 local congregations. What was a heart vision of a young man and his bride is now reality.

You have to read it for yourself! We think you'll enjoy it.

It was through one-on-one conversations that we reaped the benefit of our parents' experience as seen in the following encounter:

David had just suffered the loss of his business—a business he hoped would be an honor to God. His heart was broken, and he spent long hours discussing with his father how he viewed God's intervention in our lives.

"David, let me tell you a story," Dad said. "The long rains in Kenya had begun, and the roads—if that is what they could be called—were a sea of mud. In many places, springs were coming up in the middle of the road. In three days, we had managed to make it only 10 miles. I was exhausted and did not know if I could take it any more. I lay back in the mud and looked up at the sky. I raised my fist in the air and said, "What are You doing? I thought You wanted me to come to Africa to tell these people the 'Good News.' Instead, here I am trying to dig myself out of yet another mud hole." Dad looked intensely at his son. "God did not answer my question then. It was years later when He told me, 'I was not only trying to build a mission; I was trying to build a man.'" Dad looked at his long trembling fingers. He was now old and white haired. "I know that I had a lot to learn, but as I look back over my life…whenever I met a problem and wherever I went, it seemed God had been there first working out His plan. It was not my doing. It was His—I was just there to help Him in it. When I had a need, He met me at my point of need and He was faithful. So faithful! "

CHAPTER 1
LEAVING THE HOMELAND—OCTOBER 19,1932

One does not discover new lands without consenting to lose sight of the shore. Andre' Gide 1869-1951

"…his heart was being drawn to Africa."

The water was glassy and only a tiny breeze caressed their faces. The deck below their feet vibrated as the huge screw turned easing them away from the dock. They could see the Statue of Liberty right in front of them, holding her light high, as the Deutschland of the Hamburg-Amerika line pulled out of harbor into the gathering twilight, and New York City's lights gradually shrank to pinpoint, flickered and went out. Could it

'Deutschland' of the Hamburg-Amerika line

be that on this day, October 19, 1932, Bob and Kitty Smith were finally realizing their dream?

Bob carried this photo in his billfold until the day he died, along with a Bible verse which read, "In quietness and in confidence shall be your strength."

On the lighted deck, Bob looked at Catharine standing at the rail with their little son, John Boy. It was a time for celebration, and he wanted to take them both in his arms. But he restrained himself, as he must, for this was 1932, and public displays of affection were not acceptable—certainly not if you were a missionary on your way to Africa. So he just looked tenderly at his wife as they made their way out to the open sea and remembered….

She had been his dream girl ever since he first saw her singing at an evening service in a little chapel in Delaware, Ohio.

He had leaned over to his brother and said, "I'm going to marry her some day."

"Oh sure, Rob," Eddie had replied.

Eddie and Bob were bosom buddies. Perhaps it had been the shooting incident that cemented their relationship. Bob was walking in front when Eddie's gun had gone off accidentally, the bullet passing between Bob's arm and chest, tearing holes in the clothes but only grazing his skin along the chest wall. Scared to death that they would be caught, they had buried the evidence, but somehow Mother Smith knew, and they were duly chastised. Or perhaps it was when they decided while riding at breakneck speed, side-by-side, bareback, to stand up on their horses and put a foot on the other's horse. It all came to an end when the horses shied at a fence. Eddie was thrown over the fence, tearing his calf muscle from its attachment. Bob miraculously was not hurt. Then again, perhaps it was the two weeks during the 1918 flu epidemic when, at 12 and 13 years old, they had stopped going to school and instead milked their own as well as all of their neighbor's cows, from dawn until dusk, for two weeks. But whatever it was that they had done together, there was indeed, a special bond between the two that never diminished throughout their lifetime.

Bob winked at his brother and said, "Just wait; you'll see!"

Bob continued to look out at the vast body of water ahead of them and remembered the terrible two weeks of uncertainty…. He had known shortly after he became a Christian that he was going to be a missionary. A "call" it was, and he knew he had it. He was enjoying his experience as an engineering student and a marathon runner at the University of Cincinnati when he became very ill with scarlet fever. His illness became so protracted that he had to drop out of school. It was then that everything changed. He had heard a speaker talking about Jesus, and he could not escape the conviction that what the speaker said was true. He yearned to know more. He had not paid much attention to Christianity up to that time, but what he did know was restrictive and unappealing. As he listened now to the message, the claims of Christ were capturing his heart. He couldn't think of returning to engineering for his desire was to know more

about the One who had filled his emptiness and changed his life. He decided to complete his training at a Christian college so he could grow in the understanding of his faith, and it was there when reading in his Bible, "Go into all the world and preach the gospel," that he knew these words were speaking to him. It was as clear to him as "anything he had ever known."

But in the days that followed, he had sought out, gotten to know, and fallen "hopelessly" in love with Catharine Biesecker.

"I couldn't do a thing about it," he often said. "It had just happened." But when he realized that his heart was being drawn to Africa, he was confused and dismayed.

Ever since Catharine was a little girl, she had planned to be a missionary, and it was to China she felt drawn. He had known her now for over two years. They both lived in the same area—she in the city of Delaware, Ohio, and he just on the outskirts of town on a dairy farm.

Catharine's sweetheart

Bob was still finishing up his college work, but it was time for a break.
He was already planning a trip home in two weeks, but now he felt confused and torn. How could God have let him fall in love with Catharine when His plan for her was China, and Bob felt called to Africa?

The day finally arrived when they would see each other. He loved being with her so he had avoided the subject all day, but now it was evening and almost time for him to leave. He knew that he could no longer delay; this was the time that he had to tell her. A beam of light slanted through the window falling on her head and shoulders and turning her hair to ebony. She smiled at him.

"Kitty," he said, calling her by the name he always used, "I can hardly bear what I have to tell you. I love you so much, and today I was going to ask you to marry me. But God has been talking to me about Africa." He paused and swallowed hard. "I've tried and tried, but I can't shake the certainty that Africa is where I must be. So I have to tell you goodbye; I have to give you up." He remembered that she had gotten up from where they were sitting and started to walk up the stairs. His heart was breaking.

She paused and then turned and said, "For two years I have loved you and have been praying that God would call you to mission service. Location makes no difference to me, Bob. I would love to go with you to Africa." Then she smiled impishly, "But first, you will have to ask my father for my hand in marriage."

He grinned as he remembered how often he had teased her that it was she who had proposed to him. He was jarred back to the present. They were on their way. Could it be?

It had been an eternity for Bob and Kitty since they had announced their love and knew that Africa was their destination.

David recalls Dad telling this story. "There were many times along the way that God affirmed His direction in my life. One of those times was when I was at Asbury College as a student long before I married your mother. My aunt and uncle who helped pay for my schooling in engineering were very disappointed when I decided to go into the ministry and would no longer support me. I took on all the work I could but still could not afford a dormitory room. So, I asked if an alternative could be arranged, and the college agreed to let me stay in what had been a broom closet. I built a little platform for my mattress with drawers beneath for my clothes. I built a desktop, which folded up on hinges against the wall, and if I sat at the end of the bed, I could study there, but I had to close it up in order to open the door. I had no window, so each morning I would get up and walk to the end of the hall to look out the window. One morning, the snow was coming down hard. I felt a little sick when I remembered my shoes. There were holes in the soles...no particular problem in the dry weather...I got along well by putting cardboard into the shoes until it wore out. But now that it was snowing, I was not so sure. I went back to my room and knelt to pray. 'Dear Lord, You know about these shoes. You will just need to take care of the problem.' I got up from my devotions and went down to the bathroom. As I walked in, another student was standing there. He looked at me and said. 'What size shoes do you wear?' I told him and he said, 'Come up to my room and try on this pair.' I did. They were a perfect fit! I said, 'What do I owe you?' and he said, 'Not a thing; they are yours.' I had never seen the man before and didn't again until three years later when he returned to speak in chapel there at the school. I spoke to him and asked him if he remembered the incident. 'I certainly do!' he said, and he told me more of how God had spoken to him that day. 'Remember those shoes that are up on your shelf that don't quite fit. Go down to the restroom and ask the first person you meet there if he could use them.' You see, it was experiences like this that helped me know that God was interested in every little detail of my life."

But things weren't going to be particularly easy. In the first place, the mission organization under which they hoped to go did not as yet have a mission work in Africa. For two years at college, Bob had met at noon on Thursdays with a small group of other students to pray and share experiences. They were part of a larger group that called themselves the Student Volunteers. Because of his strong desire to go to Africa, Bob arranged for three of these friends with a similar interest to come with him to appeal to the mission under which he hoped to work in Africa.

3

THE DARKEST TIME IS JUST BEFORE THE DAWN

Meeting of the Missionary Board - May 9, 1927- Chicago, Illinois

The Committee of the Student Volunteer Band of Asbury College, Wilmore, Ky., representing 105 volunteers for the foreign field, 34 of whom are called to Africa, presented a written request to the Missionary Society ... for the establishment of work in Africa. (See document on file). This Committee was composed of R.R. Miller, Alex J. Reid, Ross O. Louthan, Robert K. Smith. The request was read by the Secretary. The Board resolved itself into a committee for open discussion of this Committee's proposition. Again the Board and the visitors went to their knees in mighty petition for divine guidance.

The first trip to the mission board

Bob described their trip as full of joy and excitement as they traveled in his old beat-up Model T Ford, "topless, windshieldless, and partially fenderless" toward Chicago. The mission board, however, was a formal, dignified and austere group. Included were college presidents, professors, ministers and a veteran missionary.[*] The board members listened patiently and then a discussion followed. The consensus was that the mission was already having great difficulty raising the necessary funds for their existing field of work and that to think of opening another was out of the question.

Mrs. Beatrice "Mother" Beezley, described by Bob as "a small woman with an enormous faith," had an opposing view. She stood and said, "I don't feel this way. If a work is opened in Africa, a new constituency will be formed, and they may even help our work in China."

The board stated they would consider it further and asked the students to return at 10:00 AM the following day.

As they left the room, now quite disheartened, Woodford Taylor, a veteran missionary to China, squeezed Bob's shoulder and said, "Bob, I believe God is in this; don't be discouraged."

But still the young collegians' hearts were heavy. The jubilation that had marked their trip to the meeting had suddenly disappeared, and reality had sobered them. It seemed like a long wait until 10:00 o'clock the following morning.

But it did arrive, and much to their surprise, when the young men re-entered the boardroom, there was an atmosphere of joy. Something had doubtlessly changed, and the truth seemed to lie in a letter the chairman of the board held in his hand. "After you left yesterday, the mail came and in it was a letter from a lawyer in Des Moines, Iowa. A client of his had passed away and in his will assigned $5,000 to be used by this mission organization if a work was ever opened in Africa."

---

[*] Dr. Iva Vennard, the mother of the mission, writer of its constitution, and founder of Chicago Evangelistic Institute; Dr. C. W. Ruth, who had been president of the mission since 1925; Joseph Owen, the president of John Fletcher College; Woodford Taylor, one of the first missionaries to China under WGM; John Paul, who was then president of Taylor University; Mother Beezley, the secretary of the mission, who from her briefcase produced the monthly mission paper called the "Call to Prayer"; and others.

But in 1927, whatever the sum (see below)[*], it was a fortune. It seemed to everyone that the answer had presented itself, and no further discussion was needed. The board then began its deliberation over the mechanism by which a work in Africa could be opened. In 1928 both Catharine and Bob, not yet married, came before the mission board.

Executive Meeting of the Missionary Board - May 7, 1928

... The President, Brother Ruth, called upon the delegaton from Asbury College to state the object of their coming to the Board Meeting. The object was to ascertain the position of the Missionary Society with reference to opening work in Africa... the following spoke: (These were all prospective missionaries to Africa) Robert Smith, Katherine Bisecker[sic], John Cochrane, Marie Goodson, Mable Mickel, Fred Alexander. For China: Clarice Morford, Julia Jenkins. From Cleveland Bible Institue Mary Helney for Africa. This was followed by a full discussion by members of the Board and the missionaries. Miss Katherine Besecker[sic] was designated by the delegation as Secretary of the Band. Address, Miss Katharine Besecker[sic], Box 23, Wilmore, Ky.

Minutes from that meeting

[*] While Dad remembered the figure as $5000.00, it was most likely $50,000.00 as indicated by the minutes from a later date when the board referred to this sum. The Quaker Friends, who took an advisory and supportive roll on the mission field, apparently did not accept the financial proposal. Instead the $50,000 was invested in bonds. This resulted in poor liquidity, a consequence that would adversely affect the missionaries in the short term.

Morning session, May 7th 1929

__The Africa Proposition was presented by Mrs. Vennard at the request of the Secretary. After a thorough discussion, a motion was passed that the Board authorize Miss Anna Spann to go to the Friends' meeting with a letter from the Board offering to the Friends for their African work now under the charge of Brother Chilson and Brother Ford in the Kenya District of Africa, the sum of $50,000.00, payable $5,000.00 per year for each of ten years; that Miss Spann be authorized to discuss this proposal with Brother Chilson and they have full power to present it to the Friends if in their judgement it is a proper action according to the spirit of the meeting, and to withhold it if their judgement it is an unwisely timed proposal.

The amount of $50,000 was invested upon receipt to yield $5,000.

THE DARKEST TIME IS JUST BEFORE THE DAWN

Bob and Catharine were married on June 12, 1929, and their first child was born on March 25, 1931. In the intervening years, the board required that they serve a pastorate in preparation for work on the mission field. They served a Methodist church in Elmira, New York.

Five whole years had passed since their efforts to get to the mission field had begun. Their application was "given favorable consideration" as they inquired year after year. Finally on June 9, 1931, they were appointed to Kenya, and shortly thereafter the basis for the beginning of a work in Africa was established.

Executive Meeting Chicago - September 1, 1931

Pertaining to our affiliation with the Unevangelized Tribes Mission of Africa it was moved and seconded that in view of the present Catholic opposition, inasmuch as this mission is so new that it cannot assure us of a government grant of territory and sanction for carrying on missionary work, and since we cannot consent to our candidates filing application with their board, we vote to withdraw from our agreement with the Unevangelized Tribes Mission of Africa. Motion carried.

Moved and carried that we accept the offer of Mr. Willis R. Hotchkiss to completely turn over to our Society the Lumbwa Industrial Misson on conditions contained in his letter of July 17, 1931 (See letter on file) and make this the basis for the beginning of our African work.

Moved and carried that the following cable be sent to Miss Clara Ford: "Board accepts Hotchkiss July letter offer. Authorizes you close deal. Advise regarding sending new missionaries."

Other minutes indicate continuing efforts were being made by the board to arrange for a work in Africa.

Now they were on their way, and what joy they felt as they saw New York's skyline disappearing into the distance!

One does not discover new lands without consenting to lose sight of the shore. André Gide 1869-1951

CHAPTER 2
GETTING ACQUAINTED AT SEA

"Eventually she knew—it was homesickness."

It was exciting being on board this stately German ocean liner. Each passing day was a new adventure. John Boy's curiosity was met with delight by most who encountered him.

Kitty hadn't told anyone about her pregnancy except Faye Kirkpatrick, who also was pregnant. As the days went by, they suffered the added problem of seasickness, and it was taking its toll. They were able to compare notes and comfort each other.

Faye and her husband Virgil (known to his friends as "Kirk") were on their way to Kenya under the same mission board. The four of them would later join Miss Clara Ford who had spent many years in Kenya as a child and whom the mission had appointed as a liaison to help find a physical site for establishing the mission. Faye and Kirk had been appointed only a few months before their departure. What a whirlwind their preparation had been, and how completely different from the long wait the Smiths had experienced!

> When Mother was anticipating something she would say, "We are on tiptoes waiting to hear." She was, by the way, always Mother—never Mom. She required that of us. Not that she ever actually gave us that rule, but it was one of many unwritten rules. It was a matter of respect and honor, and to all of us, in spite of the reality, she stood very tall. David observed, "When we children reached heights that exceeded hers, she would remark to people, "My word, look at our children all towering above me." What she didn't hear us say was, "Look at our Mother whose virtue, grace, tenderness, and most of all love, towers above us all."

Kitty was petite—on tiptoes, only a little over 5'2". She had black, naturally curly hair, was outspoken, principled and determined. She embraced life, and was captivated by history and literature, and she loved to read.

"Bob, did you know that Teddy Roosevelt also traveled to Kenya on the Hamburg line?"

"So I have heard, but it could have been another ship. This is a large line and, in fact, there was a previous Deutschland, a much larger ship."

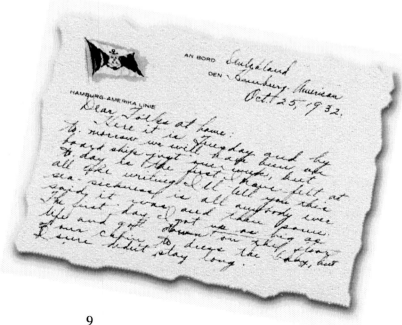

"Sea-sickness"

Kitty quoted from a book she was reading, written by President Theodore Roosevelt[*] after he had come to Kenya, commissioned by the Smithsonian to collect birds, mammals, reptiles, plants and specimens of big game for the National Museum in Washington D.C. "Again and again in continents new to peoples of European stock, we have seen spectacles of high civilizations all at once thrust into and superimposed upon a wilderness of savage men and savage beasts. Nowhere, and at no time, has the contrast been more strange and more striking than in British East Africa during the last dozen years."

Bob and Kitty found it incredible that while nearly the whole world has been affected by civilization, apparently only the borders of Africa had felt the effects of it for centuries, and that very little. Within the continent, few had any idea what was going on in the rest of the world. It was known as the Dark Continent and for them an adventure must certainly lie ahead.

Mrs. Elma Barnett, known to all as "Mama," a returning missionary who had come first to Kenya in 1907, overhearing their conversation said, "You know that Teddy Roosevelt laid the cornerstone for the mission school at Kijabi where, no doubt, your children will attend when they reach school age."

Kitty recoiled at the idea of sending her children away to school, "Yes, he mentions that in this book. It was on the fourth of August, 1909. Mrs. Barnett, how can you bear to send your children away to school? I just couldn't do that."

"You will come to that, dearie!"

Kitty's major in college was education, and she had received her master's degree in literature at Ohio State University. She felt herself quite qualified to teach her own children if necessary, but she said no more. More than anything, she wanted to do her best in what she regarded as a treasured calling, and she pursued her goals with tenacity. She had listened to every missionary speaker that she could. Daily she studied her Bible, and she read avidly, memorizing poetry that she loved. Her life was orderly, principled and fervent, and she had a deep appreciation for beauty both visible and experienced. She believed in the methodical working out of one's salvation as taught by John Wesley.

"Be an example to all of denying yourself and taking up your cross daily. Let others see that you are not interested in any pleasure that does not bring you nearer to God, nor regard any pain which does. Let them see that you simply aim to please God in everything. Let the language of your heart sing out with regard to pleasure or pain, riches or poverty, honor or dishonor, "All's alike to me, so I in my Lord may live and die!" John Wesley

Excerpt from John Wesley's famous work, Christian Perfection

As time passed on the boat, although she didn't want to admit it, in addition to the seasickness that had plagued her, another feeling was beginning to surface. It was hard to identify, but it felt like a sickness, too. Eventually she knew—it was homesickness. Her memory was filled with thoughts of home. Kitty was one of five sisters. Their only brother had died as an infant of pneumonia. Rhea, the oldest, along with her husband, a history professor, was doing mission work in Buenos Aires, Argentina. Irene, the

---

[*] Theodore Roosevelt, *African Game Trails*, New York: Scribner, 1910.

next sister, was married and had left home. Anna and Mary, the two younger ones, were still at home. Anna, indeed, marched to a different drumbeat, and Kitty wondered what her choices in life would be. Mary was a beauty. Kitty knew her littlest sister would soon have some man entangled in her enticing net. Both Anna and Kitty had contributed financially to Mary's education, but she still had school bills, and these remained a collective family concern.

"Call me 'brother'.... "

The stock market crash had occurred in October of 1929, ending six years of unparalleled prosperity in America. The depression that followed had been devastating. In the year just prior to the Smiths' going to Africa, the United States was still in upheaval. Unemployed workers had marched on the Ford Motor Company's plant in River Rouge, Michigan; New York's Bank of the United States had collapsed; unemployment was on the rise and by '32, more than 750,000 New Yorkers were on relief. Everyone the Smiths knew was struggling to make ends meet. The comfortable and somewhat opulent life that Kitty's family had known was gone as was the company position her father had held, and now Father Biesecker was trying to sell insurance. Kitty and Bob had each taken out an insurance policy with him, partially because they hoped it would help Kitty's father and partly because it seemed a sensible thing to do in light of potential dangers ahead. The cost of the policies they had chosen totaled $12.35 per month. As Kitty reviewed these choices in her mind, she worried that the cost would be too much in proportion to the salary that they were to receive. The mission board had determined what their salary would be, based largely on information they had gleaned from missionaries in Kenya. Thirty-five dollars a month was the amount deemed necessary.

Executive Meeting - Chicago - December 8, 1932

Then followed a very profitable discussion on faith. Questions concerning our Africa work were presented. A motion was made by Mrs. Vennard that under the present circumstances we allow our Africa missionaries $35.00 each per month, the balance of $2.50 to be kept on the field for whatever is needed for general expenses connected with the living of the missionary other than direct personal items covered by their allowance. Motion seconded and carried.

Board minutes discussing salary

With that goal in mind, Bob and Kitty had embarked on their deputation (fund raising) work joined by Mr. Willis Hotchkiss, who had arrived in Kenya, Africa, in 1895. He had agreed to turn over his work in Kenya, the Lumbwa Industrial Mission, to their organization.

In the eleven months that he and Bob had traveled together, they had found individuals or churches willing to share in the proposed new effort in Kenya. Each had pledged an amount to be given monthly for their term on the mission field. Additional funds were also raised for travel, and a car had been donated. It had not been without great effort on the part of Bob and Mr. Hotchkiss. In many of the churches visited, the offering plate had come back empty.

"I am in awe of your ability to speak, Mr. Hotchkiss. When I open my mouth, it seems the words just fall flat. I long to be able to speak as you do," Bob confessed.

"Call me 'brother,'" the old Quaker missionary had said kindly. "We are brothers, and we are in this together for our Savior."

"I will try to do that, Brother Willis." He felt awkward not calling him by his formal name. "My heart is full of this message. I just can't seem to get it across."

"Brother Bob, it will come. Don't be discouraged. You never know what happens to the seed you have planted. Most of these people to whom we are talking have never even been presented with a message of missions. Let's keep trying. Perhaps God will set their hearts on fire."

With each passing day, Bob and Kitty had become more attached to Brother Hotchkiss. They noticed that he read his Bible daily and consecutively so as not to miss anything. Also, they devoured the wonderful stories he told about Kenya.

"...fragments of truth...became one glorious revelation."

The days on ship slowly passed. At first, seasickness had overtaken many, and Kitty especially was finding it difficult. But now the sea was calmer, allowing plenty of time for reflection.

She and Bob thought a great deal about what they were facing. What would this new land and this new experience hold? Mr. Hotchkiss's stories were still vivid in their memory—one in particular that described the circumstances of his finding the word for "Savior" was moving:

"Hour after hour I've sat with Kikuvi and others, exhausting every conceivable illustration in the vain effort to draw out that magic word. But with agonizing persistency they would beat all about it without approaching the thing itself.... Never shall I forget the inexpressible thrill of the moment, when this wonderful word illuminated the darkness of a memorable night yonder in Africa.

How It Happened.

Let me tell you how graciously the Lord has brought about the turning over of the work in the Lumbwa Industrial Mission to the National Holiness Association. In December of 1930 Mrs. Hotchkiss had to be sent home hurriedly for medical treatment. Later advices made it appear that even though she were to recover it might be necessary for me to leave the work and remain home permanently. Now see the loving hand of the Lord. In July of last year I was asked to speak at a conference of missionaries about a hundred miles away. There I met the father and mother of Miss Clara Ford, who had been commissioned by the N. H. A. to seek a field for them in Africa. Her efforts had proved fruitless up to that time. In conversation with Brother Ford he casually mentioned this fact. In a flash it came to me that this was of the Lord. The L. I. M. was the key which could open up the door to Africa for the N. H. A. I had been perplexed and troubled over the prospect of leaving the work to which I had given most of my life and wanted to turn it over to a body which would perpetuate it to the glory of God. The two needs met in this providential manner and fitted as key to lock.

I at once said so to Brother Ford and we both communicated the fact to the Board of Directors of the Missionary Society of the N. H. A. I was summoned home soon after, only to receive a radio message in the Mediterranean that the dear companion of the years had gone on to be with the Lord. As soon as possible after my arrival I got in touch with the Board. When we met we were of one mind that we had been brought together in the plan of God and it was marvelous in our eyes.

Excerpt from "Call to Prayer"
Written by Willis Hotchkiss

"In January 1898, Mr. Kreiger, another missionary, had been attacked by a lioness, which mauled him badly. The lioness had released him briefly and was getting ready for a final spring when Kikuvi gave a shout. The lioness turned to look at Kikuvi, and in that moment Mr. Kreiger leaped into the reeds at the nearby stream, and the lioness ran off to join her cubs. I had heard Kikuvi retell the incident. Then on one particular night while seated around the campfire, Kikuvi finished by stating, 'I saved the *Bwana*.'

"'Why Kikuvi,' said I, 'this is the word I've been wanting you to tell me all this time because I wanted to tell you that....' That was as far as I got. The black face lighted up as a wonderful word, illuminated by the Holy Spirit, broke in upon and tore away the veil of ignorance from an immortal soul. I can see him still as in the light of the campfire, he turned to me, interrupting me and exclaimed, '*Bwana*, I see it now. This is what you've been trying to tell us these many moons...that God so loved us that he gave His Son to save us!'

"The next morning while I was speaking to a crowd gathered for a service, Kikuvi asked to talk a little. I wondered what he would say. Kikuvi began to tell the old, old story.

..."That flash of intelligence the night before by the campfire explained it all. In that blessed moment when the word 'Savior' dawned upon his dark vision, all the scattered fragments of truth that had been floating about in his darkened mind fell into line and became one glorious revelation.

"The two and a half year search was over. *Muthania—Savior.*"[*]

It was a story among many others that had stirred Bob's heart. He wanted so much to emulate Brother Hotchkiss, and he was grateful for the months they had had together. He chuckled as he remembered one night when the two of them were out in deputation work, visiting churches that had very little or no interest in missions. Most of these church members were people with low income and little money to spare. Nonetheless, after an evening service, they were invited to stay in a woman's home. She showed them to their room which was also the wash room and kitchen.

She pointed to one of the beds and said, "This is the prophet's bed."

Later, as Mr. Hotchkiss got into bed, he said, "The prophet must have been a strong man," and he took out his sweater to cover his face and mask some of the smell.

Other occasions just as significant provided special memories and endeared this man to Bob even more. As a result of their travels, many individuals became loyal supporters, and enough had pledged support for Bob, Kitty, and John Boy to be on their way to Africa.

Mr. Hotchkiss in Toledo, Ohio

It was in listening to Mr. Hotchkiss that their dreams had taken shape. He described Chaigaik where his home and mission were. There were six outstations where fledgling churches and schools had been planted. These places had strange sounding names: Siwot, Kiplelji, Kong'otik, Tulwetab Mosonik, Mengit, and Kimagata.

The plan was that together with the Kirkpatricks they would stay in temporary housing on Mr. H.'s station and then begin to build another in the area called Sotik or 'Sot.' The next steps would be quite simple. They would need to obtain from the British government permission to use land for creating a mission station. In Kenya they would meet Clara Ford and her father. Her mother had recently died, but her father remained on the field and, among others, would assist them. It seemed everything was ready for their arrival.

---

[*] Willis R. Hotchkiss, *Then and Now in Kenya Colony*, New York, London, Edinburgh: Fleming H. Revel Company, 1937, 142.

When Mr. Hotchkiss first arrived in Kenya, the main thoroughfares were still trails that had been used by Arab traders. Not surprisingly, along one of these trade routes, he began his work among the Wakamba, a pastoral and hunting tribe located south and east of Nairobi just before reaching the slopes of the central highlands. The Wakamba traded in ivory and rhino horn in exchange for beads, ironware and clothes from the Arabs.

Bob remembered listening to Mr. H.'s descriptions of the Wakamba living quarters.

"You enter through a thorn bush lined opening by crawling into an open space from 20 to 30 feet in diameter. This enclosed *boma* (hedge) is a protection from wild beasts. This is the cattle kraal at night and at the far side is the manure heap. Along one side of the kraal and opening upon it are the living-huts, while back of these are smaller huts used for storing grain and other food supplies. These living-huts are circular in form, shaped like a beehive, built of grass thatch over a framework of slender sticks. The only opening in the hut is a little hole two and one-half feet high by one and one half feet wide, and into this you must crawl on your hands and knees. You cannot stand erect except in the centre, so you squat on one of the low seats a few inches high and look about you....

"On one side is the wood used for cooking purposes, piled high in preparation for the rainy season. In the centre are three stones upon which an earthen pot, the only cooking utensil, sits above the fire; while on the floor amid the refuse and filth are calabashes of various sizes, which serve for plate and cup alike. Sometimes, these are washed. Do you want something to eat? The woman picks one up, brushes the dirt out with her knuckles, and it is ready for use.

"The beds are along the sides of the hut, and are made of binding slender sticks together and fastening these to props about two feet from the ground, for, of course, there is no floor in the hut save Mother Earth. Under this rude bed is usually a young calf tied, or a big goat or sheep fattening for a feast, and almost always a lot of little kids or lambs frisking about at will....

"The men wear absolutely no clothing, the women only a small apron, a few inches square, suspended from the lions [sic] by a thong of leather. The former deck themselves out by twisting brass or copper wire about the arms and legs; the latter with hundreds of strings of beads about the neck and waist.

"The body is smeared with red clay and grease, and the hair is carefully shaved off even to the eyebrows, eye-lashes pulled out, ears pierced and hole gradually enlarged, until I have frequently seen them pick up a tin can on the station, then insert it in the ear-lobe and use the can as a pocket in which to carry their trinkets."[*]

---

[*] Mrs. Hoyt's description of her approach to teaching reading.

Time continued to pass and days merged into each other as the Smiths steamed toward the "Dark Continent." By any measurable intention Bob and Kitty were Sabbath keepers. For them the commandment to keep the Sabbath was a loving *aide memoire*—at rest our souls are restored; a time when, all commonplace, busy activity was replaced by worship, rest and reflection; a day, by design, set aside to be completely different from the rest of the days of the week; a day to escape the world's contrived importance; to be still, to listen, and to know. With this in mind, they paid close attention to the commandment.

"Have you noticed that the commandment to keep the Sabbath is the only one which begins with the word 'remember' as if it were something we might have an inclination to forget?" said Bob one day as he looked up from his Bible reading.

"I hadn't made that connection, but I love the Sabbath day. I don't think I would ever forget it," said Kitty.

Nonetheless, Kitty, with great chagrin realized that a precious Sabbath day had slipped away unnoticed.

"We had been gaining 43 minutes a day and it was hard to keep track of the days. One of the days was so nice and sunshiny in the morning, the boys played and we watched the miniature horse-racing etc. and had a real wild time all day. When we came to the evening meal, the menu said, "Sunday Evening Dinner." Well, we couldn't and wouldn't believe it till we had it confirmed by the steward. You can imagine how these missionaries felt. We got to talking about it and there was a Russian who overheard. The poor man told about his hungry heart and that he'd lost his faith...we all had a chance to testify...."

"You can imagine how these missionaries felt."

CHAPTER 3—ABOARD THE WATUSSI

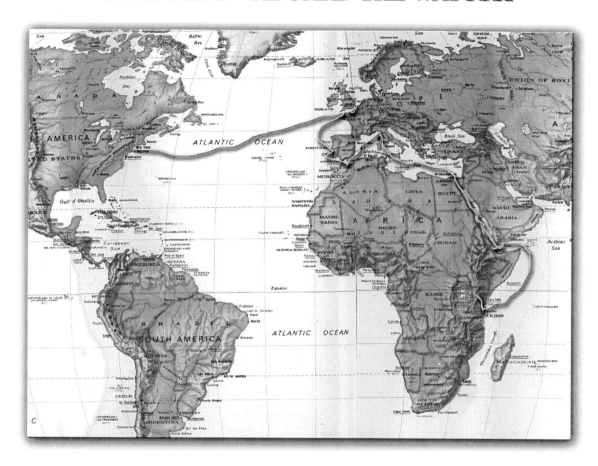

ROUTE OF SMITHS' FIRST TRIP TO AFRICA

The voyage began October 19, 1932—ended November 26, 1932.

They had been at sea for ten days. Having stopped briefly in France, they stopped next at Southampton, England. As they approached, there was animated conversation about the prestigious ocean races for which this port was famous. Some recommended seeing the museum that contained memorabilia from the Titanic, which sank on its maiden voyage from England to New York in 1912.

They wondered what to expect next, as they would be disembarking from the Deutschland and boarding the Watussi for the final leg of their journey.

October 29, 1932

Well, we are now in "Merry England" and are finding our experiences here are just as thrilling. I wish you could be here. You surely would be able to place some of Dicken's characters and also to see into some typical English shops. It seems so queer to see the cars driving on the left. Most of them are the size of the Austin at home and every once in a while they'll dart across and park on the opposite side if they happen to want out on that side.

There are two characters at this hotel I wish you could see, and I'd especially like you to hear them talk. One sounds like one of the characters in "Gene and Glue" but he's nearly as hard to understand as the Germans on the boat were....

Anna should come over here to finish up her M.A. You could bring your bicycle and be right in style. All the ladies here use them and it looks so funny to see them perched on their high cycles and pedalling down the street. It seems these English are able to spot us Americans at sight, and they can't conceal their mirth at some of the things we do. I guess we have to take our medicine but we do notice the English are worse to laugh at us than the Germans were on the boat. Or at least we couldn't understand what they said if they did make a joke of it.

We all went shopping this P.M. and found some wonderful bargains but we couldn't get all we wanted to. Especially is the wool cheap here. There are most marvelous woolen blankets here for little or nothing, great double ones for $5.00 our money. I never saw any so woolly and so heavy or rather thick through. There are some things I wouldn't want to buy here. One of them is shoes. They are so big and clumsy looking and they have no narrow sizes.

Deutschland Den Ameriki

*D. Watussi
Woermann-Linie
A. G.*

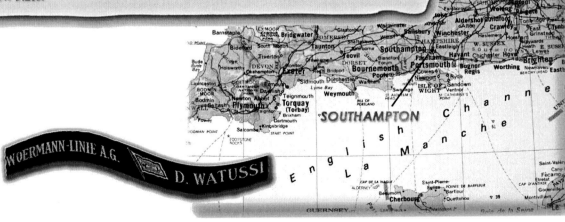

"You will like Lisbon," the old missionary who was traveling with them had said. "It is the largest city, capital, and cultural center of Portugal. It overlooks the beautiful Tagus estuary, one of Europe's most important natural harbors. Next to the harbor you will notice a low, flat area called the Baixa. It was built as part of the reconstruction of Lisbon after two-thirds of the city was destroyed in an earthquake in 1755. We always enjoy our visits here."

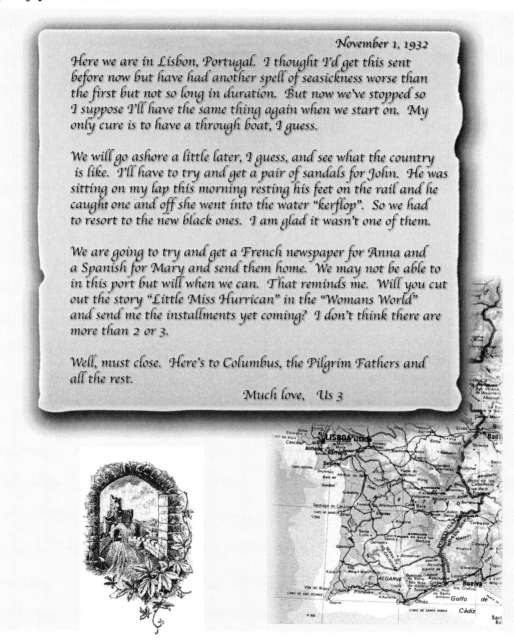

November 1, 1932

Here we are in Lisbon, Portugal. I thought I'd get this sent before now but have had another spell of seasickness worse than the first but not so long in duration. But now we've stopped so I suppose I'll have the same thing again when we start on. My only cure is to have a through boat, I guess.

We will go ashore a little later, I guess, and see what the country is like. I'll have to try and get a pair of sandals for John. He was sitting on my lap this morning resting his feet on the rail and he caught one and off she went into the water "kerflop". So we had to resort to the new black ones. I am glad it wasn't one of them.

We are going to try and get a French newspaper for Anna and a Spanish for Mary and send them home. We may not be able to in this port but will when we can. That reminds me. Will you cut out the story "Little Miss Hurrican" in the "Womans World" and send me the installments yet coming? I don't think there are more than 2 or 3.

Well, must close. Here's to Columbus, the Pilgrim Fathers and all the rest.

Much love, Us 3

THE DARKEST TIME IS JUST BEFORE THE DAWN

From Lisbon they sailed south and, for the first time, set foot on African soil in Spanish Morocco, just across the strait from Spain.

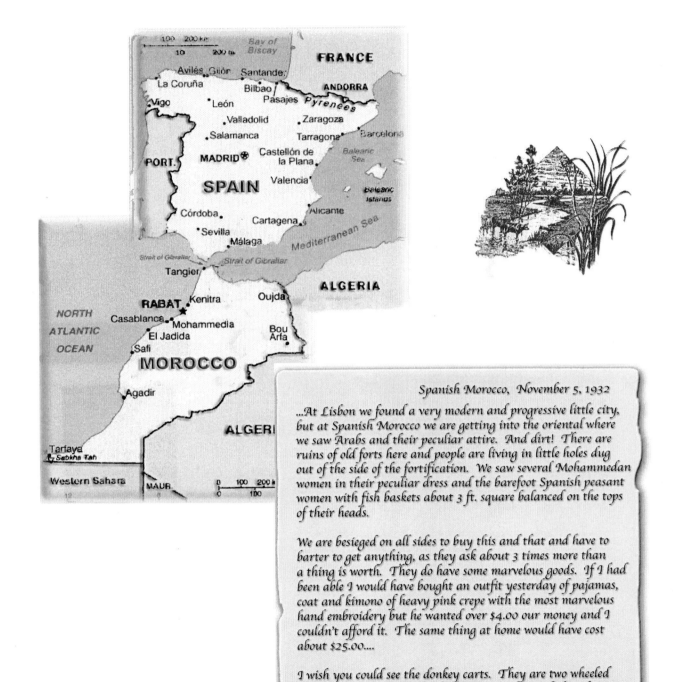

Spanish Morocco, November 5, 1932

...At Lisbon we found a very modern and progressive little city, but at Spanish Morocco we are getting into the oriental where we saw Arabs and their peculiar attire. And dirt! There are ruins of old forts here and people are living in little holes dug out of the side of the fortification. We saw several Mohammedan women in their peculiar dress and the barefoot Spanish peasant women with fish baskets about 3 ft. square balanced on the tops of their heads.

We are besieged on all sides to buy this and that and have to barter to get anything, as they ask about 3 times more than a thing is worth. They do have some marvelous goods. If I had been able I would have bought an outfit yesterday of pajamas, coat and kimono of heavy pink crepe with the most marvelous hand embroidery but he wanted over $4.00 our money and I couldn't afford it. The same thing at home would have cost about $25.00....

I wish you could see the donkey carts. They are two wheeled affairs and they hitch the donkeys one in front of the other. I saw a team of five, but they are usually two or three. They are little bits of animals like burrows....

"Kitty, how was the talk on Málaga?" Bob inquired as Kitty returned to the room after listening to the ship's program.

"I think I learned a lot. You know Andalusia is the term they use for this southern part of Spain. Málaga is its major costal city. They say that 3,000 years ago when the Phoenicians landed in Málaga, they called it MALACA (probably from the word *malac—to* salt). The harbor was used as an important center for salting fish. The Moors occupied the city until the mid fifteenth century. But I am excited to see the bullfighting rings. There are seventy in Andalusia. They used to have the bullfights in the village squares, then they built the bullrings and the events started to follow a sequence: the entrance of the bull, the *picador* (the horses), the *banderilleros* (the men on foot), and finally the *matador* (bullfighter). Many of the *picadors'* horses were injured in the early days, so now these horses wear a heavy protection. I would surely like to see where these bullfights take place. The other interesting thing is Pablo Picasso is the city's famous son, and there are several galleries showing his work. Perhaps we can see one of them. I'm excited and it will be so good to get on *terra firma* once again."

> Malaga, Spain   November 5, 1932
> written in the Mediterranean
>
> Dear Folks:
>
> I am going to try and write my impressions of the day while they are still fresh in my mind. I have enjoyed this sight-seeing day more than any one yet. We took a horse-cart this morning. It was an old fashioned topless coach and the little horse had bells on. John surely enjoyed it. We rode an hour for 5 Pesetas or about $0.45. We first went to the Cathedral but decided not to enter it then. Then we went to a real Arena and it was where they have Bullfights every Sunday. We saw where the Governor sits on his raised platform. The stadium seats 11,000. We saw the stalls where they keep the bulls and stand on a little balcony pull a rope and the animal rushes out. We saw the place where the Toreador goes in a little chapel before going into the ring and the hospital where they take him afterwards. As the Englishman said, "a place to prepare him to die and a place to keep him from it." Then we went through the residential section and saw the villas. They are perfect mansions and are surrounded by the most wonderful gardens. The milk man was delivering milk through some parts of the town. He went down the street driving a herd of goats and calling his wares. When he'd get an order he'd call out one of the goats, takes it to the back door, milks the quantity desired and drives on. Bob got a picture of one group, but it was a dull day and it may not be good.
>
> We saw one of the Municipal gardens, and John fed the pigeons, hundreds of them. He got so excited over it.
>
> We saw the home of the Argentine Counsel. It is a beautiful place.

Bull Arena Málaga, Spain

Mother referred to being on the Island of Palma as they were traveling from Spain to Italy. It seems it must have been Palma, a city on the Island of Mallorca in the Bay of Palma, one of the Balearic Islands.

Island of Palma, November 6, 1932

Saturday morning. On our way to Palma and a calm sea, so I'm not sick yet, thank the Lord. Bob is feeding John. I guess I didn't tell you that he eats first in the children's dining room then the Stewardess keeps him while we eat. At first he wouldn't stay with her but now he does pretty well. There are 11 children in our class but he is the youngest. There are the 5 German youngsters and now 5 English. John can't understand much any of them say to him but he likes to play with the German youngsters best. The English are little rough-necks.

At dinner....John got a little clown cap and looked so cute. He was excited over the youngsters. I wish you could hear some of his expressions. The other day he wanted something and I looked for it and couldn't find it. I told him and he said, "Oh! dear!" I guess I told you about his saying "Pardon me." I wish I could write it like he says it. It is extremely "New Yawk" style "Pawdon me."

Sunday we landed at Palma. We found it was an island in the Mediterranean instead of on the mainland. There is an old Cathedral there that was built during the time of the Caesars. Bob went over in the P.M. and saw it. Said there were beautiful windows and the stone pavements were worn in great groves.

We had a lovely service in the morning with the other missionaries. We met a couple of Swedish ones going to Tanganyika. We had known they were not ordinary but were surprised to find that they are very spiritual. They can't speak English very well, but they seemed to enjoy the service so much.... Our hearts were surely warmed together.

"On our way to Palma...."

"Bob, did you know that Christopher Columbus was born in Genoa? It seems like a dream that we will actually be able to see some of the mountains of the Alps. I suppose they won't be as spectacular as in Switzerland," Kitty commented.

Genoa, Italy November 9, 1932

Tuesday morning. Here we are in Genoa. We have not been allowed to land yet as those who are stopping here have to be taken care of first and we have to get our Passports from the office before going on land.

We see that the "President Roosevelt" of the Dollar line is in the harbor, and are going over the passenger list to see if possibly Raymond might have gotten this far though it is not at all probable.

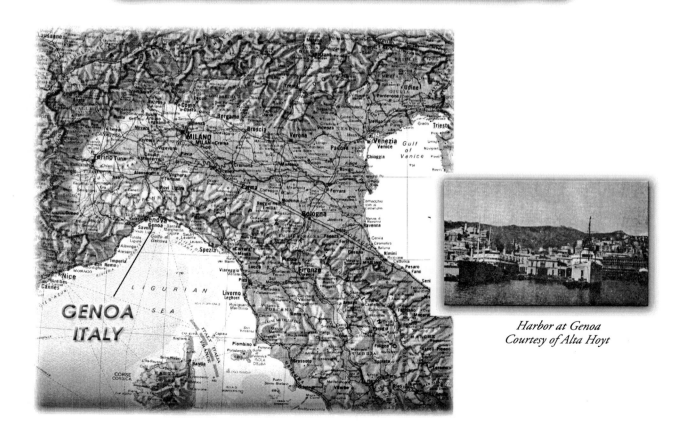

Harbor at Genoa
Courtesy of Alta Hoyt

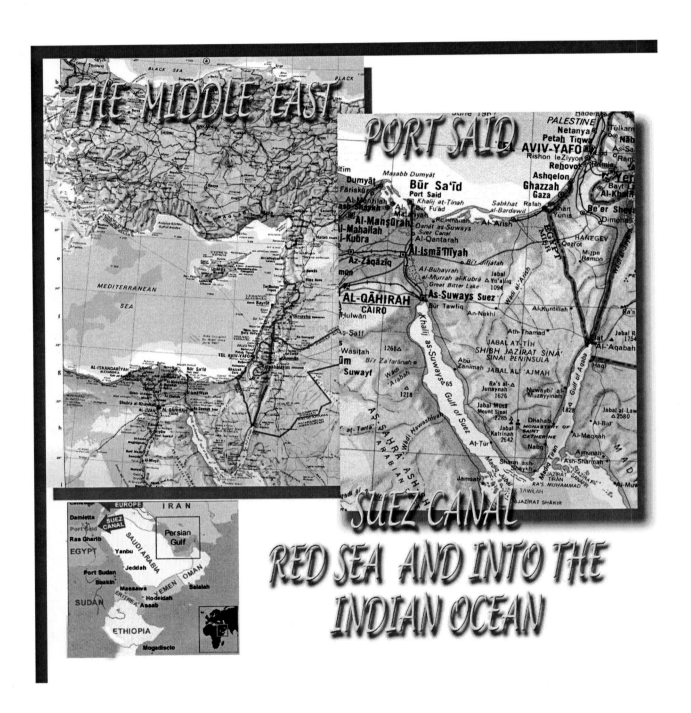

They did not find Raymond on the "President Roosevelt." But as they pulled into Port Said, they noticed some Navy ships were in port. Bob's brother, Raymond, was a medical officer in the Navy and known to be somewhere in the Mediterranean. As soon as they were in port, Bob went in search of his brother and was successful.

Raymond immediately proposed that he take Bob and go to Cairo and then on to see the pyramids. Kitty was happy to let him go and Bob could hardly wait. He preferred to go through life at full throttle. Kitty, on the other hand, preferred to take it in well-measured, well-considered bits and pieces.

The heat was appalling, oppressive and inescapable. Kitty found it difficult to get any writing done, let alone her usual knitting. She did love the absence of movement and most certainly appreciated not being seasick. Reaching down, she gripped John's sweaty little fist. "Let's go for a walk, John Boy." The child jumped up delighted for the activity.

The time of departure was fast approaching, and Bob had not returned. All of the others with whom he had gone on tour had arrived back at the dock and then had been brought out to the ship by a launch boat.

"Do you have any idea where my husband is?" Kitty inquired desperately of the people who had just arrived.

"Oh, he must have returned by train. That was our original plan, but we came back early by car. When we arrived, the shuttle boat brought us right on over to the ship."

One of the Pyramids
Courtesy of Alice P. Smith

Kitty hurried to tell the purser that her husband was still on the dock, and he agreed to go in search of him. It seemed a long wait, but finally the shuttle returned to their ship anchored out in the harbor.

"Oh look! I think I see your daddy coming." Kitty let go of John's hand as he ran to greet his father.

"Hello, little skeezix! Bless your little cotton socks! How did you and Mommy do?"

"Bob, you had us all worried there for awhile." Kitty's look spoke volumes. "How was the trip?"

"You were not the only ones concerned. Great day! You wouldn't believe how frightened I was when I saw the launch was gone but, Kitty, the pyramids and sphinx are beyond belief. I got to ride on a big camel, John Boy. What do you think of that?"

John Boy jumped up and down, laughing with delight.

"Was it good to be with Raymond?"

"Well," he paused, and his expression betrayed his feelings. "You know Raymond. He doesn't mince words. He told me he thinks we are fools. He can't understand going to a place we don't know anything about to tell people we don't know about a God in whom he doesn't believe. He particularly thinks it is wrong to ask other people to support us. The conversation left me with a heavy heart. He just doesn't know Jesus, so how could he begin to comprehend what compels us to go? Still, he is my brother. Maybe someday he will understand."

More of Egypt
Courtesy of Alice P. Smith

Bob's family was not totally in agreement with his idea of going to the mission field. His parents were supportive, but he remembered the letter he had received from his uncle when he had made the decision to leave engineering and go into the ministry. "The family has lost a great engineer and gained a poor preacher," he wrote.

Bob was one of five boys. The only girl, Verna, had died of complications from a ruptured appendix at age twenty-one. Howard, his oldest brother, was teaching in a university and made few comments. Raymond was the second oldest. Next was Roy, his dentist brother, who also thought him a bit of a fool, and hoped he'd soon get over it. He did continue to be close to his brother, Eddie, who now was busy in his medical practice.

There was a heaviness that accompanied thoughts of home, and he didn't like it. The time had come to leave Egypt, and he truly welcomed that. Bob felt Paul must have understood what he was going through when he said:

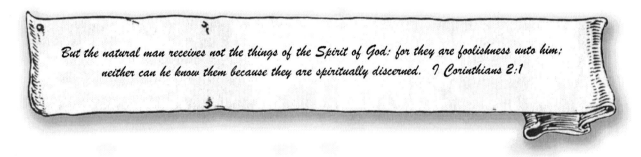

But the natural man receives not the things of the Spirit of God: for they are foolishness unto him; neither can he know them because they are spiritually discerned. 1 Corinthians 2:1

They were now in the Red Sea, narrowing the gap to their destination. Aden, Yemen, was to be their next stop; then Jabuti, on the horn of Africa, and finally Mombasa.

Dad and Mother were 29 and 30 respectively when they set out for Africa. Our Mother, as most young mothers, was thoroughly enjoying her child who was just beginning to talk. Her letters are filled with stories of his progress. Only a few are selected.

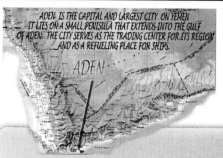

Aden November 18, 1932

We find we are stopping at Aden at the end of the Red Sea for mail, so I am writing just a note to get you word from our last port this side of the east coast of Africa. They say Aden is the hottest place in the world. I do not know but we are finding the Red Sea very hot in spite of a breeze. It seems the air lacks something and is so oppressive. We have been doing quite well, but Bob takes most of the care of John. He is getting so he wears his helmet pretty well, but the poor little fellow does get so hot with it on. However we watch him carefully as it is so very dangerous to be without the helmet now.

John has kept very well and still seems to be. He sleeps well and eats about as usual. He talks about everything or at least attempts it. The other day when we stopped in Suez it was so very hot, Bob got a lemon phosphate for himself and for me and an orange aide for John. He didn't know how the latter would be so said, "Let Daddy taste it, John." John said, "Daddy taste" and handed it over and then Bob took a sip and said, "Oh! Boy! it is good." and gave it back. John took another swallow and said, "Oh! Boy! Good." When he wants an orange he'll say "Peel oranch," and we'll say "please?" Then he'll reply "please peel oranch." He now says "tank" or "Notank".....

I suppose you have seen Raymond by now and have learned that Bob was successful in finding him. They had a wonderful time together and Bob picked up some sand at the foot of the Pyramids that he brought back in the cuffs of his trousers. So the sand in this envelope is that. After Bob left the party from the boat, they changed their plans and got back by motor car early. The launch didn't wait for the train and when they arrived at the boat Bob wasn't along. They hurried right back and found him waiting but we had some pretty anxious minutes here before he arrived, as you can imagine. However they held the boat 25 minutes for him altho' the Captain was pretty sore till the Purser explained the situation.

We land the 25th at Mombasa. Have Aden and Jabuti yet before then. We will go to Nairobi by train, have one night on the train, and one in Nairobi, then on to Kericho. We are anxious to get there as we are getting pretty tired.

Hope you are all well. You should have quite a collection of stamps by now.
　　　　　　Much love,　　　　　Us 3

"You should have quite a collection of stamps by now."

27

But how can they call on Him to save them unless they believe in Him?

And how can they believe in Him if they have never heard about Him?

And how can they hear about Him unless someone tells them?

And how will anyone go and tell them without being sent?

That is what the Scriptures mean when they say,

"How beautiful are the feet of those who bring good news!"'

Romans 10: 14,15 NLV

"It was not going to happen overnight."

And so the days slipped by, as did the water along the large vessel. Bob stared down at it, and he tried to imagine how his effort to tell these people about God's love would take shape. How would things change in the their lives? He envisioned homes in which men and women, who had become sons and daughters of the King, would enter erect rather than on hands and knees, woman would be honored and revered, filth would be replaced by cleanliness. Men and women would not be the recipients of charity but would proudly make sound choices for Christ and accept all the attending responsibilities. But how would this all take place?

> Dad often mentioned that, in the early days, he pondered over how mission work would take shape. He had had no direct training as is often given missionaries now, and so he constructed his own ideas and actually wrote a booklet, which he later abandoned when he found other similar ones had already been written.

- First, people would have to be told the Good News—learning the language would be an initial step.

- The people needed to be shown mercy, kindness and healing—hospitals and medical care would surely have to come.

- The language would need to be put into a written form—the Bible that contained the message could then be translated.

- In order to study the Bible, they would need to be able to read—schools would be part of the formula.

- When there were people who could teach and preach, they would need to be supported—natives would need to learn trades that provided income so they could support their pastors and the church could then be indigenous.

- He, Kitty, and the children would have to provide for their own needs so that they could survive in a hostile climate—safe housing would be one of the first orders of business.

- If those things were to happen, they would inextricably be linked to the necessity of travel and transport.

It was not going to happen overnight. This was going to be a lifetime commitment!

Papa Barnett˙ looked across at the new recruits, his weathered face reflecting his years of work. He remembered his first bewildering days in Kenya, and the innocence and enthusiasm of these folks was amusing. He wanted to help.

"Who is meeting you in Mombasa?" he had asked.

"We are not being met. Our goods will be transferred to the train station and we will drive up country in our car," Bob replied.

There was a long pause. "The road to Nairobi is very dry and rough now, but the rains will be coming soon, and when they set in, there is no relief. Being stuck on a muddy road is not a good place for a woman with child. I wouldn't want to be interfering, but it might be best that the women go by train."

Consequently arrangements were made for Papa and the men to take the car, and Mama, with the women, would go by train.

"I don't much like this plan," Kitty had said to Bob later. "I really don't want to be separated… and, besides, Mrs. Barnett makes me nervous."

"Kitty, I think it is the best thing. These people know what they are talking about." And so it was settled.

Little did Kitty know how much this woman would come to mean to her in the future.

Missionaries aboard the Watussi

˙ Bert "Papa" Barnett was born to a wheat ranching family in Wellington, Australia, in 1876. His work as a flour miller in the town dried up in 1902 because of a drought. Bert left for USA to seek work and his fortune. In Sacramento, CA, he had a conversion experience and a call to be a missionary. He attended Moody Bible Institute in Chicago, graduating in 1905. He left USA for Kenya in 1907 with a small party of Africa Inland Mission missionaries. At a port in Italy, a Swedish single lady going out with AIM joined the party. Her name was Elma Nicher. She had felt God's call in Sweden to be a missionary, and then attended a Bible college in New England, USA. Bert and Elma fell in love on the boat before reaching Kenya. They were both assigned to work with the Maasai people in a remote area north of Thompson's Falls in Kenya. Courtesy of Dr. Stan Barnett

Watussi, Thanksgiving Day

Dear Folks:

We are a bit behind in our schedule so we are not arriving in Mombasa today as we had hoped, but will arrive tomorrow in the morning we hope. We have heard that the roads in Kenya are dry but somewhat "bumpy" so the boys are going to drive up and we are going on the train. There is a missionary here by the name of Barnett who is with the Africa Inland Mission who will go with them and be their guide. He says they know Bro. Hotchkiss but I really don't care much for either of them.... I do think they are good, sincere people however, and I believe they are doing a good work. I rather dread the thought of her being with us, however, as she gets on my nerves most terribly.

Well I'm glad our voyage is about over. Everyone is getting tired and touchy. One poor woman at our table is really quite pitiful. There isn't a thing that is right and she'll wait till the meal is half over then she'll say Stewart, I have had nothing to eat." It is now quite a daily occurrence and we have a hard time not to laugh at her.

We have been having some good prayer meetings with all the rest of the missionaries every evening at 7:30. I haven't gone to many because of putting John to bed but have enjoyed the fellowship very much. I especially enjoy the Swedish missionary and his wife. They surely do have the love of God in their hearts and the Holy Spirit too. They have a real shine upon them.

We have had splendid sailing weather since our last two stops, but it has been terribly hot. There were two nights in which I really suffered terribly. John has been fine. We have the wool band on at night and let him run in his bathing suit in the day time. He keeps his hat on splendidly now so we don't have it to worry about.

We'll soon find out if we are good mountaineers. We are to go to an elevation of 9,000 feet and then back down to 7,000....

Much love, Catharine, Bob and John

"We are to go to an elevation of 9,000 feet and then back down to 7,000."

CHAPTER 4
ARRIVING MOMBASA—NOVEMBER 26, 1932

"Black faces were everywhere...."

Heat waves rose from the shimmering water. The air was sultry and still. A tugboat had met them and now was towing them through the channel between the coral reefs and into Mombasa Harbor. The city of Mombasa is on an island. Before they entered the channel, they had seen most of the beautiful white beaches with arching coconut palms extended out along the mainland. Along the banks were huge baobab trees, which Bob estimated to be as much as thirty feet wide. The branches looked more like a network of roots, and hanging from them in great numbers were long pods, which they later learned contained a substance similar to cream of tartar. The seeds could be used as an antidote for arrow poison; the pulp could be used to treat fever, diarrhea, malaria and vitamin C deficiencies, since its fruit contains six times the vitamin C of an orange. Additionally, they learned these trees could live up to 3,000 years.

As they were being towed into the harbor, they could also see the massive ancient fort on the bluff. Fort Jesus was built by the Portuguese in 1593. For close to four decades thereafter, Portuguese dominance was unchallenged until, in 1631, they temporarily lost both the town and the fort to an Arab sultan. By 1875, it had changed hands nine times.

The car

The sunlight sparkled on the water. Everyone was on deck as the big vessel made its way into the harbor and carefully edged its way up to the dock. Mombasa, Kenya, Africa at last!

The dry, sultry air was oppressive and heavy with smells of salt sea, fish, wet sisal rope, garlic and spices. Black faces were everywhere in this bustling place, but there were also many Asians and Arabs who had claimed this as their homeland for over 500 years. People shouted directions to each other in languages not understood by the Smiths as the precious cargo began to be unloaded. They watched anxiously as the Ford V-8 they had brought was lifted high in the air and not so gently lowered to the dock. Bob was reminded of the breathtaking news that a woman in Ohio was donating her brand new car.

This year was Ford's first V-8, and this was the first one to arrive in Kenya. It was humbling to Bob to realize this woman's sacrifice, and it reaffirmed his determination to do the best job he could.

THE DARKEST TIME IS JUST BEFORE THE DAWN

The day of arrival would have been baffling had it not been for Mama and Papa Barnett for whom Mombasa was an old friend.

Kitty remembered the first time she had met Mama Barnett at the beginning of their voyage. Mama, in her matter of fact way and in her thick Swedish brogue had said, *"Ven is dis babe coming?"*

Taken aback, Kitty had answered, "Oh! I had hoped no one would notice!"

"Dearie, you are vell beyond the stage of not noticing."

The proper thing was to be discrete about such things as pregnancy, so Kitty had carefully sewed her drop waist dresses hoping to hide her pregnancy. Obviously it hadn't worked, and now she was a little upset with Mama who, in her matter-of-fact way, was pointing that out. She really had not liked her at all, but those feelings had lessened as they approached Kenya.

Kitty and Bob on board ship

The group of missionaries had spent many hours discussing their arrival in Mombasa. Mama had agreed to travel on the train with the two pregnant women and the goods, while the men would come along the bumpy roads in the Ford.

"The rain was relentless."

The trip inland

At 4:00 PM with the women, John Boy and the goods safely on board the train, the men eagerly got into the little car and headed for Nairobi. Only six years before, the first car, a Riley, had motored from Mombasa to Nairobi successfully. Most vehicles were transported "up country" by rail since as yet there were no suitable roads.

Bob knew this would be a challenging trip and he didn't want to miss a moment of the rough and tumble of it. He also found that he was feeling very possessive of the car that he had received as a gift from the woman in Ohio since he had overcome the red tape of getting it aboard ship.

When Kirk announced that he would drive it up country, Bob had to swallow hard and agree. After all, the car had been donated for the work of the mission and it needed to be shared. So off they went with Kirk at the wheel. Dusk came abruptly but the western sky was clear and lit by the rising full moon. Weary, the men took shelter in a Hindu temple they had found along the way.

The following day, the heat quickly gave way to fresh cool air, and the coconut palms to scrubby harsh brush and fine penetrating dust. Soon the landscape changed again and became densely forested. Broken and uprooted trees betrayed the presence of elephant. In only thirty miles, the men had climbed around 1,500 feet over a twisting trail, along which

Mt. Kilimanjaro forming the backdrop for giraffe

animals began to appear. It was thrilling to see them in their natural state. Graceful giraffe ambled among the trees, nibbling the top branches of the acacias. Then giant drops of rain began to fall, pelting the little car, and changing the dusty road into a mess of chocolate rivulets. The trail dissolved into sticky gumbo and finally into a quagmire.

"Did you know that the name Kenya means 'mist'?" Mr. Barnett asked smiling.

"Quite appropriate, I must say." Bob sensed Mr. Barnett's smile betrayed information he hadn't shared.

The men were making slow progress slipping from one bank to the other and back. Finally the rains had abated, but as they were approaching the famous railway bridge at Tsavo, they heard a sickening thud. Everyone jumped out of the car, knowing that it could be hours or days before another vehicle would be along.

It didn't take long to find that the oil pan had been damaged and was leaking badly. So, Bob removed it, and he and Mr. Barnett began walking along the railroad track toward the town of Tsavo while Kirk started to set up camp. Because the oil pan was cast aluminum, the repair was not forthcoming. They were able to patch it up by riveting pieces of leather to the aluminum, but they knew this was unsatisfactory. They had no choice, however, but to return with the partially repaired pan and hoped to make do until they arrived in Nairobi.

Because the men had just read J.H.Patterson's, *Man Eaters of Tsavo*, their heads were filled with visions of ghostly lions crunching bones. As the sun slid behind the horizon, they settled into their campsite. A magical feeling overtook them as sounds evoked images, trees became elephants, and rocks became rhinos. Bob, armed with a .38 cal revolver, was excited

Large lion prints were everywhere.

to be actually sleeping overnight right where the "Man Eaters" story had taken place. As they had been advised, they burned their lantern outside the tent all night and slept little as they waited for intruders. They could hear a hyena laughing as they tried to sleep.

"Well, I'll be jiggered. Look at this little critter with a curled tail? Is this a scorpion?" Bob asked as he stepped from the tent the next morning.

"That it is. You don't ever want to put on your shoes without shaking them out first in this country, and there is the reason why, right there!" observed Mr. Barnett, pointing at the scorpion. "Come on, let's take a look at the watering hole."

They walked down the pathway through the trees. Large lion paw prints were everywhere. Little chills ran up and down their spines, as they imagined what they had not seen in the night.

The desert scrubland and tsetse fly belt had given way to more open countryside with breathtaking views of Mt. Kilimanjaro (Africa's highest mountain). The men gazed spellbound across the rolling plains, dotted here and there with twisted thorn trees. In their view were tens of thousands of wildebeests and zebra, gazelles with tirelessly wagging tails, impala closely packed with their beautiful spiral twisted horns, and eland with their peculiar dewlaps swinging back

The Great Rift Valley

35

and forth as they walked.

The sights were breathtaking, but still the men needed to make their way through the black cotton soil of the Kapiti plains to Nairobi, where they would meet their wives again. By then they would have traveled 302 miles. After joining them in Nairobi, they would continue over the bamboo covered Kikuyu hills, then down along the lakes and watercourses of the Great Rift Valley, and finally into the densely forested highlands that would become their new home, Lumbwa Industrial Mission at Chaigaik near Kericho—another 150 miles. They could hardly wait!

But the sound of rain drumming fiercely on the little car's roof was relentless. Progress was slowed and often brought to a halt as they pushed and pulled their way out of one mud hole after another. The repaired oil pan continued to leak precious oil, and although they had replenished their supply at Tsavo, they were running out. The roads had become so bad that it was difficult to even know where they were. The ground seemed to dissolve into a bottomless swamp, and anything that tried to move on it sank.

"Here we go, sinking down to Guinea," Bob said as he inspected the car, stuck once again and up to the floorboards in a mud hole.

"This, my friends, is black cotton soil," said Papa. "In the wet season, it is this sticky impossible mess. In the dry season, it bakes hard as cement, then cracks up and becomes a fine powder that chokes everything with dust. You get to take your pick. I favor the dust myself." He chuckled as he looked at the men covered with mud.

In spite of Mr. Barnett's reassurance and their gradual progress, at Makindu, having completed only about half their trip, they hit a protruding stump once more, and finally the oil pan was beyond repair. "This time we will have to take the train the rest of the way. It does make a stop here at Makindu," Papa had said.

CHAPTER 5

NAIROBI—NOVEMBER 28, 1932

"… the beginnings…of progress."

Until the late 1800s, Nairobi had been little more than a watering hole for Maasai cattle, but in 1896, construction was started on a railway from Mombasa to Uganda, which would open up the interior of Africa. After four years of energy-sapping work, frustration, disease, death at the paws of the "man-eaters" of Tsavo, and perseverance, the line reached Nairobi and then, in the following year, proceeded to Kisumu, then known as Port Florence on the shores of Lake Victoria. By now, it had become the main and most reliable means of transportation from the coast to Nairobi.

The name Nairobi (*enkare nyarobi*) means "the place of cold water" in Maasai, and it referred to the Nairobi River, which came down from the snows of Mount Kenya. At 5,450 feet above sea level, once it had been a treeless swamp full of thousands of animals and was the last open area where trains could be rearranged before climbing up the Kikuyu escarpment. As inappropriate as the place was, it curiously continued to grow into a pleasant little town with a few paved streets, in spite of bubonic plague sweeping through its sodden and unsanitary pall of shanty shacks (1902), being razed by the fire (1903), and suffering again through plague (1904).

In fact, the city of Nairobi was a kind of miracle in the middle of what used to be dark Kenya, in spite of the absence of decent roads from the coastal city, Mombasa. There were numerous open-faced Indian shops with only metal gates to enclose them at night. In the hotels, there were eating places sporting shining brass fixtures and linen covered tables, served by men in long white gowns called *kanzus* with red *fezzes* on their heads.

The grounds of surrounding hotels were planted with lovely flowers. There was the pungent sweetness of frangipani, the brilliantly vivid colors of the bougainvillea, the over-arching flame trees and the graceful purple-flowered jacaranda trees. Yet in striking contrast, the city was not without its bungalows, sheds, dust, beggars and squalor.

Nairobi and other places in Kenya had evolved because of the determination of British settlers as well as missionaries and others looking to change this country in one way or another. And it was, of course, because of the railway that the various elements required had arrived. The British settlers, an odd mixture of adventure-seeking pioneers willing to work the land plus the governing faction, all came with mixed goals and purposes, and some were slowly achieving them. The Indian coolies who had been brought in to build the railway had gone on to become the merchants.

As Winston Churchill had put it after his trip to Kenya, "Everywhere I see hard work, strained resources, and hopes persisting through many disappointments, stout hospitable hearts and the beginnings, at any rate, of progress."

As time passed, the British had created a sort of feudal system to serve their needs. The nationals were given jobs of servitude but were paid. The missionaries fell into a similar pattern of training nationals with various skills they needed to improve their chances of survival in a rapidly changing culture.

Aboard the train that had been so crucial in the development of Kenya, the women had awakened excitedly. The train, however, was interminably slow, trying every limit of their patience as it trudged along hour after hour. Finally a delicious fragrance of ripening fruit, sweet-scented flowers, spices, and warm dusky flesh filled the air—the smell of an emerging civilization. None smelled it more eagerly than these fledgling missionaries as they arrived in Kenya's capital. Mama Barnett conversed freely with the natives busily arranging transport for the women to the tiny missionary guesthouse. Settled comfortably in her room, awaiting her husband's arrival, Kitty was happy to have a chance to get back to some letter writing.

> *Nairobi, Kenya Colony, British East Africa*
> *November 28, 1932*
>
> *Dear Folks:*
>
> *As I write the date, I remember it is Mary's birthday, so I'll send her many happy returns though I suppose it will be about six weeks late.*
>
> *We are here at Nairobi waiting for the boys who are driving up from Mombasa. We expect them some time today, as they did not leave until Saturday P.M.. We just got into port Friday about 11:00 but it took so long to go through customs etc. that we barely got to come up on the 4:00 o'clock train. We rode all the rest of that day and until about 1 o'clock the next. We came up an altitude of over 5,000 ft. and progress was very slow on average of about 15 to 20 miles an hour. We often felt as though we'd like to get out and push. And everything was so dirty. We were surely glad when it was over. We are now at a missionary rest home where it is quite nice and at any rate very comfortable. Mrs. Barnett is here also and has proved a much more congenial companion than I anticipated. I surely do not know what we would have done without her as she helped us in ordering (it had to be done in Swahili and again with our baggage, getting a taxi etc.) I am also more than glad that the boys have someone with them who knows the way as they have had to camp out two nights instead of one.*
>
> *I am wondering if we have any mail in Kericho. When we got here we had a couple of letters at the boat saying that our plans were a little altered, and instead of going straight to Kericho we were to go to Fords' first and then out from there where there was a furnished house we could get. The two temporary buildings that we were going to have on Bro. Hotchkiss' place were deemed unnecessary and so we will not have the problem of furniture right away. It is quite a relief to us because we have run short of money and instead of the $300.00 we asked for there was only $100.00 at Mombasa. But the Lord has met every need thus far and finding this place where we have to pay only half as much as we would have to at any hotel and now that we have had to stay it is nice that we don't have so much expense.*
>
> *Well they are ready to go now so will have to close. I'll have to write my impressions of Africa later.*
>
> *Much love,   Catharine*

"We are here at Nairobi waiting for the boys...."

NAIROBI

Finally, the men had arrived, mud covered but energized by their adventure. Bob described it all to Kitty in detail. Here in Nairobi, Mr. Barnett had directed them to an Indian shop where a new oil pan could be purchased, and they hoped to soon be on their way again.

Nairobi, Kenya Colony, British East Africa, November 30, 1932

Dear Folks:

I have been waiting to write my impressions of Africa until I could also write that the boys had safely arrived. They got in this A.M., having come the last part of the trip, 120 miles, by train. They have surely had some experiences as the rain had just begun and seemed to follow them right up. Several times they were in mud holes where the water came in through the doors and the engine lay half-buried. They camped one night near the water tanks where the railroad building was held up so long and the next morning saw lion tracks about 75 yds. away. They saw many jackals and smaller game, two great giraffes, the largest Bob said he ever saw, easily as high as one of our telephone poles at home. They slept one night in a Hindu temple and were bitten by mosquitoes there. However they have been taking quinine and hope to suffer no ill effects. The reason they had to come home by train was that they punched a hole through the pan that holds the oil and they have gone down to see if they can get a steel pan. This one is cast aluminum and can't be soldered.

We are going on from here, if the roads permit, by car but if not we will go again by train.

I wish you could see the boys' clothes. They are caked with mud, covered with grease and what not. Bob wore his cover-alls, fortunately, but I don't know whether he'll ever wear them again or not. So you can a little imagine they have had their first initiation to Africa. But they say they wouldn't have missed it for anything....

Well we were glad to arrive in Nairobi. This is a beautiful little city. There are lovely stores that seem more like American stores and the streets are wide and very beautifully paved.... Every morning a native comes to the door with fruit and vegetables and they are wonderfully cheap. There are oranges, that are about the color of lemons, but oh! so sweet. They are very thin skinned but peel like a grapefruit and the sections skin like grapefruit also. They are surely nice to fix for John. They also have wonderful pineapples. Then there are mangoes that I can eat and papaya that is very good for one, but that I can't go yet. However, I might learn to like it in time. Apples are very dear and almost impossible to get. Other necessities are quite reasonable, some about like home, some more expensive and some less. Cornstarch is "corn-flour". While "mealie-meal" is corn meal. Everything is "tinned" instead of canned....

"I wish you could see the boys' clothes."

The rains had not let up, so Faye, Kitty, and John Boy once more boarded the train, if somewhat reluctantly, and continued their journey to Kisumu where they would be met by Friends missionaries and then taken to their station at Kaimosi. Bob and Kirk would go by car.

CHAPTER 6

KAIMOSI—DECEMBER 1, 1932

Making home among Friends

Mr. Everett Kellum and Clara Ford stood on the platform of the train station in Kisumu, the nearest town of any size to Kaimosi. Kitty and Faye knew Clara would be meeting them. "Welcome to Kisumu! How was your trip?"

"We are so glad to be here at last," Kitty replied, and she meant it.

Kitty thought back on the trip, remembering the train moving through the vast countryside, vague impressions looming out of the darkness, the jostling crowds of African vendors at each stop thrusting all sorts of wares up to the windows from the gravel platform below them. There had been men in dirty crimson blankets, children in tattered clothing or nothing at all and woman with brightly colored beads and skins as their only clothes. She thought of the train with its tiny wood-burning engine rumbling along the landscape, stopping with hardly any excuse along the way. She had written more about it:

> Well, now as to Africa as we have found it. I already told you about Mombasa and how terribly hot it was. I think I forgot to mention that the trains are English in style composed of little square rooms with long seats facing each other. These are the lower berths and their backs raise up so as to form the upper ones. The trains have an up and down motion similar to that of a spring wagon over a corduroy road. I didn't sleep much you can well guess.
>
> Oh! Yes. We rent our bedding. That is if we want to sit up all night we may or if we want to use our own blankets. But we rented so as to have plenty as the boys had taken the two steamer rugs.

Letter of November 30, 1932

Before they knew it, Faye and Kitty had been shown their next form of transportation. They climbed into the ancient truck wearily. Kitty wrapped the little woolen blanket around John Boy against the chill as they approached the Friends Mission station at Kaimosi. The cool damp air made her shiver, but once inside the Kellums' home, she delighted in the noble stone fireplace and its crackling fire which warmed and comforted her. John Boy and little Gladys Kellum cautiously eyed each other at first and soon were cheerfully running around. Kitty wondered if she looked as pregnant and as tired as Faye. It had been a long day.

She awakened the next morning to a rhythmic swish, swish, like waves on a beach as the paths on the mission station were swept. There was a melody of happy voices chattering in hope and laughter. Night was over, the sun was up, and she was refreshed and anxious to view the mission station, even though the men had not yet arrived.

Home among Friends—Courtesy of Alta Hoyt

43

THE DARKEST TIME IS JUST BEFORE THE DAWN

Taking John Boy's hand she ventured out the door and shivered again from the morning chill. Behind the station was a forested area where Kitty could see a strange-looking black and white monkey playing in the trees.

Colobus monkey

Across the road from the house where they were guests was another brick house where the Hoyts lived. Further down the road, she could see more residences, the church, and a large building called the industrial department where Africans were being taught woodworking and furniture making. Across from that was the hospital where their hostess Mrs. Kellum put in long hours as a nurse.   Back in the house, she noted that a national nursemaid watched little Gladys while her mother worked.   The idea of having someone else care for her children was something Kitty found difficult to comprehend and knew she would do her best to avoid in the future.

Clara's family was still shaken by the loss of her mother who had died the year before of a sudden and unpredicted cerebral hemorrhage. Nonetheless, her father, an accomplished missionary, continued his work here under the Friends Mission. Earlier, Clara had traveled to America with the Chilsons to continue her education shortly before Bob had made his first visit to WGM headquarters, trying to create interest in opening work in Africa. As mentioned earlier, the board had not been receptive at first, but then what seemed a miracle to Bob occurred. That very day, the mission received a check " to be used if a work was ever opened by this mission in Africa." It was then that everything changed. The minutes of meetings held in those early years indicated that Mr. Chilson, the founder of this Friends station, had visited and most likely suggested that they recruit Clara Ford to help find an area where their mission could work. And now here in Kenya, as they were getting acquainted, Kitty was finding Clara to be tough and energetic with a patient and courteous manner. She was busy teaching in the Friends school, and Kitty, herself a teacher, enjoyed hearing about the methods that were used to teach the Africans. Mrs. Hoyt later described the method:[*]

> We had twelve charts hung on the walls of the mud and thatch school house.
> Chart No. 1 just had the vowels printed on them and they were pronounced
> as in German, for the beginners. No. 2 Chart had the vowels printed
> with a consonant such as ma, me, mi, mo, mu, until all the consonants
> were familiar to them. Then on the last Chart 12, we jointed them to-
> gether thus: ma-ma=mama or ki-ta-bu=kitabu book. Then they would
> shout, "O, the letters are now talking our language." In just a few
> days they were able to read words in the primer, then short sentences.
> We found these African boys and girls just as bright and quick to learn
> as white children. They easily passed a grade a year. Very soon Afri-
> cans themselves could teach in these beginning schools and we would
> teach the advanced ones. Our one aim was to train the Africans to carry
> on their own schools all over the country side, and to train the young
> Christians in the Bible so they could conduct Sunday Schools and Church
> services themselves, at all the out-schools.

Mrs. Hoyt's description of her approach to teaching "reading"

---

[*] Alta Hoyt, *We Were Pioneers*, Self Published

At Kaimosi, Clara wasted no time introducing Kitty and Faye to their first order of business—language study—and before they knew it, they had their first lessons in hand.

Kaimosi Station
Kenya Colony
British East Africa
Dec. 1932

Dear Folks at Home:

Here we are still at Kellums', and we are expecting the boys may be in sometime today. However, there have been very heavy rains around here for the last few days. In fact, here yesterday and day before, we had real bad hail storms. It gets quite cool and we had to have a fire all day long. Mr. Ford said he remembered when they had hail near here so big that the next day there were still drifts of hail in the gutters. Imagine that on the Equator.

We have been having a very good time here and have tried to help out Mrs. Kellum in things she wouldn't have been able to get done otherwise, so Faye and I pieced her a little quilt for her baby. She is just a little over a year old. The quilt is of the bow-tie pattern and is made from some of her baby dresses. It is real bright and pretty, has 99 patches in it (that is blocks). It is 9 blocks by 11 blocks, and has a border of 2 inches of pink. I don't know just what would be the final measurements of it. We would tie it for her but she hasn't the lining for it yet or at least hasn't decided on it. I wanted to make a little dress for Gladys but she says I must not sew on the machine, so I guess I will have to give that up. She is a nurse and works about 6 hours every day, so she doesn't have much time for her house and family. I feel real sorry for her husband and see the mistake of trying to do a regular missionary's work and keep a house and family too....

Well, here it is after breakfast, and I have been doing a little cleaning up. Now I'm ready to study a little Swahili. I'm afraid it suffered for the two days while we were making the quilt. We are on an especially long lesson now, and it is hard to keep at it. It includes all the numerals, cardinals and ordinals, all the days of the week and ways to write dates, and also all the various verb forms and conjugations with the different classes. So you can see it is some job. We thought we would try and keep up our study so we wouldn't be too far behind when we have to leave for our "vacation." We have been learning some things about the hospital, and I find it will not be like the one at Elmira. We have to furnish our own baby clothes, and someone to wash them for us, also our own nightgowns. The towel and bedding is furnished.

While we are here, we have access to a piano, and I have surely enjoyed what little playing I have been able to do. The rain has kept me in some and, then as I said, the quilt has occupied a great deal of time.

Well, the mail came this morning, and I didn't get a single letter. That is quite heartbreaking as Faye and Kirk got about 30, including Christmas cards.

The last word we had from the office, they said they had been doing without their salaries in order to send money to the field. And Faye had a letter this morning saying that Mr. Hotchkiss had stayed at their house during the Mansfield Convention, and he had seemed so worried about something. She said he didn't eat like he should. I wonder just what his worries are.

Well, I expect you'll have a message by the time this arrives. I am hoping for a little girl, but anything will be o.k. I am not sure what we would call a little boy, but perhaps Robert Edward.

Do write often, all of you.

Much love,   Catharine

"Mr. Hotchkiss...seemed so worried about something."

THE DARKEST TIME IS JUST BEFORE THE DAWN

Just over two months had passed since they left home. Christmas was just 15 days away. Kitty loved Christmas, the fine gifts that, in the past, her family had been able to give each other, the snow, the singing, and the laughter.

It was hard to accept that Faye and Kirk had thirty letters and cards waiting for them in Kaimosi, and she and Bob had had none. Kitty tried to be cheerful about it and hoped that soon they would be getting word from their loved ones. There were clearly differences between the Smiths and the Kirkpatricks. The Smiths had waited for five years from their first appeal to the mission board, and then it had taken another eleven months to raise their support before they were on their way. The Kirkpatricks, on the other hand, had raised their salaries and were on their way within months and, in that short time, had developed an excellent constituency. Faye and Kirk had contact with well-established Christian communities, but for Bob and Kitty, the supporting churches had rarely assisted any missionaries. Bob was a new Christian without a strong church background. Kitty's family were strong Christians but had very limited resources, though they contributed generously to Bob and Kitty's support. Kitty knew some of these things made a difference, but the lack of letters was demoralizing nonetheless. She was determined to turn her attention to other things.

What would Christmas in this new land be like? There would be no snow, of that she was sure.

As time passed, a shadow began to loom. Initially it wasn't something they could touch or measure, but with time, it was becoming increasingly palpable. Comments Kitty made about Mr. Hotchkiss, their friend and mentor, were received with a raised eyebrow or silence. She had experienced it when she spoke with missionaries on the ship coming out, and she began to understand that, in part, her negative feeling for the Barnetts had grown out of their strange responses to her comments about Mr. H. during their trip on the Watussi.

> Mother no doubt would have been trying to sort this all out in her mind and, when Dad arrived and began to tell his experiences, would have interrupted thus:

"Bob, what are you saying?" said Kitty urgently, still not believing her ears.

"We are not wanted in this area for some reason. The District Commissioner seems to have a campaign going against us," he said, trying to hide his concern.

"How can that be? He doesn't even know us! Who is this District Commissioner anyway, and why does what he thinks affect us?"

"He is the British government representative who makes the decision whether to approve our work or not. Apparently there is a great deal of animosity."

"How did you find this out?"

"Well, it was like this, Kitty. When we stopped at Lumbwa Station, a missionary from Africa Inland Mission, Sam Anderson told us that not only is the District Commissioner vocal about his opposition but also many missionaries in various parts of Kenya agree with him. They have never heard of our organization, and they don't want confusing views being taught to the Africans."

"What about the temporary houses that were supposed to be built for us at Mr. Hotchkiss's place, Chaigaik? What happened there?"

"Well, they are not completed. With all these rumors, Mr. Scouten, the man who is caring for Mr. Hotchkiss's place, wasn't sure we would arrive, so things are at a standstill. We did get to meet Mr. Andrew Andersen at Litein station. He is the man Clara has arranged to be our advisor. He is also the one who checks on the schools that Mr. Hotchkiss started in Kipsigis land. The government requires that those schools be supervised by a missionary, so he has been doing that in Mr. H.'s absence."

"What is he like? "

"Oh, he seems like a great guy. He has a wonderful Danish accent. I think you will like him. He was very congenial, but he is not well. He has a heart condition."

> We can imagine how troubled Mother would have been that things were not as expected and Dad would have reassured her. He was always full of buoyant energy and good humor. Even then, he would characteristically have been seeking the positive.

"Does Clara know about all of this trouble?" Kitty asked feeling a little overwhelmed.

"Now, Kitty, don't you worry," he said reassuringly, "These people don't know us. It is natural they should be leery of a new group. Just you wait. In six months they will be begging us to stay." He patted her shoulder.

> What could be the problem? They would likely have been very anxious to get to know Clara better and Mother would have been looking forward to having a long talk. There had to be more to this, but at this juncture they had no choice but to let the matter drop.

For Bob, the Kaimosi station was a model of what he dreamed he would be able to develop. He delighted in the ingenuity of these missionaries. Mr. Chilson had created a sawmill about a mile from the station. Many Africans were employed there, and the lumber produced created further opportunity for students in their industrial school to learn. Bob was very impressed also with the brick kiln and paid close attention to the process as he hoped to duplicate it on their station some day.

Log roll at Kaimosi—Courtesy of Alta Hoyt

THE DARKEST TIME IS JUST BEFORE THE DAWN

Mr. Hoyt's 62-inch saw at the mill—Courtesy of Alta Hoyt

Mrs. Hoyt had also described this kiln in her book:

... Fred trained men to make bricks by hand moulds, lay them out carefully in a drying shed to dry. Then after weeks of drying he helped them make a brick kiln laying them up carefully, with openings at the bottom for firing. After mudding the kiln all over, they brought the slabs of sawn logs from the saw mill and it was an exciting time when the big fire was started under the bricks. African workmen would have to take turns staying right there all night replenishing the fire, and Fred would go down two or three times a night to see that the proper heat was kept steady. After three or four days when the bricks would glow red hot, we women folks would go down too, to see the sight. It was tedious work but necessary, as the termites were so bad they would destroy houses built with wood. There were just a few hard woods that the termites would not touch.

Courtesy of Alta Hoyt

Their brief time at Kaimosi had come to an end, and they now must make ready to move on to Malava.

48

Beware of letting your care degenerate into anxiety and unrest; tossed as you are amid the winds and waves of sundry troubles, keep your eyes fixed on the Lord, and say "Oh, my God, I look to Thee alone; be thou my Guide, my Pilot"; and then be comforted. When the shore is gained, who will heed the toil and the storm? And we shall steer safely through every storm so long as our trust is fixed on God.

—Avis B. Christiansen

CHAPTER 7

MALAVA—DECEMBER 15, 1932—MAY 30, 1933

"… they would be reassured by the letters…."

Kitty awakened and, as usual, Bob was up already outside walking around the V-8 checking the tires. How muddy and dirty the car was, but now that the new oil pan was in place, it had performed beautifully. He was pleased. He was already beginning to understand that bringing the message of Christ to Africa would include waging war against the almost impassable roads with their black cotton soil or slick red clay. Kitty was happy to see his smile, and her thoughts turned to what the next step would be.

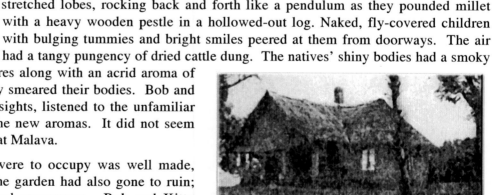

Since temporary housing was not completed, arrangements had been made for an unoccupied house at the Friends Mission called Malava. The two couples would stay there until the babies were born. Here they would study the language, assist in the church services, and work with the native staff who provided first aid to people in need. Clara, also, would join them but not until her teaching duties at Kaimosi were completed. Kitty realized that her talk with Clara would have to be delayed.

Pounding millet—Artist unknown

Nandi girl

On this beautiful sunny day, it seemed less important. The new station was not far from Kaimosi, and the drive was uneventful. Along the way, they could see natives walking along the road, some working in fields. Round windowless huts were clustered in villages, and they saw women with long dangling beaded earrings hanging from their pierced and stretched lobes, rocking back and forth like a pendulum as they pounded millet with a heavy wooden pestle in a hollowed-out log. Naked, fly-covered children with bulging tummies and bright smiles peered at them from doorways. The air had a tangy pungency of dried cattle dung. The natives' shiny bodies had a smoky smell of bush wood fires along with an acrid aroma of the fat with which they smeared their bodies. Bob and Kitty gazed at all the sights, listened to the unfamiliar sounds, and smelled the new aromas. It did not seem long until they arrived at Malava.

The house that they were to occupy was well made, though neglected. The garden had also gone to ruin; plants were shaggy and overgrown. Bob and Kitty were eyeing all of these things with anticipation of their potential and were pleased.

By evening, with the sun disappearing, there was a sudden chill in the air. John Boy's teeth were

House at Malava from "Call to Prayer"

chattering, and Kitty hurried to find a sweater. Bob rounded up some firewood, and soon the fireplace was ablaze warming their bodies but also healing their souls.

It was good for Kitty to be able to share in letters with her mother, but the wait for a reply seemed intolerably long. They had yet to receive any mail from home.

Dear Folks: Malava, British East Africa
                                                               Dec. 15, 1932

We are glad to report we are about settled in our temporary home. By that I mean we are here temporarily but we are living in a very nice permanent house. The temporary buildings Bro. Hotchkiss ordered made were not completed and we are very happy about it as we have seen several such and I'd hate to have to live long in one of them. They are made of sticks covered with mud with a grass roof. But the roof is not sealed at the top so often the lizards etc. fall down "kerflop" most anywhere. They are made circular and usually have mud floors and are consequently very damp. This little house where we are staying is one belonging to the Friends and has been unoccupied for 4 or 5 years so it was a mess to clean up, but we have it now in pretty good order. It goes a little hard to put up with the way the African boys do the work sometimes but we will make the best of it in time, I guess. We did not bring all our things here because of the expense of transportation but we have enough to make it homelike and comfortable. I will try and draw a picture of our quarters so you can see us in your mind.

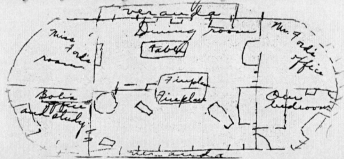

We have our little curtains up in our two rooms and they surely do look pretty. Bob is sleeping in his office and John with me for the time being as the bedrooms are small with the round sides. They are cozy but not very spacious.

Perhaps I should go back and begin with our leaving Nairobi. The boys got the car fixed up there and we left on Friday, we by train and the boys driving. We met the Barnetts again at Kijabi. They had gone the day before. They got off at Nicuru [sic] and we had gotten ready and gone to bed, as we were very tired, when who should appear at the window but the boys. They had beat the train there and had pitched their tent for the night. They went to El Dama Ravine where Barnetts have their place, had breakfast and then went to Lumbwa and then to Kericho. They found the man Bro. Hotchkiss has in charge and also saw Bro. Andersen whom they asked to be our advisor for a year. He, however, is very sick with heart trouble and they do not know whether he will ever recover sufficiently to go on with his work. We are all praying that the Lord will touch him because we need him so much, and the work needs him more. The boys found that the conditions here had really changed since Bro. Hotchkiss went away. In the first place, the District Commissioner who has to grant permission for work to be started, heard of our coming and said, "They'll not come if I have any thing to say about it." Humanly speaking he has the "whole" say, so it looks rather difficult....

Well, we left the boys at Nicuru[sic] as I said, and came on to Kaimosi station and waited there for the boys who arrived on Monday. We talked things over and decided to come here for the present, so Kirk went to Lumbwa on the train and there got a truck to take the stuff we could get along without over to Kericho and store it, and then bring up here what we needed. Bob, Faye, Clara and I drove over, and then Bob and Clara went to Kitosh with the car to get her things they could bring and then again when Kirk came with the truck. Then she was called back to Kaimosi to finish her teaching, and we hopped in and did the work, and, as I said, are quite nicely settled now.

I forgot to tell you our house is brick and although it isn't finished as to casings etc., yet it is plastered. It has a thatched roof, or rather a grass one, but it is very nice grass....We have a nice yard and a place for a lovely garden, but, of course, the place is neglected because it has been so long without care.

We are looking longingly for some word from home.... I cannot realize that it is December. We have the windows open and a lovely breeze coming through.
I am sending this to you and asking you to share it with the Smiths to save postage.... as it is quite high, and we have so much correspondence now. We are all well and by the time you get this we may be able to speak a few words of Swahili.

Lots of love, Kitty

"It has a thatched roof...very nice grass...."

"…divisions among the missionaries…."

In those days, adults were addressed by their formal names and never by first names until they were very familiar. In trying to piece the story together ourselves, we conclude that certainly they, too, would have been trying to understand the history of these missionaries, and the discussion may have gone as follows:

"Clara, her father Mr. Ford, and Mr. Andersen are all going to be here this evening. Maybe we can learn some more," Bob commented to Kitty. They were increasingly aware of how much planning had accompanied their arrival. The interaction of the various missions and the necessity to placate the government all seemed complex. With each contact, a multifaceted story that both united and divided the various groups became clearer.

It was late when the visitors arrived, but after a little refreshment, they all decided to sit out on the veranda.

"You've heard the one about the Quaker man, a pacifist of course, who heard a robber in his home on the lower floor?" Bob started. "He went down stairs and, pointing his gun at the robber, said, 'Pardon me, sir, but thou standist where I am about to shoot.'" Mr. Ford, himself a Quaker, laughed heartily at Bob's joke.

They exchanged more pleasantries, but quite abruptly Kitty asked, "Mr. Andersen, will you tell us how it was you came to know Mr. Hotchkiss?" She was anxious to get this story straight in her mind.

When Mother told stories of Mr. Andersen, she would mimic his Danish accent.

"It vas in 1903 vhen I came to America from Denmark vith my friend. After a vhile I came to study at da Cleveland Friends College. One night, in 1906, Mr. Hotchkiss spoke there to the students and when he asked for young ones to go back with him to the mission field, I found myself standing up. When I left that meeting, a lady put a little paper into my hand."

Everyone looked at him in anticipation.

"It said a woman named Miss Nunn would like to meet with me. So we met. She said she was going to buy clothes for me, and also my boat ticket, if I would go and work with Mr. Hotchkiss in Africa. This she did. I came here in 1907 along with Mr. Swenson from Sweden."

"Did you go then to the Lumbwa Industrial Mission?" Kitty tipped her head to one side as she tried to take it all in.

"No, it was not yet. Mr. Hotchkiss arrived in 1895 and was first working with the Africa Inland Mission. He left the AIM in 1899 and returned to the U.S. to find staff for the mission he hoped to establish under the Friends Church. In 1902, Mr. Hotchkiss brought back to Africa Mr. Arthur Chilson and Edgar Hole. They made the Kaimosi station that was then called the Friends Africa Industrial Mission with the Kavirondo people. But in 1904, he came to the United States; then that was when I was recruited."

"Did Miss Nunn continue to support you?" Kitty wondered.

"Yes, she did continue all along, and in 1923 when Litein station where we now live was finally granted, it was time for my wife and me to go on furlough. Miss Nunn was again going to supply the funds. Since the government required that we occupy the station immediately, we asked her if she would be willing to send the funds she had set aside for the trip and instead let us use them to start the new station. She agreed, but we never saw her again. She died before we were able to go on furlough.

"But long before that time, when I was still single and working with Mr. Hotchkiss, he asked the government for the Lumbwa station, but the land was not granted until 1909. At first, he wanted to work with the Nandi folk. They were a warlike tribe and very difficult, so he resigned himself to work with the Kipsigis tribe who are similar but more approachable. I stayed with the Lumbwa station while Mr. Hotchkiss went back to America.

"What is the cost of these mission stations?"

"The Lumbwa station was 1,685 acres of land on a 99-year lease for an annual rental fee of Kenya shillings 202/32… believe it or not."

"This would be about $30 per month depending on the exchange rate?" Bob questioned.

"That's right. But getting back to Mr. Hotchkiss. When he came back in 1911, with him were the Hoyts, the Kramers, the Estocks, and Mr. Smith."

"The Hoyts were with Mr. Hotchkiss also?" Kitty seemed alarmed. She had recently met the Hoyts who were now with the Friends Mission. "When did they leave him?"

"Mr. Chilson offered them the option of joining the Friends Mission, and not long after they arrived, I think about nine months, they moved to Kaimosi."

There was a long pause; then Bob queried, "Clara, how does your father fit into the story?"

"Well, he was at the Cleveland Bible College and actually introduced Mr. Chilson (whom Mr. Andersen just mentioned) to Mr. Hotchkiss in 1908. But my parents didn't come to Kenya until 1914 when the Chilsons returned for their second term."

Kitty sighed, "It is hard to take all of this in. Did none of those people continue to work with Mr. Hotchkiss?"

"Not a one." Clara answered and looked away.

"It is troublesome that there were such divisions among the missionaries," Bob said as his face clouded with concern.

"But there were. That there surely were!" Mr. Andersen's voice was grave.

The lanterns flickered and the air was becoming chilly. Kitty and Bob could tell that this subject was best left alone for now. As they tried to fall asleep, they pondered the information they had just been told. They still had a great respect for this man who had been their mentor. Accordingly, sleep did not come easily. There was so much to learn, so much to understand.

Dear Folks: Malava, Broderick Falls, Kenya Colony, British East Africa, Dec. 26, 1932

Christmas has come and gone and it surely hasn't seemed like the Holiday Season. We have had roses out of our garden and other flowers and green vegetables and oranges etc.

But there have surely been celebrations here after the African fashion. Yesterday there were between 500 and 1000 here at this station and they had a Union service. We sang Christmas pieces for them and they seemed to appreciate it so much. But about the most thrilling, after we were through, the Big Chief over all this section and his 6 favorite wives and about 4 of his officers were entertained in the parlor at tea.... Today the rest of the Christmas celebration went forward with native wrestling etc, and now and then a free-for-all fight when some few would lose their tempers or become displeased with something.

I spoke about the "patients." We have quite turned into a hospital. We have on hand now a boy that had an epileptic fit and fell into the fire. The natives think they have a devil and if they touch them they will get it so they just let them lie. Consequently this poor lad is terribly burned, legs, arms and back. Then there is a woman with a tiny baby and she has an ulcerated breast. Then there are two babies with cases of nearly pneumonia and a woman also with a bad chest cold. And there is a little girl with a terrible hand, I don't know what is the matter but have been poulticing it for two days. We took one woman to Kakamega for a tooth extraction and another to Kaimosi who had burned her foot to the bone, that is all the flesh was burned away. The natives are hearing of our work all over and a man came in tonight 8 miles for quinine for his baby. I could go on and on but you can get a little idea of how much we need a doctor....

Now I must tell you about our own Christmas and especially John's as we had no money to exchange personal gifts. We got a little tree, not much to look at until we doctored it up a bit.... Then we got out John's things we had brought and your gift. Faye and Kirk gave him a drum.... He surely enjoyed everything but I wish you could see him with his little car. He takes it to bed with him at night and for his nap. And seldom puts it down through the day....

Tomorrow Miss Ford goes to the hospital for an appendicitis operation. Kirk will drive her and Esther over and see what arrangements he can make for Faye. In the meantime we have been and are studying Swahili and it is some job. Here is the first part of I John 2:1 "Watoto, wangu, wadogo, na waundikia liaya illi msitende dhanachi." "Children my little, I am writing to you that you do no sin." A "toto" is a child. We learned the rest of it but I am not sure of all the words now. One word we have so much fun with is "chakua" and here chakua means "to carry."

It goes like this in present tense, positive: The negative goes like this:

Ninachukua	Thunachakua	Sichukui	Hatuchukui
Unachukua	Muachakua	Huchukui	Hainchukui
Anachukua	Wanachakua	Hachukui	Hanachukui

Pronounce all the vowels long and each one a separate syllable and you will see what a tongue twister this one is – for example the first Ni(nè) – Nä – chü – kü – (ä) All "i's" are like long "è."

Well, I must close.. Much love, Catharine

"...we...are studying Swahili and it is some job."

56

Learning more than Swahili

Kitty, Bob and the Kirks had been at Malava for a month now and were getting into the routines of mission life. They found that the nationals entered into their lives at many levels. They helped with cooking on the wood stove. They also assisted in supplying water brought by ox cart from the nearest river or lake. A few homes collected water from their roofs into huge round corrugated iron tanks. This water was saved for cooking and drinking primarily. There was no electricity. For washing, clothes were frequently taken to the river where stones were used as a scrub board.

In their new home at Malava, nationals, who had previously worked for missionaries, offered to help in their home. They were of the Ragooli or Maragoli people[*] — one of the eighteen sub tribes or "houses" of the Luhya tribe. While Kitty at first resisted the idea, she soon came to understand that this would be the only way she could have time to accomplish anything beyond her activities of daily living. Already Bob was working daily in the shops. Kitty was holding sewing classes, attending church services and playing the pump organ for services.

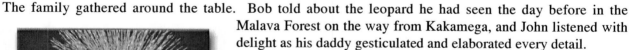

Anna Verne writes what might have been a normal day for Mother and Dad.

The day began early for Kitty—around 6:30 AM.

She requested warm water of the cook who had arrived to get the fire going in the stove and prepare breakfast. Bob had already left for the shop. A young helper built a fire in the fireplace and set the breakfast table. Breakfast consisted of *posho* (corn meal mush) or *bek* (millet porridge), as there was no cold cereal nor were there eggs to boil or fry.

"Come wash up in the warm water." Kitty slipped the little bathrobe on John, that she had bought in Nairobi, and washed the sand from his eyes.

"Is breakfast ready?" Bob asked as he came in from the woodworking shop, having assigned the workmen some jobs, and sharing a brief lesson from the Bible with prayer—a pattern he would always follow in the future.

The family gathered around the table. Bob told about the leopard he had seen the day before in the Malava Forest on the way from Kakamega, and John listened with delight as his daddy gesticulated and elaborated every detail.

Kavirondo crane

"It was a good breakfast, Muddie," John Boy said.

"Let's have a little devotional reading from *Streams in the Desert*, and then Daddy will pray."

A baby sitter arrived to help John Boy dress, brush teeth, and prepare for the day, so Kitty went to the kitchen to instruct the cook regarding menus for lunch and supper. Then, it was off to

---

[*] The Friends were the first missionaries to work with this tribe, starting in 1902, but the first "white man" the Luhya had contact with was probably H. M. Stanley as he voyaged around Lake Victoria in his search for the missing Scottish missionary, Dr. David Livingstone, in the 1870s.

language class. Not everyone in the Maragoli tribe knew the Kiswahili language that they were learning and trying to use whenever possible. Clara spoke both fluently and was proving to be a good teacher, but

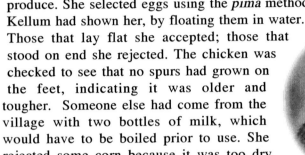

Kitty knew that eventually she would need to know the Kipsigis language if they were to work in the Sotik area, the initial plan when they came to Kenya.

Teatime mid morning didn't come any too soon! It was Kitty's opportunity to be with Bob and the family again, and she welcomed the break.

Before she returned to her study, someone came to the kitchen door selling produce. She selected eggs using the *pima* method Mrs. Kellum had shown her, by floating them in water. Those that lay flat she accepted; those that stood on end she rejected. The chicken was checked to see that no spurs had grown on the feet, indicating it was older and tougher. Someone else had come from the village with two bottles of milk, which would have to be boiled prior to use. She rejected some corn because it was too dry,

Rooster for sale!
Courtesy of Richard
Adkins

explaining to the vendor that she would buy corn only if milk was still in the kernels. There was enough time left to get to her last class before lunch at 12:30 PM.

Grey monkey

She was learning that food could best be preserved by canning since there were no refrigerators, so she would do some canning later in the day and catch up on her correspondence. She also needed to help with the dispensary work and check on dinner.

All homes had unlocked doors that were entered as the visitor called out without knocking. *"Hodi!"*

"Karibu!" The person within would call back as he came to welcome the visitor.

"The post has come!" was by far the most welcome news.

They all ran out to greet the post runner who had come on his bicycle all the way from Kaimosi. The mail came in a heavy canvas sack folded at the top to accommodate a lock. Only one person on the station had the key and the responsibility for distributing it. Mail was treasured, and it was with great joy that they read and reread each letter. If one came from America, John Boy also got to hear the news. Kitty tried hard to enhance the memories of his grandparents and other relatives from whom he was now distanced.

Bob had returned to the shop, and Kitty had time now to spend with her child. He went with her to the flower garden to gather some roses for the dinner table. In the absence of electricity, before evening came, the lamps had to be filled, the wicks trimmed, and the candles made ready for carrying to the bedroom.

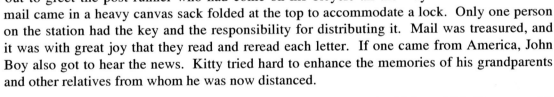

Around the mission stations, it was not unusual to see animals of various types. Grey monkeys (the Boscoe toy was made to look like them), as Mother mentions in a later letter, and Kavirondo cranes, named for this (Kavirondo) region and also known as golden crested cranes, were always a delight to see.

Dear Folks: January 8, 1933

Here it is Sunday again and I hardly know where the week has gone. We have been studying the language and taking care of sick folks etc. etc. and the days have slipped away. We received Mother's letter of Nov. 26th last week. It surely does seem to take a long time to reach us. It doesn't seem that you are now just receiving our letters written at Thanksgiving time. I think we will wait and get a whole lot of news and then send it airmail. That way you will get it in about two weeks.

We have had so many new experiences in the hospital.... The burned boy is healing nicely and the old father is quite well again, and several others of the patients are up and around who had been sick in bed.

We are laboring away at Swahili but will be pretty glad when Clara gets back to go on with our lessons.... I don't know whether I told you that Clara Ford went to the hospital two weeks ago Thurs. for her operation, so we expect her home sometime the latter part of this week...

...Bob took Esther to meet her father at Kakamaga on Clara's motorcycle. It has a sidecar and they took John with them. Coming back, he rode in the sidecar all by himself. He surely did look cute. We will try and get a snap of him in it. He loves to ride in it and you'd imagine he would get afraid. Yesterday we went out where the boys are cutting up some wood and the place was alive with monkeys. They'd come out to watch us and would chatter at us and at each other. John could hear them but he couldn't see them. He has his little monkey he got at the Christmas tree and he calls it Boscoe. So he called these others more Boscoes....

Next Sunday is our week to go to the miners' service. We haven't succeeded in getting the S.S. started yet but are still hoping it may materialize.

Last week we got part of a beef and cold packed 13 cans of meat. We opened a can this a.m. and found we had cooked it too long. It is good but falls to pieces very easily. Bob planted a garden, and it is now beginning to come up. Everything grows luxuriously here. We have wonderful American Beauty roses. If they were taken care of properly, they would be great. Mr. Ford said he had seen them 8 inches across....

Well, the day is over. The supper work is done up, and Bob is putting the baby to sleep. Over across the way, the native children are having a great old sing, and every time they pause, John says, "More." They have very obligingly continued each time, but they can't keep it up all night.

This afternoon an old, old woman came to the porch begging. There was an old rag, a piece of Bob's shirt, that had fallen down off the railing, and she wanted it. She was surely a sight, had a hole in her lower lip as big as a quarter and holes in her ears. She had wires around her head and breasts and a blanket and skin around her. She called me "mama" and jabbered away asking for something, I suppose to eat, but I couldn't tell what she said, of course. Anyway we gave her the cloth.

Well, I must close and get to bed. The mail goes tomorrow, so I hope this letter will come through in good time. I hope also to hear from you folks again then.... Hope all are well, and a prayer crosses the continent and the ocean and on over to Ohio that God may take care of you all.

Love from us, Catharine

" The burned boy is healing nicely and the old father is quite well again..."

"…confused by…stories…innuendoes."

In the morning, Kitty saw Clara coming down the path to the house. The day before she had asked her to drop by for tea.

"It is so good to have you home, Clara." Kitty was amazed to see how quickly she had recovered from her appendectomy.

"I'm glad to have that behind me! You will enjoy the hospital at Kampala. The people are top notch. They will take good care of you when your time comes." Clara was always matter-of-fact and without an ounce of self-pity.

"That is reassuring. I had a difficult delivery with John Boy, so it is encouraging to know I will be in good hands." Kitty poured the tea she had prepared for Clara and looked at her co-worker. While they were alone together, perhaps, finally, Kitty could ask about some things that continued to haunt her.

"Clara, will you answer some questions for me?" She started, "I would like to know what has caused such a great division among the missionaries. I'm confused by the various stories and innuendoes."

"It is complicated. I don't know everything, but I'll try to tell you what I know. Africa Inland Mission is the largest of the Protestant missions in all of Kenya. Preceding the arrival of the AIM missionaries, there were the Scottish missionaries Livingstone and Stanley, then other missionaries arrived in Kenya from the Anglican Church in 1844 as the Church Missionary Society."

"That's the British mission?"

"Yes, Britain's official Anglican church. But in addition, the British Methodist Mission started a work in 1887. The Scotch Presbyterians and then the Lutherans followed in about 1891, while our friend Mr. Hotchkiss came in 1895. He was one among seven under the Africa Inland Mission. Within a year, Mr. Hotchkiss was the only one remaining, as four had died, and the remaining two women had decided to return to the U.S. In those days, there were no railways or roads, so people traveled in long caravans with porters carrying their goods. They had no defense against malaria, black water fever, and dysentery, and many died, including the leader of the Africa Inland Mission, Peter Scott. Living in this country was very tough then. The tsetse flies killed oxen and mules, so the use of animals as beasts of burden frequently failed. The native people were very hostile, especially the Nandi and Maasai tribes. In fact, many stories are told about the Nandi tribe among whom Mr. Hotchkiss had originally wanted to work."

"What a sacrifice it took to get missions started! Do you know any of the Nandi stories?"

"Yes! By that time the railway and telegraph services were being developed in Kenya, and the *morani*(the warriors of the Nandi tribe) made great sport of spoiling the European efforts to build the telephone system. They would cut lengths of the beautiful telegraph wire and give it to their women to use for jewelry. They did such things as burn a telegraph office and a rations store, they attacked railway personnel and murdered white settlers, and successfully hid from the *askari* (police) expeditions sent to right the wrongs they committed. The British spent a great deal of money trying to subdue them."

"Where do these Nandi live?"

"Not far from here, northeast of Kaimosi, is the town of Kapsabet. It is in the Nandi district."

"I have heard of the Nandi hills and the Nandi forest. Mr. Hotchkiss has told us many stories about those early times. When he was coming up from the coast, he had to shoot rhino that were attacking his caravan. He also told us about a time when the natives were not allowing him to get any food. He was starving. A woman passing by his hut each day tipped her head to allow cassava root to fall out of the basket on her head. This supply of food kept him alive until he was able to win the hearts of the people."

Clara nodded, "For awhile, he was the only AIM missionary in Kenya, and then when he returned to the U.S., he resigned from the AIM for reasons I don't know. He was very strong willed and independent, and there must have been some demand with which he could not comply. That is when he began to recruit from the Friends Church. He had a vision to establish an industrial mission where natives could be taught to grow coffee, plow with oxen or be taught a trade. He was impressed with the devastation that the yearly famine caused and tried to find ways to help the Africans look ahead and overcome their tendency to live only one day at a time.

"In any case, Mr. Hoyt, a builder, Mr. and Mrs. Kramer, Dr. and Mrs. Estock and a single man, Mr. Smith, joined him in 1911. Having carved out his work, Mr. Hotchkiss demanded the leadership position. The talented men whom he had recruited became discouraged by his rigid restrictive requirements for timeliness and precision. Also, although he had clear-cut goals and plans, he would not communicate adequately with his helpers, and when their efforts to communicate with him failed, they became discouraged and all defected. Later, Mr. Andersen came out as a single man to help Mr. Hotchkiss, but he, too, found him impossible to work with, so after he married his wife who was here under the Pentecostal mission, Mr. Andersen joined the Africa Inland Mission. My family has been aware of this history and has witnessed the behavior of Mr. Hotchkiss that alienated missionaries and government officials as well. His dream was ruined, and he became a bitter and broken man."

"That is not the man I know, Clara. He is so tender and kind. It is just impossible for me to believe all this."

"He did change; I saw the change in him. When his wife became ill, and he prepared to go again to the States, I spoke with him, as you know, because our mission had recruited me with the express duty of finding a location for them. Of course, Mr. Hotchkiss was brokenhearted over his wife's illness. It was then he offered us his mission. He was truly a changed man at that time. He also met with several missionaries he had alienated, but it was difficult to believe his contrition, so attitudes did not change significantly."

"The hurts must have been very deep." Kitty struggled to maintain her composure.

"Well, for example, it was believed that he misrepresented his mission structure. He was required to have a board to make his organization legal both in this country and in America. When Mr. Hoyt and others investigated this, he found Mr. H. to be the only representative on the board and all the mission assets were in his name. Mr. Hotchkiss acknowledged that he was not a business man and claimed it was only an oversight, but nonetheless, the British Government no longer recognizes him as a legitimate missionary, and therefore, his assets apparently cannot be turned over to us."

"Does our mission board know all this?"

"Yes, I have written confidential letters to them as I've become aware of problems."

"Then how is it that our mission has let him join us? It is his intention to return is it not?"

"Yes, it is. The information was not all available at the time. Also in 1931, after Mr. Andersen realized that Mr. Hotchkiss's assets were not available to our mission, he wrote a letter to his (the AIM) asking that the Litein station be turned over to our mission, as the AIM was short of funds to continue. I was very hopeful that that would be our solution, but the home board of AIM disagreed and refused."

"The opposition has come because of our association with Mr. Hotchkiss then?"

"That is certainly part of it. Additionally, no one has ever heard of our mission, and some new missions have been very disruptive to the point of confrontations with the Africans. In one case, people were killed. The body that serves as a liaison between the missions and the government has recently become very reluctant to accept new groups, given what happened," Clara continued.

"That is part of the reason we will be going to Kijabi to again seek an affiliation with the AIM in hopes that we can still become a part of the Litein work. But because they had these unfortunate experiences with Mr. Hotchkiss, and we are affiliated with him, they also are reluctant. Both Mr. Andersen and my father feel that we should still pursue that avenue."

"I see, but if that fails, we still have to acquire an entirely new plot." Kitty felt like something was twisting inside her stomach. She could hardly breathe. She still dearly loved Mr. Hotchkiss and believed this love could be sustained with understanding. "I'm afraid I can't handle anymore, Clara. Mr. H. has meant a great deal to us. We have held him in such high regard that facing his failures is devastating."

"It is a very hard thing. Perhaps this upcoming meeting at Kijabi of the Kenya Mission Council[*] will solve some of our problems."

Kitty could feel the baby moving. John Boy was awakening from his nap, and she was jarred back to the moment. In her heart she prayed, "Lord, please help us all." As Clara left, Kitty turned her thoughts back to the coming baby and the preparations she must make.

Bob, Kitty and John taken just before they left for Kenya

---

[*] This inter-mission group served as a liaison between missions and government. It was first known as the Kikuyu Mission Council; in 1924 it became the Kenya Mission Council; in 1943 the Christian Council of Kenya and now is the National Christian Council of Kenya.

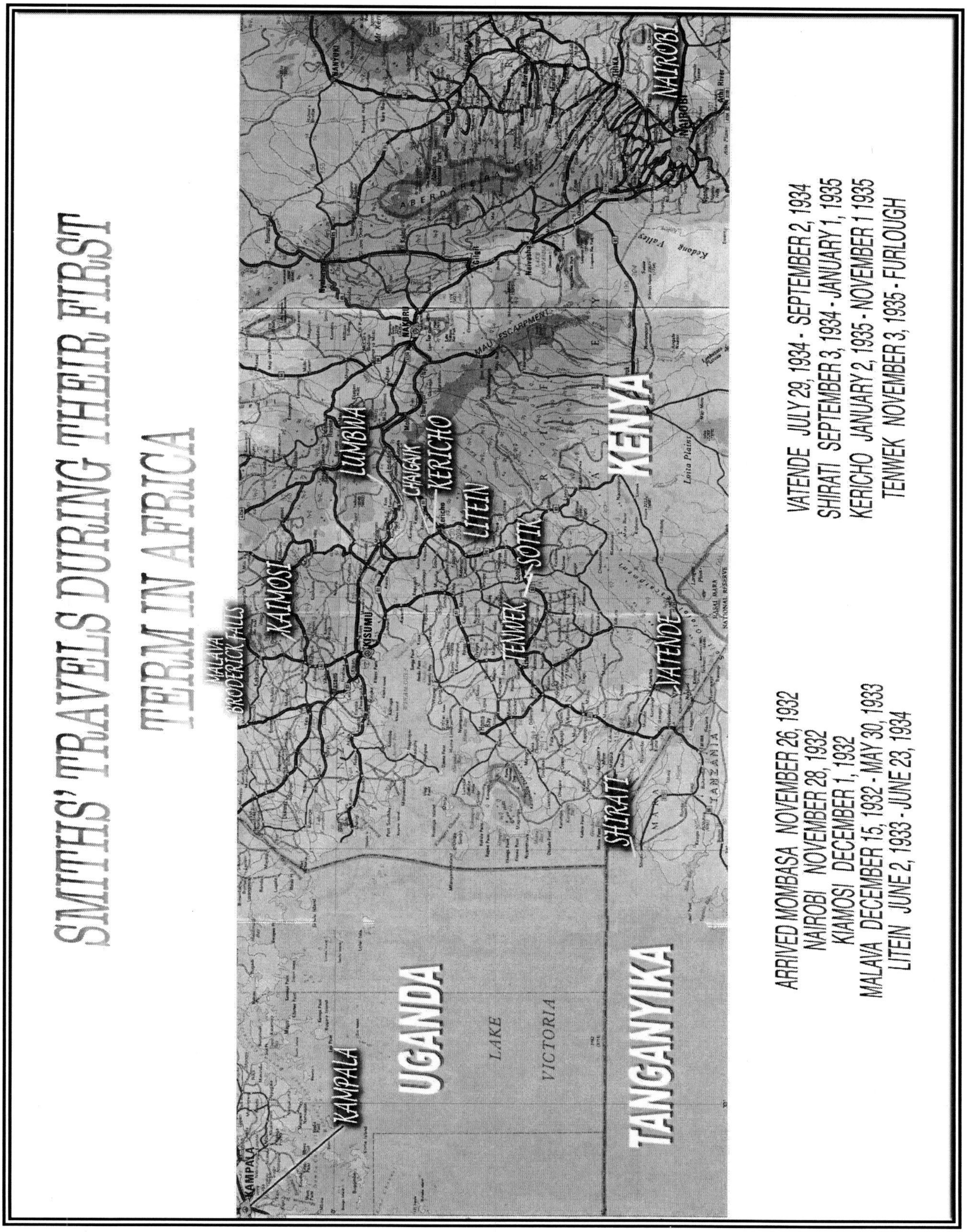

SMITHS' TRAVELS DURING THEIR FIRST TERM IN AFRICA

VATENDE JULY 29, 1934 - SEPTEMBER 2, 1934
SHIRATI SEPTEMBER 3, 1934 - JANUARY 1, 1935
KERICHO JANUARY 2, 1935 - NOVEMBER 1 1935
TENWEK NOVEMBER 3, 1935 - FURLOUGH

ARRIVED MOMBASA NOVEMBER 26, 1932
NAIROBI NOVEMBER 28, 1932
KIAMOSI DECEMBER 1, 1932
MALAVA DECEMBER 15, 1932 - MAY 30, 1933
LITEIN JUNE 2, 1933 - JUNE 23, 1934

UGANDA

KAMPALA

LAKE VICTORIA

TANGANYIKA

KENYA

NAIROBI

KAIMOSI

LUMBWA

KERICHO
CHAIGAIK
LITEIN
SOTIK
TENWEK
VATENDE

SHIRATI

MALAVA BROEDERICK FALLS

KUSUMU

Dear Folks at Home: Kaimosi, Kenya Colony, British East Africa, Jan. 22, 1933

We received your Christmas letters last week and were surely delighted to get them. They were written Nov 26th, but we also received one from Mother Smith written Dec. 4th. It came through quite well. John was very much pleased about his little "Doggie." We received quite a bit of mail at that time. It had been forwarded to us from Kericho. I guess that is one reason it is quite late in coming. I am anxious to know how long it takes for a letter to come from us to you....

As you see by the address, we are at Kaimosi again. The council of the A.I.M. met in Kijabi, and the boys were supposed to meet with them, and Miss Ford was to go also. She returned from the hospital on Monday but had recovered so well that she seemed able to take the trip. So that would have left us alone on the station with no means of transportation and no means of sending quick messages, and as the doctor said Faye might have two weeks more and she might have six, it was a little risky. So we came here and are staying again with the Kellums. They have been so nice to us, and I am sure this is quite like an imposition, but they don't make us feel like it for a moment.

...The Kellums have a little girl just a year old but she walks all over and plays quite nicely. Then there is a little boy two months younger, and a boy and a girl (10 and 11), so it is quite a new experience. John is minding much better than he did.... I wish you could hear him read his "Mother Goose" book. He can say about half the rhymes.... He says "sunbean" and "birdies"- he likes especially the last verse "sooty black bird on-a-wall." He can pick out Jesus in most of the pictures and he says, "Jesus in-a-sky." Once in a great while he'll, of his own accord, get very affectionate. Then he'll come and say "kiss, Mummie," and put up his little mouth all puckered.... He misses his Daddy, as he's quite a companion of his. He dearly loves to go "out sop" (out in the shop) with Bob when he is working. He's such a help.

Bob shot a deer last week. It was quite a joke, however, as he picked out the biggest so he would get a buck but he got an old cow. My but it was tough. But we cold-packed some and are making dried-beef (venison) out of the rest. If it gets like some we tasted, it will be delicious. You soak it first in a salt brine and then hang it up to dry....

We have been studying Swahili, and I have been doing some crocheting. Otherwise, we have been quite lazy since we came here. We are invited out to tea this evening at the doctor's, so I guess I will have to go and get ready. We have a service tonight at Hoyts' again, and so we will go to it. It is the only European service.

My, I wish you could see this spot. It is certainly beautiful. We have had two showers so everything is lovely and green. I am on the veranda writing and just at my side is a bush about as big as three ordinary lilac bushes, just covered with large lavender blossoms. I don't know what it is called. Then they have great geraniums and lilies and wisteria and all sorts of plants.

My how I wished for your button box and rag box and patch box!

We had a tiny baby last week.... It looked starved but must have had more the matter than that, as it died. Our dispensary still continues.... Dr. Mitchiner came last week on his monthly call and said they had done very well, especially about the burned boy.

Well, I must close. Will try and write again from here. Will have a great deal to write after the boys get back as this council will settle some things of very great importance to us. Keep on writing often. Hope you are all well.

Much love, Catharine & John

"...this council will settle some things of very great importance to us."

Waiting for the babies

At her mother's knee, Mother had learned to knit, crochet, and tat, and somewhere along the line, perhaps from her father, she had learned to name and appreciate many varieties of material. She was a skilled seamstress, working primarily by hand except when she had access to a sewing machine. It was only on rare occasions that she could use her knowledge, as her choices were few—missionaries were most often sent printed flower sacks to use for material and all of us children wore clothes made from them.

Kaimosi Station
February 3, 1933

...I am going to try and get some fine material and make some more little dresses as I have only 2 new ones and some of John's will be too large at first. His were all short dresses except his baptismal dress. I think I shall also crochet and tat a little as there will be no trimming otherwise. Five-cent and ten-cent lace isn't one of the things we can get. I shall put on some little embroidery also.

I wish you could hear some of John's cute sayings. The other day when he was getting ready for his nap he was talking to Boscoe. That is his monkey and they are inseparable companions. He said, "Look, Boscoe, Don make a goose" and sure enough he had his little hand up to the wall where its shadow could be seen and was crooking his little finger up and down saying "Clack, clack." Pretty soon he sort of whined and I looked over to see why. He had both Boscoe's hands up over his eyes and was saying "Boscoe cry, Boscoe cry." Then he said, "Now Boscoe, let Don get dat booger man." The other day he began calling us Bob and Kitty. We didn't even notice it. Just said, "John, who is Bob?" and finally got him to say "It's Daddy and Kitty is Mummie" and that's all there was to it. Once in a while he will revert to it but not for long. Sometimes he has called me "Mudder" and it surely does sound sweet. But he is wild about Bob, cries when he leaves and when he returns won't let him out of his sight. Bob has his wish for someone to trail him around when he works too, as he is at his heels constantly. He dearly loves to go to the "sop" (shop). I am not sorry he is so attached to him, however, as he will not be so lonesome while I have to be away.

"John...is wild about Bob."

Two or three more weeks remained before the babies were to arrive. Kitty and Bob worried about the coming of this new baby. Kitty's delivery with John had been traumatic, and she had never completely recovered, so in this new environment, they felt vulnerable and uncertain as the day of delivery approached.

The expectation that they would move to Sotik soon thereafter was dimming. It still was not clear to the Smiths that before the government would approve a mission site, their organization had to be accepted by the other mission organizations already working in Kenya. Still that seemed a minor hurdle compared to getting approval from the Local Native Council, the District Commissioner and finally the Kenya government body. But in January of 1933, Faye's and Kitty's husbands and Clara returned from Kijabi with the unwelcome news that the issue of their acceptance had effectively been tabled rather than approved by the governing body called the Kenya Council of Churches.

Malava Station, Kenya Colony
British East Africa, Feb. 12, 1933

Dear Folks at Home:

Here it is Lincoln's birthday. I have been thinking of his great sacrifice for the black people at home, for their emancipation, and for the greater sacrifice of Jesus for the emancipation of humanity and yet so few know of it, and of those who know, how few have received.

It is Sunday again and we are planning to go to the women's service. We have a little folding organ now, and I can play for their singing which they seem to enjoy so much. But it all seems very little so far.

We are planning to help the wives of our boys to make some clothes for their children and also for themselves next week. We got some shorts for the boys, as they were both pretty ragged, but especially Sami's wife needs clothes. He used to be a teacher, but he backslid and lost his job and had no money. Then he was reclaimed, and Mr. Ford was anxious that he have a chance again so we hired him to do our washing and house work. He is a very good worker and washes very well, so we are anxious to help him all we can. Twiolli's wife is very much advanced. She can sew and has several very nice dresses that have been given to her. She has two quite small children while the other has four children, two boys and two girls.

Well, Faye and Kirk went to Kampala last Friday. We are all very anxious to know all the developments etc. She is not due until tomorrow but the trip might have hurried things up a bit. When we ask John about where Faye is he says, "gone to Kampala to get little babies budder." I wish you could hear the inflections, He says the last three words way up high as if it were the emphatic part. He is quite faithful in his prayers also and prays over and over for different ones in his, "God bless etc.." When we are having family worship or grace at the table, and he thinks we have prayed long enough, he'll say, "Amen."......

John has a very decided will of his own and doesn't always give up his notions easily. He is quite heartbroken when he gets a spanking, however. He'll come to me --Mudder sank, Daddie sank." And then when I'll say, "Why did Mother spank?" he'll usually tell the reason. If I make him sit on a chair, he'll stand it so long then he'll say, "Mudder, Don good boy," and I'll say, "John do you think you can be good if Mother lets you get down?" And he'll say, "Yes Mudder." If I ask him to do something he doesn't want to do, he will say, "No sanks oo- Mudder." ...He is as polite as he can be. If he accidentally hits you or something of that sort, he'll say "Pardon me, Mudder" and he'll look at you so earnestly with his head on one side.

...Last night we took a little ride (in the motorcycle) around the big woods near here and even though the road was pretty bad, the thing rode fine and John and I both got to see three colobus monkeys. They are a very rare specimen even in Africa, and Malava forest is one of the few places where they are. They are a large monkey...and they are beautiful white with black stripes on each side. They have a great flowing tail as long as and shaped like a cow's tail, but it is much more hairy and wavy at the end..... There are also large baboons here.

Colobus monkey

66

> *The boys and Clara and Esther, Mr. Jensen and Mr. Andersen took the trip down into Sotik to meet with the chiefs etc. and to see about a location. Their trip wasn't as successful as they had hoped, but they feel as if good were going to come of it in the end. When the D.C. I spoke of before found they were going, he sent a native runner to all the chiefs and told them to refuse permission, but the boys heard that the people are trying to get rid of this D.C. and so the next one may be better. It may be the Lord's way of removing the difficulty. They have two men working down there now and hope they may have some influence with these chiefs. So get the folks to praying about this....You probably won't hear from me again until after I go to the hospital. I am not sure whether we can afford a cable or not, so you may get the news via air also.*
>
> *Much love to all, Us 3*

"I'm not sure whether we can afford a cable or not...."

When Kitty and Bob arrived at Kampala, they checked the location of the hospital and then decided to look around. Uganda was much like Kenya in some ways, being part of British East Africa, but in other ways they found it quite different. Arab traders had moved inland from their enclaves along the Indian Ocean coast of East Africa and reached the interior of Uganda in the 1830s. At that time, there were several African kingdoms with well-developed political institutions dating back several centuries.

Kampala, which was the capital of Uganda, was still regarded as a town rather than a city. It spread over ten hills and derived its name from a Luganda expression *kasozi k'empala*, "the hill of antelopes."

The origins of the Kampala city went back to 1891 when Kabaka of Buganda had his court on Rubaga and Mengo hills. But earlier, in 1877, Anglican missionaries had arrived with the Christian message and, in 1885, in a place nearby Kampala called Namugongo, King Mutesa had executed several Christians, and by 1887, the number of martyrs had grown to 45. Memorials to these martyrs were erected in Kampala as well as Namugongo, and Kitty and Bob were able to visit some of these areas.

67

...Uganda (the country we are now in) is quite different from Kenya in many respects. The people here are very zealous to cover their bodies. They adopted a sort of style of the dress of India and wear yards and yards of cloth, beautiful silks some of them. Those who wear a rather plain dress put on plenty underneath until it looks like they had on hoop skirts. As to length, they touch the ground, but their arms are often bear and the necks, back, and front are very low. There are many prostitute women, and I suppose that is where they get their money for finery. They are not heavily ornamented nor are their faces disfigured or tattooed. The people have been in touch with civilization longer than in most countries....

Bob and I walked to the Cathedral the other morning. It is a beautiful building made similar to all the Episcopal Churches and quite elaborately carved. It was erected in memory of those who were murdered, and the tablet is there with the names of them on it. A man passing through here fell in love with the place and decided to make it his home. He built a little cottage and gave a pipe organ to the Cathedral. I imagine it is the only one in the country. It is not large and has just two manuals, but it is wonderful to find it way in the interior of Africa....

"Bob and I walked to the cathedral...built in honor of those who were murdered." Excerpt Feb. 23 letter

Dear Folks:

Malava Station, Broderick Falls
Kenya Colony B.E.A., Feb. 23, 1933

My heading should have been Kampala, as I am here waiting for "the little man or little maid," whichever it may be. The "doc" says the former and, as he was right in Faye's case, I guess he knows. In case it is a boy, we have decided to call him Robert Edward. We are hoping to send a cable if we can afford it, but don't be alarmed if you haven't received one as we find that they are most unsatisfactory and often delayed.

Faye's baby arrived last Sunday at 5:30 P.M. She had a "bit of a tussle" as the doctor said. The membranes ruptured at about 1:00 A.M. the night before. They tried to have it without instruments but she got very tired, and so they used them at the last. It is a boy, Donald Craig Kirkpatrick, weighed 8 lbs exactly, and looks a lot like Kirk. He has a wealth of dark curly hair, and rather small blue eyes....

Bob is here but has opportunity to go back Saturday with expenses paid, so is anxious that it be over with by then. John is with Kirk at Malava. I get so lonesome for him, I don't know what to do, but all reports say that he is doing real well and seems perfectly happy. We came over last Thursday and brought him but found that there was no place to stay here and the hotel was too expensive, while to camp out would have been very dangerous as this is a very bad malaria section down within town. The hospital is up on a high hill, but even so, everything is screened and we sleep with nets to be sure no mosquitoes can get to us....

Feb. 24th - Got lazy yesterday and did not finish. Bob was in a few moments this A.M. and was quite disappointed that nothing has yet happened. So am I for that matter, but I expect we must let "patience have her perfect work...."

The doctor was just in to see me. He says they are too busy today to have a baby, so I must wait till tomorrow, but not to put it off until Sunday. They said when Faye's baby arrived on Sunday they were going to write our board that our children wouldn't keep the Sabbath nor let anyone else keep it.

Well I must close. I am surely anxious to hear from you. It seems so long since I saw any mail from home. Hope all are well.   Much love,   Catharine

"...waiting for a little man or little maid...."

In Kitty's view, a Christian did not defile God's temple (i.e. one's body) by smoking, although she thoroughly loved the smell of some types of pipe tobacco. She was just becoming acquainted with British customs and having her first exposure to an Anglican mission.

> I like it here quite well, though it is English and consequently quite different from what we are used to. They are also very strict and at times, I think, quite foolish, but we are glad to put up with a few inconveniences because we are glad to have such a reliable place to go to....
>
> There is no doubt about their skill here. Bob hears almost every day from someone or other down in Kampala of some quite wonderful operation or black water fever or something they have pulled through here. They seem quite devout in their way. One of the doctors smokes a pipe, but for that matter many of the English clergymen do that and they seem not to think a thing of it...I've found the nurse (sisters they call them) quite idealistic about her mission and really serious about her call as a missionary.... They are very formal here, by that I mean, they go through prayers every morning etc. regularly and religiously. The native nurses are often seen praying with the native women. I don't know how the Lord looks at it all. I'm glad I don't have to decide.... Well, I must take a nap now and will continue later.

Excerpt from Feb. 23, 1933 letter

> Kampala, Uganda
> February 25, 1933
>
> Dear Folks,
>
> Anna Verne was born this A.M. at 5:30. She weighs 8 1/2 lbs. and is apparently all splendid. She came naturally in every way and without the need of ether. The doctor did the repair work in a very few minutes with Kitty under chloroform. She is now resting and I shall return in a few hours to be with her. There was no loss of blood and her color is splendid. The whole thing has been a marvelous success and we are rejoicing. We cannot afford a cable so are sending air mail. Be perfectly at ease for all is well. I might say that there was no tear this time. The repair work that I had reference to was the old trouble. Doc says she will be in better health than she has ever known following this second child with the repair work done. We are happy, and I trust you are now too.
>
> Your Kids.

"Anna Verne was born.... Be perfectly at ease for all is well."

THE DARKEST TIME IS JUST BEFORE THE DAWN

Bob left Kampala to relieve Kirk and Faye who were caring for John. When Kitty with the baby arrived home she wrote:

Malava Station, Broderick Falls
Kenya Colony, British E. Africa
March 20, 1933

Dear Folks:

Here we are at home again after being gone for just a month. We came back a week ago yesterday. The trip was such a long one that the doctor didn't think it wise to undertake it until we were quite strong....

I wish you could see John with the baby.... I have allowed him to hold her for a little and he is as proud as a peacock. Tomorrow he will be two years old and Anna Verne will be one month, so I am going to take their picture together....

Bob surely had everything fixed up nice when we got home. He had a dear little bed for the baby made.... I made a kapok mat for it....

"Bob surely had everything fixed up nice when we got home...."

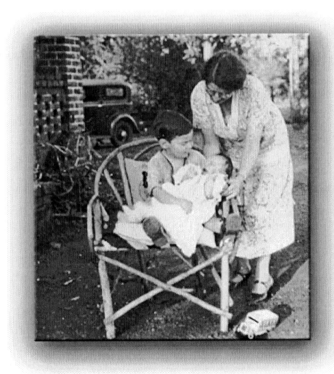

John, Anna Verne and Kitty

70

Mileage—Insurance—Salary

"…our worry not yours."

Malava, Broderick Falls
Kenya Colony, B.E. Africa
April 27th, 1933

Dear Dad B.
    Several days have passed since we received your letter. We have not sent nor received many letters directly from you. Mother B. has been quite regular in her weekly letter. One at home can hardly imagine how isolated we are from friends. One can really have fellowship with an Englishman under these conditions and that is saying something. So we do watch the weekly mail to see if....

    Glad to see the report of your January sales. Keep it up. I always felt you would make a go of it. I suppose insurance is difficult now as well as any business except a cash grocery business. I trust that you are keeping the old bus running as usual. I imagine you will fall over when I tell you that we have over 12,000 on the V-8 already. More than that, we have had no wrench on the motor yet. Sometimes we get as high as 28 mi. to the gallon. In 700 miles we do not have to add more than a pint of oil. We have broken a back spring and had some headlights go out but aside from that she rambles right along. As for power, well, the other night we started for Kitosh to get a load of goods for Miss Ford in a borrowed truck. We had gone about 10 miles from home and the truck ceased running. We tested the ignition and it was all right. We adjusted the carburetor and still she wouldn't run, so Kirk left me just at dusk and started to go the 10 miles to Malava on foot to get the car and tow. While he was running, a chevolet truck came along. I begged him to tow me, so he tied on and we started for home. After 5 miles, we overtook Kirk. But when almost home, we came to a hill and behold the Chev. truck (and it was as good as Chev.'s are) couldn't pull the truck up the hill. We untied and Kirk went on for the V-8. Well he was back soon and tied on and without a kick purred right up the hill truck and all. It sure has the power. We bring in logs from the forest with it -- logs we can scarcely roll. They talk about the rear end being weak and the clutch going bad. We have certainly given it a test. They say that cars that go 30,000 miles here are worthless after that. Well the V-8 is almost half worn out according to that but I know that it is good for 100,000 yet. It is some car!

The hardeat part about it is that, when we fill the tank, it is 28/- or $5.60. We have driven 6,000 miles in Africa at an average of 20 miles per gallon. We have then consumed over 300 gallons of petrol or gas. At 3/30 per gal. we have spent 990/00 in transportation. Don't think we are joy riding. When we took the girls to Uganda for the babies, we drove over 500 miles each time. Even at that, it was far less expensive than the railway. We are driving all hours of the night with patients who are too bad for us to care for, taking them to the hospital 38 miles away. Then our occasional runs for provisions and our safaris, ("i" pronounced as "e" -- each syllable given equal emphasis) or long journeys, on mission business have run mileage up. We are expecting to move very shortly now to Sotick [sic] where we will build the new station at one of Bro. H's out schools. This week we are going down with a truck load of our goods. As soon as we can arrange suitable quarters for babies and mothers, we will all move.

Little Anna Verne is developing rapidly. We expect to have the boys hanging around before long. She really is a sweet child. Her muddie is so pleased that she has the privilege of nursing her, no bottles, etc. But oh boy! we sure have sails in the wind....

Have over 800 on mailing list so I am writing almost constantly. Every time I write around, I spend about $50 on postage. That is one place spare change goes and oh how much of that we havc. There is very heavy expense in spite of the low cost of native food stuffs. Our traveling expenses with the baby cost $50, the hospital was $64, our taxes $24 – ammunition permit $2 –license for car $28 – expences other than hospital at Kampala $60 – living expenses per month $35 – after insurance was paid last check amounted to $32 so we were not even able to pay our board last month – now Africa is not free from financial burden either. Well that is our worry, not yours. Keep a stiff upper lip, and some day our troubles will be over. We expect under separate management we will be able to live cheaper in Sotik. I inquired what salary a C.M.S. missionary was receiving and he said 1500/- We received 300/-. We are not objecting but we find it very hard to get on with our present salary.

Well, will write again and send some more news maybe next time. Give our love to all.

Your son, Bob

"… over 800 on our mailing list so I am writing almost constantly."

CHAPTER 8

LITEIN—JUNE 2, 1933—JUNE 23, 1934

"You are not welcome."

It was May of 1933; almost six months had passed since their arrival at Malava. It had been a good interim time. They had learned some Swahili, the trade language; the babies had both arrived safely; and they had learned a great deal about mission work.

Mother told of the arrival of Mr. Andrew Andersen, along with Clara and her father at Malava. *Bwana Fundi* (Master Craftsman) was the name the Africans gave Mr. Andersen because of his building skills, and Mother often referred to him by this name. Also, when she told these stories she used Mr. Andersen's accent.

Mr. Andersen was tall and muscular, a typical Dane with blond hair. His bright blue eyes were unforgettable, and they twinkled as he said, *"Vell, de leetle babes are here now, and I tink de time has come dat you all should come to my mission station at Litein."*

And continuing in his delightful Danish brogue though not reflected here, he explained, "Until things are worked out with the government on where you will be, there is no reason that you cannot stay with us and help until a site for your own work can be established. We don't have housing, but you can live in two rooms in the hospital until Bob can build a place. Kirk and Faye can use an office and an annex in the hospital or rent a little brick home that belongs to my wife's mother, Mrs. Waldron. Clara can use a room in our home at Litein. My health is not good, and I could certainly use Bob's help on the station. Kirk, you can use Kericho as a base and do work in the jails there."

As early as July of 1931, Mr. Andersen had been notified that the Smiths would be coming to Africa and, on October 25, 1931, he had written a letter suggesting that AIM work with WGM until a site could be found. After their arrival, Mr. Andersen had gained approval from the AIM field director for them to help on the Litein station.

He continued to support the original goal, which was for the Smiths and Kirkpatricks to take over the work that Mr. Hotchkiss had started. Even though that was not working out at the moment, he believed it would in the end. There was significant utility in their coming to this place called Litein because the tribe with whom they hoped to ultimately work lived in the surrounding area. Here they could learn the tribal language and also begin to understand the customs of the Kipsigis tribe, quite different from the Luhya tribe at Malava.

On the 23rd of May, they were packed and on their way. Kitty at first shrugged off the chill and the feverish feeling she was having. She had worked hard to get everything packed, the house cleaned, and things put in order. But as they reached Kaimosi, there wasn't any doubt. Her teeth chattered, and chills ran up and down her spine. It was malaria.[*] She was so grateful to climb in a bed provided by the Kellums. How kind these missionaries had been to them on so many occasions, never making them feel that it was an imposition. It would be two days until she was able to continue on the trip to Litein. Meantime, Kirk and Faye were settling in their brick home in the town of Kericho several miles away.

On the day of their arrival, Mr. Andersen was away. As Kitty and Bob drove onto the station, they noticed a building on the right that was the schoolhouse. As they rounded the corner, they saw another building they later learned was the girls' home and above that a rectangular building that was the hospital. To the left was a small house and beside that what looked like a workshop. They gathered the children up, walked to the door and knocked. A lady appeared at the door.

"Hello! We are the Smiths," Kitty said.

The attractive lady's hair was nearly black, and her dark eyes were piercing. "Yes, I know," she said somewhat timidly. "Andrew told me you were coming, but as far as I am concerned, you are not welcome…."

There was a long pause. "Come in, though; we will make do until Andrew returns, and then we will discuss this some more." And so they did. There was no other choice!

"We hoped to be of help," Kitty stammered, dumbfounded by the reception.

"I understand that, but we are almost entirely out of food, and so crowded already." She held an infant in her arms, and two other little girls peeked out around their mother's skirt.

Mrs. Andersen served them tea and then pointed out their lodging. Instead of the two rooms in the hospital, they were directed to a one-room mud house. They began to settle in.

> *Dear Folks:*
>
> *Letein [sic] Station, Kericho*
> *Kenya, B.E.A., June 2 1933*
>
> *Here we are at last, and I wish you could see us. We will have to take a snap shot of our one-room house when we get a new film. It is sumpin! It is 14x14 and this is what we have in it: One double bed, John's bed, Anna Verne's bed, my large trunk, 2 steamer trunks (under large bed), my cedar chest, a chest of drawers, library table, cupboard for dishes, book rack (3 shelves) small round wicker table, two chairs, sewing machine, carpet sweeper, slop pail (2 potties), large basin (John's bath-tub), Bob's 2 guns, 3 suitcases (2 under John's bed, one on my trunk, with baby's things in), John's kiddie-car and little red wagon and sundry toys. This is all except four people. Now have you any idea how it is done? We are becoming experts at football, the huddle formation. We have to go outside to change our minds, and that little poem "Our two-by-four" is appropriate except that we can't teach our baby to creep upon the ceiling when we want to use the floor because the ceiling is simply two strips of matting. The walls are plastered in native style with mud and cow (?) (you know) and we smell like a nice clean stable, which really isn't so bad….*

We are becoming experts at football, the huddle formation."

---

[*]Malaria was caused by four different plasmodia: *P falciparum*, *P vivax*, *P ovale*, and *P malariae*. Humans acquire malaria from the bite of a female *Anopheles* mosquito. The dreaded black water fever is caused by *P falciparum*.

"You are not welcome." The words kept echoing in Kitty's head as she tried to arrange all of their belongings in the room that had been assigned to them. This was the first time she had actually heard it spoken even though it had hung around them like a heavy shadow ever since they had arrived in this wonderful and mysterious land. She looked at her husband who was whistling as he brought in all their earthly possessions.

"Kitty, don't you worry. She does not know us. Give it some time."

Anna Verne's twinkling eyes looked up at her, and her beautiful smile enveloped her face. "You precious baby." Kitty's heart swelled in love. She began to feel a growing assurance that they were going to make it all right. She realized that she could not know what burdens caused Mrs. Andersen to feel that they would only be an added burden.

"Don't you worry, Muddie," John Boy chimed in.

The plan was that Bob would soon build a small home out of material that could eventually be moved to their final place of work.

But things seemed to have a way of going haywire. It would be three more months before their little house would be completed. They were behind three months in receiving salaries, not to mention the decline of the dollar. There was no such thing as a general fund, and so the materials for the little house had to come from the Smiths' personal funds. Thirty dollars per month or, depending upon the exchange rate, 300 shillings was their expected salary, but this was more of an illusion than a reality. Occasionally they received a little money from friends or family or would borrow some in anticipation that their salaries would soon arrive. Moreover, they had had to go further into debt for the delivery of their baby. The accumulating burden of their finances continued to rest on their shoulders like a heavy weight, and there appeared to be no solution.

For lack of funds, the little house stood incomplete while all four of them lived in the 14x14 room. Kitty found it hard to believe that the mud and dung walls, the forest of wattle poles lashed by creeper twine and covered with thatch, and even the rustling insects and lizards hardly fazed her anymore. She spent a great deal of time washing diapers by hand. They seemed endless, and her hands were chapped, but the washboard worked well, and she was grateful for the use of it.

When her children were sleeping, she could leave the manure and cedar-scented warmth of her tiny room and step out into the moonlight. The star-studded sky faded against the bright tropical moonlight. Trumpet-shaped flowers on the nearby terraces were wonderfully fragrant, and the little hillside fell gradually away in front of her. She could make out the outline of their vegetable garden plot with its emerging plants. Bob joined her and slipping his arm around her said, "My stars! Kitty, what are you doing out here?"

"It's just so beautiful!" She loved the moonlight and the cool air.

Bob gazed past the garden at the shadow of the two-room house he was building. "In your new house, you will have windows to look out, and I'm going to put a little fireplace in each room, Kitty. We'll be nice and warm, and you won't have to go outside to look around. Come on in now. You need to get some rest."

Our little two-room house is coming along nicely and we hope to be able to move in soon. They are not going to make it out of mud because it takes so long for it to dry out, especially in the rainy season. Bob is going to try and get sheet iron for the outside, part way up, and the rest grass, and the inside matting for the walls, and cheap unbleached muslin for the ceiling. It won't be so bad, and the rooms will be 14'x14' each with a nice fire-place in each. Then there will be a little mud cook-house at the side and a little brick stove arrangement until our stove gets here.

We are to start in learning Kipsigis here and helping on this station. Kirks are living in Kericho in a little brick house, and he is to do some sort of work there in the jail and a sort of mission church. Then through the week, they will be in Sotik and will visit Bro. Hotchkiss' schools and have prayer groups here and special Swahili Bible Classes. Miss Ford is carrying these on.

I like it here so well and the country is beautiful. We are 7700 ft. in the air but I don't seem to mind the altitude. Both children are well, although John has been having a cold.

"I like it here so well...." Excerpt—June 2, 1933

Bob, usually up early, would continue to work through the heat of the day, but today he was not succeeding. "My head, my head," he groaned. He scooted sideways through the small space between their beds where he collapsed. By that evening, he was rolling around in bed and moaning. Kitty tried desperately to help, but he kept getting worse, and in two days, he was delirious.

Fearing spinal meningitis, and that it might be contagious, the children were hustled up to the Andersens'. Then the doctor was called.

Bob was more rational Wednesday, but I was about crazy with everyone suggesting it was something else and prescribing remedies so I was ready for a doctor.... When he came he assured us that it was nothing like spinal trouble and advised that we both take the cure at once as it was Bob's 6th attack. So we are taking Atebrin [sic] to be followed by Plasmaquine. The latter is very hard on the heart so we have to be completely quiet at that time. But it is guaranteed to cure 90% of the cases and if we are not one of the 10% we will be through with this old fever and I surely will be glad. I have had about enough of it. These past days have surely been a test to me. Brother Andersen said one day, "Many are the afflictions of the righteous but the Lord delivereth him out of them all." My how I did hang onto that verse through these days. My heart would have failed me many times were it not for that.

"...I was about crazy...." Excerpt—August 6, 1933 *

By now it was not hard to understand why Mrs. Andersen had opposed their coming to the station. She had grave concerns about her husband's health. Food was scarce. Everyone was struggling to survive and desperate to find ways to keep the work going. Mr. Andersen had come to Kenya as a single man and soon after met Vivian Waldron in Africa, working with another denomination. When they married, they had left their respective missions, joined the Africa Inland Mission (AIM) and since they no longer had a definite means of support, the AIM supplemented their income with monies from their general fund, when there was any available, but they were rarely available. Soon after they were married, Andrew had built a home that burned to the ground with everything they possessed. Destitute, they had gradually gotten back on their feet, aided by some nearby settlers. For years they had gone from one place to another establishing stations, but now they were settled at Litein and continued to subsist from one month to another. When there was nothing in the AIM general fund, Mr. Andersen would work for the tea companies until he could build up some reserve again. Along with everyone else, they suffered from the recent depression in the United States and the frequent devaluations of the dollar. Therefore, they were continuously wondering what the next day would bring. There simply was nothing to spare.

Since Kitty and Bob had arrived at Litein, they all were pooling their resources where they could. Kitty smiled as she thought about the seeds they had brought along. Not all the seeds grew well here, but how the peas had produced! Everyone on the station had had peas. Peas for lunch, peas for supper and then again, day after day, since there was little else. One evening as they were all gathered for worship they began to sing, "Peace, peace, wonderful peace, coming down from our Father above." Kitty began to smile and then as she looked up at the others, everyone was smiling and then laughing. "Peas, peas, wonderful peas." There were indeed blessings coming down from the Father above.

---

* Atabrine (quinicrine) was developed by Germans in the early 1930s and surprisingly was already available in Kenya at this time. It treated not only malaria but also parasitic diseases. It was later found that Atabrine was soaked up in muscle fiber and the liver, causing uncomfortable side effects before it was able to build up in the blood. By changing the dosage to a first-day big dose to saturate the tissues followed by small daily doses that would then go right to the blood, the problem was circumvented. Plasmaquine (cloroquine) is one of the older treatments, as is quinine.

As previously mentioned, the Kenya Mission Council had met in January of 1933 to consider their mission's approval. There had been a vote taken in which they agreed to consider but not to approve the mission.

Bob and Kirk made periodic visits to the Sotik area visiting the schools and churches that Mr. Hotchkiss had started and getting acquainted with the people. Kitty was working alongside Mrs. Andersen and learning from her the customs of the Kipsigis people.

In the meantime in America, the Board was meeting as early as April of this year, but Kitty and Bob would not learn the results of that meeting until at least six weeks had gone by.

> **Meeting of the Missionary Board - April 26, 1933**
>
> A motion prevailed that we take the motion regarding Brother Hotchkiss' case off the table and give it further consideration. After a lengthy, thorough discussion and prayer about the matter, during which time Brother Hotchkiss was called in, it was moved by Bro. Bishop that as a substitute to the original motion we, with deep and sincere regret, accept the resignation of Brother Hotchkiss. Motion seconded by Bro. Anderson. Carried.
>
> By common consent it was agreed that the Secretary should formulate a resolution expressing our appreciation to Bro. Hotchkiss for his services and our regret that it is not possible for him to continue with us.

Brother Hotchkiss resigns.

They still held out hope for Mr. Andersen's plan for them to become affiliated with the Africa Inland Mission. They received the news of Mr. Hotchkiss's resignation with mixed emotions, and letters filled with concerns had arrived from folks at home who asked for clarification. Kitty decided it was time to tell them as much as she could understand.

Litein Station, Kericho
Kenya Colony,B.E.A.
July 2, 1933

Dear Folks at home:

Your good letters arrived in last week's mail and we were so glad to get them. I hardly know just how to answer the one part, that in regard to Bro. Hotchkiss. I have purposely refrained from writing some things in hopes that the break might not come, but now that it has, I will try and explain so you will not be too hard on the Board. In the first place, when the Board took over his work, it was with the idea that he was not going to return to the field at all. They took it in order to get an opening into the country. You know one cannot just come in and settle; there is a lot of government red-tape to go through in getting permission, a grant etc. Well, if we came to a work that was already established, we could settle on it and then ask for a further grant. When we first arrived, the District Commissioner was on the war path, so instead of going directly at the thing, we had to go in a round about way. He said he would not grant anything to the party who were coming to the Lumbwa Industrial Mission, so we were left high and dry. We sought an affiliation with the A.I.M.(Africa Inland Mission) because A.M.Andersen, our field advisor and the one in whose charge Bro. Hotchkiss left his schools, is a member of that mission and advised us to do so. This mission already occupies Kipsigis and could petition for the land grant and then turn it over to us. So the boys went to their Field Council Meeting with Bro. Andersen, and there the first difficulties arose. They absolutely refused to have anything to do with it or us because we were Bro. Hotchkiss's missionaries, and thereby hangs a long tale.

When Bro. Hotchkiss first came out, he brought a party all of whom died but himself and two women whom he took to the coast and sent home. At that time, he was alone and the only white man in Kipsigis if not in Kenya. He remained here for several years longer, two anyway, and then returned to America where he set the land on fire, and collected a second party to come out. In it was this Mr. and Mrs. Hoyt who are now with the Friends' Mission, and later this Mr. Andersen came out to join him. He had a doctor, a preacher, a farmer and an engineer. (Mr. Hoyt the agriculturist and Mr. Andersen the engineer). It was the latter who put in the turbine, the dynamo etc. It was at that time that Mr. Hotchkiss raised $10,000.00 for the Expedition and received his wonderful constituency. Well I can't go into the details of it all, but there was a terrible misunderstanding and a split up in the party. Bro. Hotchkiss settled down in the one little spot and put his farmer, his doctor, his preacher and all to work growing coffee. They felt his vision was terribly short and so it proved to be and then the funds that had been given, it is said were expended foolishly and invested only to be lost etc. Finally when the trouble began to brew, Mr. Hoyt went to him and told him the whole situation and that his party was threatening to leave, and they and his wife begged him to listen to reason, but he refused. The result was, the whole bunch packed up and left. These were terible times for his poor wife, I guess, and she lost a baby, and the older son said if missionaries fussed like that, he didn't want any of their religion etc., but Bro. H must have set his jaw and he'd have his way. Well, some of his party went away entirely, some joined the Friends, and some formed the A.I.M. From then on, there was open hostility. Bro. H's work went on but kept getting less and less, and he had to depend more and more on his coffee, then corn etc. She went through terrible privations, but he wouldn't give in. The other works then began to broaden and enlarge until they have spread throughout Kenya in different sections, the A.I.M. being the strongest outside of the Roman Catholic. This went on until Mrs. H.'s illness and return home. Then a change seemed to come over him, and he made friendly overtures to those with whom he had refused to have anything to do, and he joined up with the Prayer Conference and made everyone amazed at his attitude. This was just before he sailed. Mr. Andersen was one who helped raise all that money etc., and all these whom he had treated so shamefully rallied to his aid.

But because of past experiences, they would not join a work that he was to head. However, they were assured that he was not to be the head but just a part, one factor. So they agreed to ask for the grant and drew up jointly with the boys articles of affiliation.

All this was reported to the Board, necessarily, but it did not influence the final decision they made, according to Bro. H.'s written statement to Mr. Andersen; it was the fact that he (Bro. H.) could not endorse their policy which is that the main aim of the N.H.A. is to spread holiness. Their split raises a new and serious problem here, as we are here now under false pretenses, and if he returns and takes over his own work, it only adds to the difficulty unless we can go into the Vitende [sic]. I am heartily sorry the break came because I believe a real change has come to Bro. H. That is the only way in which I can reconcile the man I know and the one I've heard about here. I do hope we may work out an affiliation on the field if he does return. There is another difficulty. Bro H. in the past has compromised himself and has allowed his teachers to compromise with the heathen. It makes a serious situation as some have run away from stricter missions, and have joined him....

...We are now just waiting for the grant, and the D.C. is balking us at every turn. We think the Roman Catholics have applied perhaps for that very site we want. However, Bro. Andersen says he's not through yet, and there is to be another meeting of the men down there next week.

In the meantime, Bob is still working on our house. The idea is to put in such material as can be used again when we go to Sotik, as the Board does not have the funds now for permanent homes.

We are all well. Bob and I have finished one course of medicine and are supposed now to be free from malaria. We have another kind to take which is supposed to make us so we can't give it to anyone else.

I can't help but wonder about how things are there. I remember that this is July and the taxes are due, but I suppose before you get this, that will be settled, and you will have written us about it....

Our money came for which we are so thankful. Well, I must close and type a letter to Bro. Bishop for Bob. I do hope he can be at the camp Missionary Day, and you also. And I hope Bro. Terry will see that he gets a hearty reception.

Much love, Kitty

"The result was that the whole bunch packed up and left."

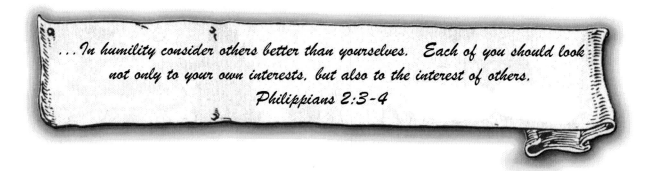

"...Tension among us...."

The following summarizes comments made to her mother in Mother's letters. The tensions had been building from the time that they had begun this trip with the Kirkpatricks, and grew steadily as time went on. It became a source of frustration and bewilderment as they tried to discover how to deal with it. Such disputes embarrassed and distressed them all, and they spent time discussing and praying for their resolution.

"How is the house coming, Bob?" Kitty set his meal in front of him.

"I've been working like a one-armed paper hanger with the hives."

"No, I mean really." She grinned at his oft-repeated expression.

"I'm still working away. The corrugated iron pieces came in, so I picked them up in Kericho while I was there. When I got home, I got the walls up. The roof will be grass but it will go up before you know it."

"Did you see Faye and Kirk in Kericho?"

"Yes, I sure did. Kirk is planning some meetings. He wants me to stop what I'm doing and go with him."

Mrs. Waldron's brick house in Kericho
Courtesy of Mary Honer

"Bob, you aren't going to, are you?" Kitty longed for some more space. The new little house would provide that, but they had already waited for nearly two months, living in the mud house, and more delays were not welcome.

"It's hard for them to understand our situation, since they are settled in their brick home."

"Why is there always this tension among us?"

"Kirk feels that the meetings are the most important thing. They are important, but other things are as well. But, I'll be jiggered if I can get that across. If we are ever to get a mission going, we will need a means of transporting building materials and goods. I want at least a two-ton truck; Kirk thinks, if anything, a pickup would do just fine. People ask what our needs are, and he writes and says we need a tent for his meetings…and now, that money has been earmarked for the tent. I feel we so much more desperately need a truck, but we never seem to agree on anything."

"I heard Clara say that tents are rarely used here for meetings. Large meetings are held outside if it is nice, and if it rains, no one comes anyway."

"Her father told me the same thing."

Tent purchased in 1933

"Does Kirk know that?"

"Yes, but he feels a tent would be a novelty and would draw in more crowds."

"Well, he may be right."

"But, Kitty, if we don't invest our money in the means to build a mission with schools, what will happen to these people who respond to the message of Christ in the tent meetings. They need nurturing and fellowship and teaching!"

"I agree, Bob. Do you think Kirk sees that?"

"We go around in circles about it. If I just had enough money, I would make the decision unilaterally. What I have to offer in this effort requires a truck. Kirk is an eloquent speaker; what he has to offer would be enhanced by a tent. And so spins the tale!"

"How does Clara feel about the truck?"

"She agrees we need one; in fact, the other day, she said she was considering buying it with her own funds. You know that the Barnetts are leaving and have one for sale. Also the Chilsons are moving to the Congo, and if we had a truck, I could be reimbursed for transporting their goods. I just wish we could all agree one time. Remember when we shot that 18-foot python at Malava?"

"How could I forget?!" Kitty mused.

"Well, we even disagreed over who should have the snake skin. He put the first shot into it so he felt it was his. But I actually killed it so I thought it was mine. I did let him have it as it wasn't that important." Bob shrugged and shook his head. "Why such a thing should be an issue, I can't imagine."

"Isn't it just the limit? There are so many things I didn't expect to face on a mission field," said Kitty wistfully, trying to comprehend what this all meant.

Eighteen-foot python

84

August 6, 1933

Dear Folks:

...We are now in our new little house. We celebrated Anna's birthday by having a house warming. We invited all the people on the station and Kirks from Kericho and Mrs. Andersen's mother from there, Mrs. Waldron. There were ten adults and six children. I had pressed chicken, potato salad, sandwiches, jam, tea, cocoa, two kinds of cake, fruit salad, cookies and candy. We had a very nice evening, and everyone said things tasted fine. I hope they told the truth.

I wish you could see the baby and have your wish granted to hold her. She is such a little darling and laughs constantly. She has such sweet and dainty baby ways, and my how she and John love each other. He isn't the least jealous of her and wants to share everything with her. Did I tell you about singing to her "There little girl don't cry, they've broken your doll, I know" etc. John was sitting on the floor and he looked up and said in the most surprised voice "Muddie, who broke Baby-sisser's dolly?" In the mornings he talks to her so cute. He'll climb up on his bed and say, "Look up here Baby sisser. You know who dis big fellah is up here. I'm John-boy."

We received a lovely letter from Brother Hotchkiss displaying the most beautiful spirit and saying that his break with the N.H.A. need make no difference at all among us and in the work out here. I am so glad he said it. He also sent us a gift of $10.00. I am believing that the Lord has "all things in His hands and is working this out His way."

"I wish you could see the baby and have your wish to hold her."

Kitty was learning many things about cooking. She was grateful for Isaiah[*], the African helper who, in the smoke-filled hut-kitchen adjacent to their little home, created at just the right moment—food, hot and wonderfully tasty with no other resource than a pot, three stones and a fire. She had learned how to search for greens called *keldichek* and could create a large variety of stews and soups that mixed well with the African staple *posho* (cornmeal mush). A frequent gift from the nationals was a gourd of the Kipsigis drink *mursik*[*] (clabbered milk mixed with charcoal). Politely drinking it at first had been a daunting challenge but eventually became a pleasure. With no refrigerator, they depended on the "jerked meat" both wild and domestic. In the high altitude, canned meat was not always reliable as the boiling point was lower and the longer cooking time required was sometimes overlooked.

Mursik gourds

---

[*] Isaiah A. Misoi began working with the Smiths on the Litein station. He traveled with Bob assisting with driving and food preparation. As a convert, he later became an elder and pastor in the church on the Tenwek station.

[*] *Mursik* is made by pouring fresh milk into a gourd in which a fern like plant has been burned to create an ash. The gourd is sealed with a leather lid often decorated with bright colored beads and left to stand (often placed in the rafters of a hut) while the milk sours. Every day or so, the gourd is shaken to mix the ash through the milk, giving it a pale gray color. When the milk has soured and sufficiently clabbered, usually three weeks, it is ready for consumption. Periodically the gourd is shaken and the consistency of the *mursik* is determined by how often this occurs.

Above: Smiths' tin house
Below: Dining room and
woodshed

August 1933

Bob is now finishing pouring the concrete on the stove. It is one he worked out the plans for and he built a form and is pouring in the sides now. The base and firebox are of brick, the oven of an old can and the top of sheet iron. It is going to be a nifty little thing and ought to work too, I think.

The babies are safely in bed. John had growing pains in one leg tonight. He plays so hard at his "working" through the day. Anna Verne is trying to get her upper teeth, I believe. She just bites on everything and scolds at things....

Tomorrow and I'm 31 years old. I guess that many years ago tonight you (Mother) weren't feeling so extra good. Does it seem that long ago? I found such a sweet thing about mothers young with paths before and mothers old with it behind, the paths of the little feet entrusted to their care. I'm so glad that the angels brought me to you when they were looking for a mother for me. You and Dad have given me a splendid heritage and a godly home. I hope Bob and I can pass such on to our children. The wise man said, "Her children rise up and call her blessed." I hope I may be such a mother to mine.

"It's going to be a nifty little thing...."

Ants…frustrations…disappointments…dependence

Kitty peered through the newly built window and down across the beautiful valley. She could feel her spirit being renewed. She set down her knitting when the baby cried and went to her. She had felt feverish when Kitty put her down for the night, her little cheeks rosy and eyes overflowing with tears. It was just a year since they had arrived in Africa. So much and yet so little had transpired.

Kitty held the baby to her and patted her back. Christmas was coming, their second in Africa. In these twelve months, they had received only six of the twelve monthly salaries. What was even worse, the value of the dollar had dropped, giving them an exchange rate of Ksh 3/- as compared to the Ksh 6/- they had first received. It seemed that no matter how hard they tried, they could not make the money stretch. She wanted desperately to make this a memorable Christmas for the children. The baby had fallen back to sleep, her feverish head resting on Kitty's shoulder. As she laid her back in bed, she prayed, "Dear Lord, keep my child safe from this illness that threatens her. I can only rely on Thee."

John Boy slept soundly in his little cot. She pulled the covers up and tucked them around his shoulders. Bob had just returned. It seemed he was always away, and she so enjoyed the times he was home.

> A mother's work seems to be the same the world over: to keep the house clean; to prepare wholesome and nourishing food for small bodies; to wash little faces, hands, and feet; to kiss bumped heads and bind up cut fingers, to invent new games and to have time to hear about troubles; to mend little socks and bigger ones, sew on buttons, make little dresses and suits, and enlarge outgrown ones. But greater than all that, she must help mould true characters, bend into the right channels strong little wills, and somehow reach the young hearts with the message of God's love. Then too, she must be a real wife and share life's problems and responsibilities and to make even a tiny cottage a real home. A missionary mother must be all of these and a missionary besides. I wonder if I will ever measure up to that standard, and am praying that I may be what the Lord expects of me.
> Yours for Africa,
> **MRS. R. K. SMITH**

Excerpt from the Children's Page of the "Call to Prayer"

"Kitty, have you heard about the driver ants? The African's call them *siafu*. My stars! You wouldn't believe the stories about them. They are like tiny soldiers that are insatiable marauders clinging tightly to one another and moving in massive colonies of 10,000 to 500,000. They travel across the land looking for food and attacking any animals that get in their path. Instead of stings, they have sharp pinchers that slice."

"Can they kill people?" Kitty wondered out loud.

"People have found tethered animals dead. The insects swarmed in through their ears, mouth and nose. They talk of babies being killed as well. The swarm moves forward like a monstrous seething black tide, around 15 meters wide at about two to three feet per minute. I saw them the other day out in the countryside, and everything in their path was scurrying away. They don't even stop at streams, but they walk over each other creating a bridge of their own bodies until the whole bunch have made it across."

"Bob, you're mixing British metres with American feet."

"Well, I'll be jiggered! This British influence is making inroads, I guess."

"You be careful now. Just because I married you doesn't mean I'm going to stop being your English teacher." Kitty smiled as she recalled the days at

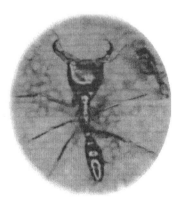

African pincher ant

Asbury College when she had actually been his teacher. One day she had corrected him in class, and spontaneously he had said, "But, sweetheart!" and then realizing what he had said, turned crimson.

September 1, 1933

We have been to a prayer conference at Barnetts and had a spirit of unity for the most part....

We had some experiences with the mud going and returning, but got through safe and sound. The only real danger was one when we skidded into a bank and got thrown around a little. We thought the wheel was broken off but not a thing was even cracked. John bit his tongue and cried a little but neither baby was hurt....

I must tell you of an experience we had just before we went on this trip. We are getting initiated into Africa "one by one." We were all sleeping and suddenly John began to cry. I asked him what was wrong and he said, "I want a gink water." So Bob got up and got it for him but he seemed to just fret and wouldn't take it. Then Bob said, "Something is biting me and slapped himself two or three places." John still fretted and I said, "John what is the matter?" He said, "I don't know Muddie, pray, Muddie, pray." So I started to pray as I always did after he finished his prayer, thinking that he had simply missed it as Bob put him to bed that night and prayed with him. Then he said, "I want your hand," and I stretched my arms out to give it to him when I felt a sharp sting. All this time Bob said he was being bitten, so I said, "We'll make a light," and he did, and we threw back the covers and there in rows around us both were the soldier ants. We both leaped out, and I slung off my night gown and grabbed my clothes. Bob grabbed John and wrapped him in his bathrobe. I threw a blanket around the baby and we ran. The other room was a mass of them. We raced down to Andersens' and began the hunt. We found seven on John, three on the baby and any number on ourselves. Mr. Andersen said we were surely fortunate to get out so soon, as they could kill a child in time. Well, they held sway for two days, and then suddenly they lined up and marched out. But they do clean house. That morning the boys killed a snake they had evidently run out of the roof and the little worms and crickets and lizards are gone too. We went over the place with kerosene and then with "flit" or "whiz"...we haven't been bothered since. They say they surely clean things up, so we did not mind so much. But it would have been pretty bad if we had had no place to go. Mr. Andersen says he has had them come into his tent when it was pouring rain outside and there was nowhere to go except out in the bush. The next morning after this happened, John touched a poison caterpillar, and we had to keep his finger soaked in bluing. That is a splendid remedy for any insect bite, by the way. It is best to make a paste like starch and keep it well moist. It drew the poison out in less than an hour.

"We are getting initiated into Africa 'one by one.'"

Bob and Kitty had been impressed with the results of Mr. Andersen's effort to help the Kipsigis by producing a primitive type of water mill for grinding flour. It was so simple that it could be left to grind on its own without supervision. Corn would drop slowly from a bin above into the middle of a millstone. The stone was turned by waterpower and the ground corn would make its way to the periphery where eventually it was collected, bagged and returned, with a fee attached, to the native who had brought it or sold it to the tea estates. It was his idea that, in this way, Christians would have income that could then be tithed, and pastors could be supported, thus promoting an indigenous church. Equally appealing was the fact that these mills could be left unattended for hours. The idea had been well received, and many of these gristmills were already present over Kipsigis land.

Recurring famine was another problem and one for which the missionaries hoped to have a solution.

Dad characteristically conversed, whenever there was an opportunity, with those around him trying to glean any information he could. Based on his discussions in the tapes, we think his conversation may have been something like this.

"Bro. Ford," Bob asked, "Why was it so difficult to get African men to use oxen to plow?" Bob remembered Mr. Hotchkiss telling him about Petero A. Ng'etich, a man whom he had sold on the idea. His fellow tribesmen, however, mobbed and nearly killed him for daring to use oxen.

Jefferson Ford, Clara's father, was a giant of a man, both figuratively and physically. He often stuttered, but it was worth waiting for what he had to say. "Wa...Wa...Well, of course it was an entirely new concept. Can you imagine seeing yoked oxen for the first time? It seemed to the natives a crime to castrate so valuable an animal as a bull, let alone yoke the animals together with a wooden pole, and whip them into submission. They were certain that this kind of behavior would surely displease the spirits. But an even greater deterrent was that the raising of crops was women's work. Men were thoroughly disgraced for doing such things."

"How does one overcome this?"

"Persistence and showing results, all the while understanding the African's reluctance. These are people whose behavior is ruled by customs and beliefs that may be very illogical to us, but it is all they know."

"I can see that." Bob looked across the hillside. He tried to imagine what it must be like for a native to be confronted with all these changes. And Kenya was indeed changing rapidly.

Bob and Kitty continued to stay engaged in the work at Litein. They had just learned that Bob's aunt and uncle were sending stoves, one for the Kirks and one for them. They tried to remain hopeful for their future, but the discouragements seemed to prevail.

Dear Folks:

September 7, 1933

We received your letters of July early and latter part (last date 31st) this week. We are so glad for all the news....

You can't imagine how wonderful Uncle Ed's and Aunt Mary's gift seems to us. We are now 3 months behind in salary and no prospect of any before the middle or last of October. And we have not had anything for the general fund for the last two times, so we have been trying to carry some of that besides our own expenses with the result that we are heavily in debt. Even with Bob doing all the work, the house cost $125.00 about. We got the folk's letter saying that the money order was on the way but we haven't received it yet. By the way, that is the best way to send money to us as we get the most for it. We don't have to pay for the exchange. If the dollar depreciates, as they say it may, it will surely be hard on us. The exchange is just normal now that is about 4 shilling to the dollar....

I guess we little realize what conditions are like these days at home. Kirk got a letter containing 10 cents, the tithe on $1.00 which were the first wages a certain man had had in several months....

Well I must close and get to bed. Had a hard day. Many discouragements. Site in Sotik has been refused. A.I.M. home council has refused affiliation and with the break with Bro. H. we are in the "soup." But the Lord is able to deliver us out of all these the afflictions! So we are down but by no means out. Thank the Lord....

"...with the break with Bro. H. we are in the 'soup.'"

Litein Mission
Kericho, Kenya Colony
B.E.Africa
Oct 10, 1933

Dear Daddie B.

I was strongly criticized by Mother B. in the last letter for neglecting the answer to your letter. Since I have no other claim on the day, I'm getting this off to you.

I'm enjoying some of your experiences. Little Anna Verne claims some of daddy's time like John Boy did his grandpa's. She is down on the carpet tumbling about. She certainly is one sweet little girlie. All through her journey of life up to now she has preceded normal development. Kitty, just now, reports that the double teeth are forming. Her teeth have fairly jumped through. She has eight through.

I suppose you have read the article in "Call to Prayer" which Kirk wrote up concerning our last preaching safari. We traveled around through the tribe and held services. One service was outstanding. Eighty-six seekers stayed to pray for victory. I think that most of them got through to the Lord. This was a stimulating experience to further effort along this same line. Kirk and I went on a motorbyke safari to Kaimosi. We were returning home from Kisumu on Victoria Lake when we ran into a storm, got completely soaked and night came on and found us miles from home. We pushed our motorbyke and sidecar over near a native hut and put the contents of the sidecar in the hut. Then we crawled in and squatted around a little fire on the floor and attempted to dry and warm ourselves. Unfortunately there was no food in the house, not even tea. We had had some breakfast but no dinner or supper. So we lay down on a stiff cowhide on the dirt floor with nothing but a smoky little fire to keep us warm while the temperature dropped toward the freezing point. Early next morning the native woman roasted an ear of corn in the fire and Kirk and I had one apiece for breakfast. Then after scraping about 100 lbs. of mud off the bike and loading up we went on home. By the time I was back with Kitty and the youngsters I was next to starved and badly exposed. I have spent two days in bed with a hot-water bottle on my chest trying to counteract what appeared to be more than an ordinary cold. However I'm on my feet today.

John just awakened from his sleep. He called, "Muddie, come here. I want to tell you what is the matter." She inquired what the trouble was and he very apologetically said, "I tored my pretty picture." He thought he had best explain, for perhaps the consequences would not be so bad. Just now he spelled "spectrascope" and pronounced it. He is quite the favorite of Capt. Oulton, Game Ranger of Kenya. He has been teaching him large words. Already he counts to ten. He follows me everywhere I go. If I start on a safari, and he thinks he should go, and we disagree, it breaks his heart. All afternoon it has rained and it is quite cool. We have to have a fire in the fireplace to keep warm, and if we step out of the house without our helmets we are liable to get sunstroke. Doesn't this seem a paradox?

As yet, we have not heard from the stoves. We expect to get a letter before long saying that they have arrived in Mombasa. However, we hope to hear from the N.H.A. with funds before it arrives. We feel the everlasting grind for finance here, too. The funds for mission expense never come and all the needed funds come out of our pockets. But we have kept our heads above water and not much more. Kitty wants to write, so with these last pleasant words, I will say adieu and relinquish the quill to my devoted frau.

You son, Bob

"We have a fire in the fireplace…and if we step out of the house without our helmets we are liable to get a sunstroke. Doesn't this seem a paradox?"

Grandfather Biesecker was a poet. Our grandmother had met him when finding his name on a poem he had written and observing it to be the same as hers had contacted him. He also was a traveling salesman, and when he came to her town looked her up. After finding they were in fact not related, he married her, giving her the same married name as her maiden name had been. Through the years, we each received letters and silly poems from our grandfather written in beautiful calligraphy. This is one he sent to John at the time of this story.

Dear John:

JAMBO! I suppose you know what that is. You will be the master of two languages and probably beat your father and mother in speaking Swahili.

There was a little boy and his name was John,
He went bye-bye and took his pop along:
He took his grandpa and his grandma too
And he wore a little coat that was made of blue.

Now he's gone on a long bye-bye
And his grandparents here almost cry
When they think it will be a long, long while,
Ere they hear him talk and see him smile.

But they are glad to know he has a sister Anna
Although she is an Africana;
She is not dark but is quite fair,
Judging from the lock of her auburn hair.

You'll both get along I know just fine,
If you both are good and always mind;
What your parents tell you both to do,
Be kind to folks and sister too.

Don't be a fop or yet a dude,
Be ever courteous, never rude;
Help your daddy all you can
And you'll grow up to be a man.

When you get big and learn to hunt
The tiger and the elephant,
Don't forget when you take your aim
To pull the trigger and get the game.

When the rhinos charge you don't wait,
Don't get cold feet or hesitate;
But take quick aim – sure and true,
And drill the rascal through and through.

And so my laddie keep your nerve,
From the narrow pathway never swerve;
Do a kind act when you can,
And you'll grow up to be a man.
                                        Grand-dad.

"My few stammering remarks…."

Kipsigis is a language with many tonal qualities. Mother told us about the time she was explaining, in Kipsigis, the fireplace Dad was building in their little home to a young African who had questioned what it was. When the African appeared terrified, she had sought out and discovered that she had told him that Dad was building hell!

Back at Litein, days went by and waiting continued, but no resolution seemed in sight. Word had come that Dr. Hotchkiss would return, and they looked forward to that with mixed emotions. Kitty had now studied two languages, the trade language Swahili and the tribal language Kipsigis. The meaning of a word changed with only a slight inflection. Her Kipsigis was improving, and she had been asked to give a sermon for the first time.

Dear Folks:

Litein Station
December 2 1933

If I do not write tonight I am afraid I won't get a letter off to you this week as tomorrow is my great day. I am to preach my first sermon in Kipsigis. It is some sermon, as you may well believe. I am having to practically learn it by heart. I had it all worked out and written out and took it down to Mrs. Andersen to see how much was wrong and found I had expressed in Kipsigis many things as we think them but not as they do. For example they never "need" anything they have. I wanted to say I have some dishes I need very much and some I don't need. But they don't say it that way, they say, "I have some I want and some I don't want." And they have a word that means stranger friend and one that means hog with just a very slight difference in inflection, so when I say I have some dishes I don't use everyday but just when strangers come, I have to be careful or I'll say when the hogs come.

Dec. 6.

You see it is Wednesday, and I haven't finished this yet and now in order that you get this anywhere near Christmas, I'll have to send it airmail. I got through Sunday all right and everyone seemed to understand me. My few stammering remarks furnished a theme for the native evangelist, and when I had finished, he enlarged upon them and preached a beautiful sermon. I have the distinction of being the first in our group to preach in the native language, small as my attempt was….

Here it is Sat. P.M. and I must finish this letter to you to get off tomorrow. I have been doing something this A.M. you would love--? Hunting cockroaches. We are being eaten out so to speak. Nothing but our books, however. They seem to like the starch in some of the covers. So I have put powder around for them instead. It is supposed to kill, but will it? I cleaned cupboard, bookcase, dresser drawers and clothes closet today. Last, we did the cedar chest. They love it in there as it is nice and dark. I had families of them from grandpas to great grandchildren, but I trust I am rid of them for awhile. Mrs. Andersen said what we needed was another dose of driver ants. I think I wrote you about our first experience, didn't I?

I got some leather and made the baby some little shoes to last until some come from home. They look quite clumsy but will serve the purpose. We had a pair made for John by an Indian, but they charge about $3.00 and that seems high, so I got the leather for $.80 and saved the rest….

The other Sunday Bob and John took a walk. When they returned, John said, "Muddie we had such a nice walk." I said, "What did you do?" and he replied, "Daddy prayed to Jesus and I covered him all up with leaves." The other day something didn't go just right and Bob said, "I can't figure out what's wrong with this crazy thing." And John looked up and said," Well, Daddy, you'll be jiggered." And he is learning Kipsigis so fast. Last night he jabbered something to our two native girls that sent them into gales of laughter, but I don't know what he said. What would I do without my two babies?....

You will never know how dark and discouraging this first year in Africa has been. All hopes, all plans, frustrated. Even as I write a dark cloud hangs over us; we seem unable to pray through and just what the future holds, the Lord only knows. But He is teaching me the lesson of utter dependence upon Him and also the importance of victory in the smallest things these days. Some days are one continual grind and seemingly no victory, Others are beautifully peaceful and victorious. And is that not life? I often wonder if the Lord really has a work for us here....

We got a letter from Mother Smith telling of their move from St. Paul's church into S.D.A. We were pretty sick about it at first but are more reconciled now. She also said Father S. was out getting money to pay transportation of the stoves from Mombasa. It is sure wonderful how the Lord has heard our need. We have been wondering how in the world we would be able to pay the duty and transportation when they came, and behold, it is all done. We received notice that the stoves are to arrive in Mombasa today....

Love, Kitty

"I often wonder if the Lord really has a work for us here...."

John remembers when he was a small boy and the family, having just returned to the United States, were living with Grandma Smith in the old farm house with its foot-thick, brick walls—so cool in the summer—and the beautiful surrounding pastures. It seemed that life's sparkle had gone out of Grandmother when Grandfather had died. She sat quietly listening to the radio, often staring into space. But on Saturday mornings, she became more animated. She would dress for church and wait excitedly while a family came by to pick her up. By the time the Smiths arrived home to America, their attitude about Seventh Day Adventism had changed, and that had largely been due to an encounter they would have later in Tanganyika.

By now the little tin house had endeared itself to Bob and Kitty because of the many experiences they had had there. She wrote for the Children's Page in the "Call to Prayer":

"We have been routed out twice at midnight by 'soldier ants' and had to seek refuge with the other missionaries. Soldier ants, however, are our least troublesome guests. First we had a siege of fleas. Both the children were covered with bites, and we could not blame them for being cross, as our own itched as no other insect bites ever did. We had everything taken out of the house and sunned, the rugs scrubbed, the floors all washed with a strong disinfectant fluid called 'Jeys.' Then we had our mud walls replastered, and the floors revarnished with the time honored insecticide natives and missionaries have found most effective for mud houses. Thus, we were free from the fleas for a time. They regularly return,

however, and we repeat the process. Next we found that everything we possessed was infested with roaches. We asked everyone we saw what to do, and took the advice of all, but they seemed to thrive on even Glodders salts. Matting, grass walls and a grass roof must be favorite places for roaches to live. So it was with thanksgiving that we read Mr. Anderson's article in the last "Call to Prayer" and found a real remedy. We went to Nairobi at once for borax and camphor gum.

"Yes, we need the latter for we have ants also, the little black pests he mentioned. For three nights not long ago, it was a question as to who would occupy our quarters, colonies of ants or the Smiths. They came in droves, each carrying a white egg or larva as large as itself. We were able to kill and drive out most of them with Flit when the first division arrived. This process we repeated for two more nights until the little insects were at last persuaded that we had first right to the premises. Since then we have not been troubled so much in the house, but the kitchen is full of them, cupboards, etc., in spite of the use of tins."

Broken all to pieces

As children, we were unaware that there were personal conflicts with other missionaries. They simply were not discussed in our presence, and although we came to know that there had been conflicts, we never knew what they were nor does that truly matter.

The purpose of including the reality that is in Mother's letters is not to place blame—certainly there must have been enough of that to go around—but rather to acknowledge that conflict existed and to highlight the difficulty, for them, of sorting through the perceptions they had developed as to the reason for their dilemma. They were not perfect either! Mother was criticized as being arrogant and outspoken, Dad as reckless and competitive.

But as children, what we experienced as the mission family grew was an amazing sense of unity and love and belonging. There is little doubt that much attention was paid to recognizing and dealing with interpersonal relationships through prayer and personal attention to alignment with God's purposes.

Anna Verne recalls: the annual mission retreats were times of spiritual revival for missionaries. We were together as a group from all the stations and were intent on maintaining unity. If something had arisen, this was the time to clear our hearts and give the Lord His rightful place. When David (her husband) was Field Director, he had to mediate for individuals in some issues, but great emphasis was put on clearing the air through prayer.

Jan 4, 1934

Dear Folks:

My first letter of the New Year! And what will the New Year bring? We do not know but we are trusting Him who holds all our lives in the hollow of His hand. This past year has been such a hard one. I am going to write plainly now what we have withheld before because of the feeling that all would surely come right in a little while. But your last letter demanded some explanation, and so we will tell you now as best we can. There is nothing you can do but pray, and that is all we want you to do, but we do want you to do that, as we need it badly. Furthermore, I would not write this now if I did not have complete victory over what has happened. Of course we need more grace daily as things are constantly coming up, but somehow the Lord is holding us steady....

Of course you know we have no real leader. Miss Ford was to have sort of over-sight for one year and Mr. Andersen to be our advisor. That was with the supposition that we would have a work to do, but we have none. Had Bro. H. remained with the N.H.A., everything would have been very different, whether any better or not we cannot tell.... Well, to proceed. It seems there is an age-old feud between the A.I.M. and Bro. H. over this territory. Bro H. was here first and so there is a sort of gentleman's agreement between him and Mr. Andersen, but the A.I.M. doesn't recognize him at all. The field council saw the advantage of an affiliation and urged it with the Home Council, but they absolutely refused to agree.... So far, the Board knows almost nothing of this, and therein lies one of our hardest battles....

Faye was made the treasurer by the board, as she has had business training. But all the time we were at Malava and for some time after we arrived here Kirk has handled all the funds. There has been no N.H.A. money to speak of and he has put his own into the general fund time and again, which is very commendable. So have we, but we haven't had nearly as much to give as we have left, after the insurance is taken out, barely enough to live. This and the fact that we still owe him for the trip out puts us under decided disadvantage....

But now for the part that breaks me all to pieces. All this and the sickness etc. has done something to my "sunny" Bob. He seldom is like his old self. He has borne it all like a man but it has told so dearly on him and I often look at him in amazement and say, "can this really be my Bob?" If we could once get free from the galling knowledge that we owe Kirk so much money it would help, I feel. And I believe Bob is going to come out one of these days when he feels sure of his ground.

None of this has marred our Christmas. We had a beautiful time, and the children were beside themselves with delight....

Well, I must close. Remember all is well with us, for we are under His care.
Much love, Catharine

"...we have no real leader."

"How I'd love to be out of this mess!"

What a year this had been! A year of conflict and confusion, a year of coming to terms with the shortcomings of treasured friends, a year of complete uncertainty and disappointment. One milestone had been reached: Early in 1934 the Kenya Mission Council met for its Annual General Meeting in Nairobi. Clara Ford attended the meeting, again petitioning for recognition of their mission. Several individuals spoke on their behalf, one of whom was an individual who had become acquainted with the treasurer of their mission, Dr. Iva D. Vennard, when she had brought deposits to the bank in which he worked. He vouched for the professional approach to their financial dealings and the stability of the organization. Others spoke to the dealings they had had with the organization since the arrival of their missionaries in the country. The Kenya Mission Council had then finally agreed to the petition, this time with only two dissenters.

Dear Mother: *Mar. 3, 1934*

I'm afraid we are late for your birthday again, but it seems the days go by so fast I can't realize it....I believe you will be writing your age 65 now.....I wish I could say more than just "many happy returns" but I sent lots of love from us all....and we all blew you kisses, so you must let the breeze give them to you.

We are still uncertain about the site. We have written the D.C. again, but in the meantime we had a native report that he had been killed by elephants, and we have not had authentic word since....

We are expecting Bro H. here a week from tonight. It doesn't seem possible. I told him in a note I put into Bob's letter to reach him at the boat, please not to think anything of it if I cry when I see him. It will be so like seeing some one of my own.

Bob has gone to Eldama Ravine to see Mr. Barnett about advancing the money for a truck. (He is the one who came over on the boat with us) They are moving from their station, and he thinks we can get the job of hauling the stuff, and they have a good second hand truck they could get for a little over $350.00. They expected to be back today but yesterday going in had a breakdown and had to stay all day in Kericho getting repaired. So they went on today and will perhaps return tomorrow.

Our rains are beginning again so it will be harder to get around, and we had so hoped to get settled before it rained. But the Lord knows best.

...How I'd love to be out of this mess! But I feel the Lord is leading if we can just hold still a little longer.... Will write more next week as there will be heaps of news, I expect.

Much love, Catharine

Mar. 14, 1934

Dear Home Folks:
Tomorrow the mail goes, and I want to send this by air, so I'll write a few lines tonight. We have at last realized our hopes. Bro. Hotchkiss is here. And how wonderful it was to see him and what a wealth of happiness he brought! I don't believe I ever saw so much packed in a box...I can't tell you one by one the things as it would make the letter be overweight....(She lists many items Mr. Hotchkiss has brought and tells how they will be used.)

Mr. H. left tonight to return Friday. We talked until two o'clock his first night here. As to the outlook, the Lord knows. We'll let you hear as soon as we do. If there is anything I forgot to mention, it isn't that it wasn't appreciated. All we feel about it is very unworthy.

Much love, Catharine

"Bob has gone to Eldama Ravine to see Mr. Barnett about advancing the money for the truck."

Now Mr. Hotchkiss was returning, but even that would provide no solution for them. In fact, the complexity of their situation seemed to increase with each passing day. Of one thing they were sure—others saw Mr. Hotchkiss differently. Yet the Smiths were discovering things they could not tolerate about him and, although they loved him dearly, would never be able to work with him on the mission field. They longed for a simple solution but continued to seem to be going in different directions even with their fellow workers. Finally, the need for a truck had become so evident that Miss Ford had decided to help finance it. For the first time, Bob had decided to step into a leadership role and take the initiative to do what he knew needed to be done. The Barnetts, who had come over on the boat with Bob and Kitty, had become dear friends and made suggestions to Bob in regard to the truck, as had Mr. Andersen and Mr. Chilson.

P.O. Box 144, Nairobi, Kenya Colony,
East Africa, March 26th. 1934

Dear Brother Bishop,

The other day Mr. Smith and Mr. Andersen came to Nairobi: Mr. Smith to advise with me regarding the feasibility of buying a truck for the N.H.A. Mission. Mr. Andersen came down to meet his son, Earl, who had just returned from USA.

Brother Smith had in mind the buying of a used International truck: get it in good condition, then install a charcoal gas producer instead of running on gasoline, which is so expensive out here. I advised him to do so if he could see his way to finance it. After the truck is thoroughly over-hauled, it would be practically as good as new and cost less than 1/3 what a new one would out here.

I had about completed arrangements to go in with a friend here and buy a cheap truck, he to take my goods over to Congo, I to pay the gas and oil for the trip, then he return to Uganda (where there is greater demand for trucks) and sell the truck–making his profit that way. But just as it was looking as if we could not find just what we wanted for the price we wanted, Brother Smith, who wanted to visit the Congo anyway, offered to take our goods over on about the same terms as I expected to pay my friend–namely, I pay the expense he would incur going over and back and an advance of $100, which is to be returned as soon as possible. This would be an accommodation to me and at the same time enable him to visit Congo without expense to your mission.

Brother Smith and I have been working on the truck for the past week while the Firm was installing the gas producer. We hope to be leaving for the Congo not later than this coming Wednesday.

We are greatly enjoying the fellowship with Brother Smith. He is staying with us here in Nairobi. We are planning on buying a truck with gas producer as soon as we can. I feel it is the most practical thing to do rather than spend a large share of building funds in transporting goods and materials....

Yours for Christ in Africa,
Arthur B. Chilson

Letter written to the President of the Smiths' mission on their behalf

"Well, Kitty, we found the truck. It's a 1 1/2 ton flat rack International. We got it for 700 shillings." "That's wonderful, Bob. I can't imagine the price."

"Well the Indian insisted it was a good buy. Clara, Mr. Chilson, and I went to pick it up at Kipsonoi with the firm belief that with our toolbox and a little work, we would have a jewel. The truth is, I'm not sure it has any similarity to jewels. Before we got very far, the drive shaft dropped down, and to our astonishment, we found there were no bolts in the assembly. In all the bolt holes, baling wire had been fed through and twisted. We also found that one of the rear wheels insisted on coming off."

"Didn't you check these things first?" Kitty's face had gone pale.

"We knew it had problems, but the price was right, and I thought we could fix them. But they are more extensive than we thought. Mr. Chilson suggests that we take it to Nairobi and have it checked. They have an International Harvester Company shop there. His idea is that when he and his family get ready to move to Kivu area of Urundi where they plan to start a new Friends Mission station, we can use this truck for transport. That will be occurring soon. In the meantime, if we get it fixed, we can use it to transport things of our own, particularly when we move to our new site."

"When will you be going to Nairobi with it then? And where will the funds come from to fix it?"

"Right away. Clara actually used her own funds to help buy the truck for the mission, and she is contributing to the repair as well."

Bob, many years later, wrote the story like this:

"So without looking into our 'kitty,' we proceeded toward the big city under the guardian care of Mr. Chilson and family who decided that the repair time could be used by them in purchasing equipment for the new station. As we proceeded toward Nairobi and rounded the corner at Lumuru, our left rear wheel

came rolling down the road past the sliding truck. With wire and tin shims expertly placed by the driver, Bob, the truck arrived at the shop. When the foreman looked it over, there were 'ohs' and 'ahs' as he proceeded checking. If we were to keep the wheels on, we would have to have new axles, which had proper key-ways and nuts. He also advised us that new hubs were a necessity as well as the brakes. He pointed out that several of the spring hangers were also fitted up with baling wire – and so it went.

Watutsi warriors

"With much salesmanship, an agent of a Swedish charcoal burner system convinced us that this was the ideal time to fit up our newly improved vehicle with this new equipment. In came pipes and a tank that looked like a boiler, radiators, cleaner box and valves. Again we should have looked into the 'kitty,' but being told that they would cheerfully let us make monthly payments, we proceeded. (In America, terrible, but in Africa, inexcusable, as missionaries of old can report that receipts in the treasury know nothing about monthly regularity!) So, fitted out, we rolled away with our hubs, brakes, hangers, smoke rolling out of our charcoal boiler, and with new ground valves helping our engine to run smoothly. One thing we forgot: the worm gear of the steering wheel had not been adjusted. So away it would drift first to one side and then to the other. It wasn't dangerous but very exhausting to the driver.

"The Chilsons had loaded the truck. Things were roped down and covered with a beautiful tarpaulin, which was purchased by Mr. Chilson who had other plans for its later use. Over our cab, charcoal bags were conveniently tied so that they could easily be placed into the tank. In the cab with me was my faithful Isaiah. His major interest was that I have food and clean, well-pressed khakis. The Chilsons were driving a Chevrolet safari car. Their daughter, Rachel, who was continually vibrant and cheerful, did almost all the driving. One of the experiences I had with them on initiation into one of the customs of the Quakers was really interesting. They were of the old school. Rachael would buzz off and leave our truck behind moving at about 15-20 miles per hour, and traveling about 40 miles on a bag of charcoal. We would roll along and just at noon or camping time, we would arrive where there was a table set and chairs placed around. It always looked good to a hungry driver and his helper. We would seat ourselves, bow our heads, and I would wait for the blessing. One time it would be *Bwana* Chilson, another *Memsahib* Chilson, and then Rachel. Seeing I was disturbed because no one was asked to pray, *Bwana* Chilson gave no explanations of Quaker procedure but invited me to pray when I felt led of the Spirit that I should.

Grass homes in the Congo

"*Bwana* Chilson felt responsible for locating our camping grounds, then searching the dukas and community for a supply of *makaa* (charcoal) for the next day. We might set up our tents and cots for the night or use a government camp where the rooms were provided. There was always a spirit of urgency about *Bwana* Chilson. His very actions said, 'Move on—let's move on.' He was always walking about as though he was unwilling to sit down and take it easy. His whole nature seemed to change when we dropped through a bridge or had truck trouble. He was immediately able to adjust attitude to caring for the problem and meeting the demands of the situation. He grew to be a great man to me, deep in understanding and rich in faith. Mrs. Chilson was also a character of faith and sometimes determined in her manner of purpose. She was a 'Mother in Israel.'

"We moved west via Kisumu and the border village of Busia into Uganda. From there we moved over the hallowed roads that Bishop Hammington had traveled to his death. We progressed to Jinja where we saw the Jinja Falls (no longer there now), which poured water from Victoria Nyanza into the Nile and started it toward Kampala and the Mediterranean Sea. From there we drove west toward Kampala and the Congo Border, at Rhusuru. We had been traveling for days through banana groves and kapok trees (which produce filler for pillows), and beautiful oil palms. I was learning that bananas (even if they were very small, or very green) were delicious. They could also be red. As we drove south, we were traveling in high country with gorgeous mountains rising into the clouds. We were meeting pygmies, seeing elephant, and being told that gorilla were in the forests above us.

"Rolling along one day, we suddenly dropped through a small bridge, which we discovered was covered only by small sticks covered with dirt. It was good enough for their small carts. We didn't get out easily, but the senior missionary was there and directed operations. We were constantly on guard from then on, as were the Chilsons. Many times we would come up to their safari car waiting to see if we could make it over a questionable bridge.

"Our reasonably moving safari suddenly came to a halt in southern Rwanda. There our clutch went out! We were in fairly level country and one in which the people seemed to be living comfortably.

"We also found that we were in a Catholic area. We removed the clutch in our camp on the side of the road and found we needed a new one. We learned that the only place this part was available was back in Nairobi at the…shop where we had had so many interesting days in the early part of our safari. Our problem was also that the shop was many hundreds of miles away. The chief of the tribe seemed to sense that we were in trouble and came to see us. He said he would supply a runner if we wished, which seemed a hopeless prospect. The runner arrived, looked at the clutch, rolled a sort of grass donut, put it on his head and the clutch on top of it, and with a letter to Motor Mart, Kampala, giving instructions, started off without a penny for expenses. The chief informed us that this was no problem. He would have friends who would house and feed him.

"Isaiah and I got out our books to read during the long wait while the Chilsons went on down to Burundi to the place where they expected to start their station. We waited while the days became weeks. It was during this time that a Catholic priest in the area sent me a ham, milk, vegetables, and water. I never had the privilege of thanking him personally, but his kindness was greatly appreciated and acknowledged by letter.

"Then one day the part arrived, a complete clutch on the head of our runner. We learned that because we needed it as soon as possible, he had run on a dogtrot at an average of about 70 miles a day. I have always considered this to be fabulous. What the chief asked us to do was equally fabulous. The chief would not let us give the runner anything for his service but eight tablespoons of course salt. He explained that money was of no value to him but that the salt could be used and appreciated, and with that our obligation was complete.

Watutsi chief

"With the clutch installed and our camp broken up, we proceeded to Burundi country. We had met the Watutsi, the tribe with men and women over six feet tall, seen the fabulous hillside gardens and lovely grass houses. We had found that *makaa* was now *makala*, and that sheep, which used to be called *kondoo* were now called *kondor*. So the nature of the country changed, as did the very appearance of the people.

"Finally we arrived at the chosen spot where the elder Chilsons felt God would have them literally give the rest of their lives in service. The truck was unloaded and in the place of this much valued cargo was put a liberal amount of *makala* for our return trip. I shall never forget the sight of the little family standing beside their pile of goods, which was again covered with the tarpaulin that had covered it on the journey. Their arms were raised high in farewell as we drove away. There was no house—only a pile of goods, great hearts and a vision that led to the Friends Mission of Burundi.

"Isaiah and I started for home. We spent the night with the District Officer, a Belgian. He wakened us early and told us that we must travel fast until we had passed a barrier that the government was building across the road some 20 miles away. He insisted that we must hurry, as there was an epidemic of tick fever, and if we did not get across the barrier, we would have to remain in the area for an unknown period of time. Isaiah had cooked an aluminum pan full of the famous calico beans we had found in Burundi, so after passing the barrier which might have been padlocked except for a letter which we bore from the District Officer, and finding a shade tree, we sat and ate our beans. Again we hurried north to get away from the affected area. By four o'clock, I was feeling distressed in my tummy and lightheaded. We stopped by the side of the road, and Isaiah set up our tent and cots and made camp. By this time, I was on the cot bloated and insensible. Some time in the night, I was awakened by a great disturbance. A truck had rumbled down the road, and Isaiah was talking loudly to the occupants. Then, as though in a dream, a long white beard and a turbaned head was peering down into my face. Isaiah was holding a lantern and frantically explaining that I was about to die. The Indian was comforting him and preparing a whole bottle of Epsom salts to be poured down into my screaming stomach. Some garlic pills about the size of large beans followed this. With assurances that the *Bwana* would live, things quieted down and I passed back into oblivion.

"At an early hour, I was internally urged to arise from my couch and seek a measure of privacy. There with the early birds singing, I moved into an era of relief and restful anticipation of a good trip home. Isaiah was awake and anxious to see my condition. Already he was cooking rolled oats. This we ate with butter and sugar. How good it tasted to me! We were on our way early, retracing our steps toward Kenya. Isaiah informed me as we went along that he had never expected to get back home with his *Bwana* dead in Rwanda. We did get home! We had years of retribution for the lavish expenditures.... It was a lesson that became a guideline for the economy of our mission: 'Look first into the kitty.'

"There was never any bitterness over our experiences. Nothing will ever take away my first contact with this lovely family. The memory of that lonely hill, the pile of goods under the tarpaulin, the waving hands and the evident spirit of the pioneers who stood there are precious. One other memory remains. That was the busy ant spirit of the daughter, Rachel. Day by day she drove along, always cheerful, always singing. That has been the keynote of a great life of service. After mother, father, and others are gone, she still picks up her guitar and, with a group of Africans about her, sings the hymns of the gospel to those black folks she had always loved. Even now I see her driving along in the safari car singing at the top of her voice, 'My father was a Spanish merchant,' etc. Then, before we ate, with the great dignity of the soul that she is, she would break out in the prayer of thanksgiving."

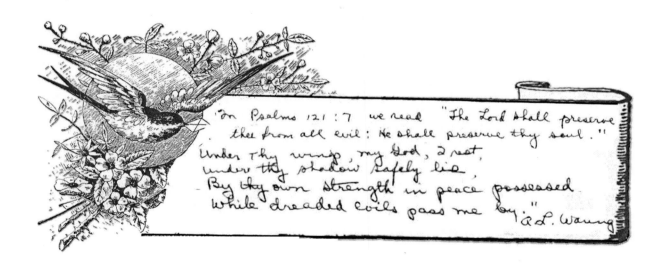

In Psalms 121:7 we read "The Lord shall preserve thee from all evil: He shall preserve thy soul."
Under Thy wings, my God, I rest,
under thy shadow safely lie,
By thy own strength in peace possessed
While dreaded evils pass me by." A.L. Waung

Dear Home Folks:

Mar. 17. 1934

I have already written you an airmail letter about the wonderful things you sent....Mother and Father Smith's came later...I slipped away some things....I think I'll save them till next Christmas... However I may weaken. They loved them so much. John carried the doggie all over with him and Anna Verne loved her dollie and called her "toto" and "pretty" and every endearing term she knew.

We had two lovely days with Bro. H. We accompanied him back to Chagaik [sic] (his farm) and had tea with the Stantons who are on his place. Then we returned, and he came back on Friday of this week for prayer day. He gave the morning message to a packed house, and it was a wonderful message. He was completely overcome in his greeting, so moved he couldn't speak for several minutes. It was a beautiful sight and quite a victory, as it was the chapel he had refused in the past to enter due to the old feud.

Well, we had some long talks. The first night we talked until 2 A.M. He seems just the same. Of course our hearts are full. Our gratitude to him for all he has done for us in bringing all these things and his own personal gifts is greater that we can express, and yet we are absolutely powerless to act in his behalf.

Many things have transpired, and I can't go into detail except to say that the A.I.M. is planning to work all of Kipsigis, and there is no place for us and really no place for him here other than what he has done before. The government wants 400 acres of his farm for an air drome, and that leaves 12,000 acres he can sell. We think his idea was to sell it and buy Litein, but it can't be done. He has filed application for Tenwek in Sotik, the one we wanted and didn't get, but several have grave doubts of his getting it. Should he, I don't know what it would mean to us....

One hope we have is that he will not be able to get the site. He does not know the A.I.M. plans and we were honor bound to tell no one. However, we feel for his sake, too, it would be ever so much better if he didn't get it. My heart is simply broken for him, and I don't know when I ever was so torn. I'm like the Psalmist said, "making my bed to swim" most of the time these days; I never was so "weepy," I'll tell you it is something for a bunch of youngsters like we are to go through such a flogging. And had we unity ourselves it would be bad enough!

Now my Bob has gone on a long ""safari" into Kongo[sic]. He will be gone at least three weeks and the baby has whooping cough. If John did have it at home that time you and Mother S. thought so I'll surely be happy. So far he hasn't shown any signs of it. But if he didn't have it, he will get it now, as it isn't possible to keep the children apart.

Today we had a regular hailstorm. My was it cold! Talk about gloom! Doesn't this letter radiate it? But I've still got my nose above water. I guess if it goes deeper I can flaot awhile! And we're claiming victory.

I wonder if you understand my seeming contradiction. I said in a letter before that we would have to wait until Bro. H. got here to see if he could get us the site as we had failed. That was before the A.I.M. decided to occupy it. Now there is no place for us. They have at least five families for it now, and they told us in committee session that they could not now recognize any claim of ours here as the home board had refused recognition.

It is so hard to write! Wouldn't it be great to have a long talk! As such I have filled up everything. I must close and get to bed. Hope all is well. Catharine and all.

"Talk about gloom!...But I've still got my nose above water."

Mother was very particular about speaking correctly and she often corrected our grammar but she was never known for her ability to spell. We are amused to see that she misspelled almost every location to begin with. Dad used to tease her by saying, "I tell her how to spell it and she tells me what it means."

"We are simply left high and dry."

Meanwhile, with Bob away in the Congo, Kitty had waited alone with the children and her thoughts. What was to have taken three weeks was extending into six. Bob's whereabouts were not clear, and it was long after his expected return that she finally received information, but even that was inaccurate resulting in more uncertainty. The maps she looked at daily were still spelling the Congo as Kongo.

When Bob returned, she welcomed him with relief and great joy. He told her exhaustively about the trip and added, "I'll have to tell you this one on Isaiah. On the trip home one day after I had finished my morning grooming and was cleanly shaven he said, '*Bwana*, you do not smell very good.' I smiled at him and said, 'Well, Isaiah, you don't smell very good either.' Then we both had a good laugh."

Unpacking the stove

Isaiah washed with water but no soap, so with time the acrid smell of body odor, added to the smoke from the fire that saturated his clothes, became intense. But in comparison to other natives who made a practice of smearing their bodies with fat and ochre, which created a rancid musky smell, Bob thought this quite tolerable; moreover, he loved his friend and helper. When Isaiah and Bob returned, the stoves had arrived. They were particularly appreciated in that the aunt and uncle of Bob's, who gave them as a gift, had in his college years withdrawn support from Bob in disgust when they learned of his new found faith and plan to become a missionary.

Excerpt from a letter written to Rev. Lee Downing from A.I.M. home council and in the hands of the Miss Ford, Kirkpatricks and Smiths by at least February of 1934

Mr. A. M. Andersen has written to us under date of Aug. 8 1933. We gave his letter careful attention. We have also your own letter and other letters sent to us by Dr. Davis when he was on the field. The gist of the matter is that our Council desires in every possible way to cooperate with the work of God, but we have not been able to see, and do not now see, any good reason why the A.I.M. should unite with the N.H.A. Our council believes there is plenty of room in Africa for the other work without entering upon a field already occupied. Looking beyond the immediate present, we feel that the future is full of uncertainty and promises some confusion, if this union were entered into. It would be best for the N.H.A. to begin right and establish a legal identity and get recognition for themselves from the beginning. This is the attitude we have held in this business and I am instructed by our Council to say that we see no good reason why our attitude should be changed. We have every desire to work in absolute fellowship with the Field Council, and we trust this decision will be taken as of the Lord, and some other way out of the N.H.A. difficulty be found.

Of the many hurdles that stood in their way, the biggest for the Smiths had been erected prior to their arrival. It had arisen out of the longstanding issues that had never been resolved between Mr. Hotchkiss and the Africa Inland Mission. Mr. Andersen had worked with Mr. Hotchkiss from 1907 until 1912, when he had married Mrs. Andersen. They joined the AIM and worked opening new stations including the Litein station. Prior to this, Mr. Hotchkiss had opened other out stations in the area. To comply with the government's requirements, these outstations had to be supervised by a missionary. Accordingly, when Mr. Hotchkiss returned to America, he had asked Mr. Andersen to represent his outstations to the government, but he had been absent for so long that there was a growing consensus he no longer had a legitimate claim to them. These among other issues needed resolution, and Bob remembered the two men disappearing into the brick house at the foot of the station. Finally when they emerged, they each had an arm around the other. Mr. Hotchkiss had decided then, and would later make the proposal to turn all of his schools over to the AIM in Belgut and Bureti in exchange for their two schools in Sot. But the feeling of the AIM that there was not room for two organizations in this area prevailed.

The main thing about Christianity is not the work we do, but the relationships we maintain and the atmosphere produced by that relationship. That is all God asks us to look after, and it is the one thing that is being continually assailed. Oswald Chambers, My Utmost for His Highest

Dear Mother and all,   *April 4, 1934*

We received such a lovely mail on Sunday. There was your letter, Mrs. William's, one from Mary, one from Anna, one from Eddie and Mary Eva and several from friends besides a lovely long letter from Mr. Warner, editor of the "Call to Prayer." I have such little time this week, I am going to write the family all together....

We told you about the truck. It was a splendid buy at $325.00. It cost something to get it in shape to run and it cost $375.00 for the charcoal burner. That is an invention, which is used in Africa, because of the high cost of gasoline. It costs $0.75 (American) a gal. And for a truck 15 miles on a gal is high mileage especially over bad roads. This burner cuts down the cost to between 1/4 and 1 cent (American) a mile. It burns the gas from the burning charcoal.... It is a tremendous responsibility for us to take, but we feel it was absolutely necessary. Had Bob been allowed to do it before, he would have been able to get enough transport to have it partially paid for by now. As to Bob's spirit etc.: Since I wrote, we have had several long talks in which he explained some things to me, which it seemed he hadn't felt free to before, and sharing again our spirits have both been revived. Then too, since he has taken his stand, he has sort of thrown off the bonds of servitude. All of these steps of sheer faith have been his, and he has felt so clearly the Lord's leading that I couldn't bear to have him defeated.

Now for the home folk. Baby is better. I am not sure she had whooping cough. She talks a lot and knows everything we say to her. The other day John was naughty so I sat down to talk it over with him. Finally he said, "It is a bad shauri (Swahili for affair) when I'm naughty. Jesus is sad." "Yes," I said, "Jesus is sad and Mother is sad, but you don't seem sorry at all." "No" he replied, "I don't know how to be sad." How is that for an answer?....

I surely will be glad when Bob returns. He has been gone 19 days now. I don't expect him for another two weeks and perhaps more, however. We got a wire from him yesterday morning saying all was running well, but he wasn't as far along as he had expected to be.

Mr. H., Mr. Andersen and the members of the Field Council of the A.I.M. have met to decide what they will do about the Sotik situation. Bro. H. has shown us a very beautiful spirit, and we are hoping that the breach of years standing will be healed. He has offered to turn over his Sotik schools to them. It is the logical move, but sometimes things like that are hard when one has been bitter toward an organization for years. If they can only get together now, it will be one of the biggest victories this colony has seen in years.

...Someday when we can talk over all this, you will understand better. Thank you, Mother, for the wonderful check. I can't tell you what a blessing it has been.

Love to all,   Catharine

"I couldn't bear to have him defeated."

The recurring years of drought, plague after plague of locust, and the harshest years of austerity Kenya had faced affected the missionaries in equal measure. Bob and Kitty's debt remained a looming presence that demanded harsh personal sacrifices. They were not alone in their financial concerns. Everyone was desperate to find ways to survive, let alone to keep the work going. Other things also had gone from bad to worse. Andrew Andersen had aged rapidly. He breathed heavily with any exertion, and his ankles were swelling daily. Still he dreamed of getting his old truck running. Bob saw Andrew cranking the motor again and again, desperately trying to make it run, hanging over the fender trying to get his breath, then trying again. Bob grimaced when he saw him. "Please, let me do that for you," he said. But the old truck stubbornly refused to cooperate and never did start. Notwithstanding, Andrew continued his efforts in quiet desperation, his hope being that his son Earl, who would soon be returning from the United States, could use it as a transport business and then channel the funds back into the mission work.

In 1987, Sarah, (the Smiths' youngest) was in the middle of a crisis—a troubled partner in her neurology practice was threatening to commit suicide and his whereabouts were unknown. She had just hung up the phone after a call from the Seattle police discussing the situation and stepped into a room to see a patient, when another call arrived. This one was from her father telling her of her mother's death. Minutes later, the news arrived that the partner had finally checked himself into the hospital where he had earlier agreed to receive rehabilitation.

A few days later, Sarah still numbed by all that was happening stood at her mother's graveside. A woman named Mary Andersen Honer stepped up beside Sarah and said, " You don't know me, but your mother saved my life." Seeing Sarah's surprised expression she added, "I'll be seeing you this evening; you are coming to my sister's house for dinner. We'll talk more about it then."

That evening as the family relaxed in Margaret Andersen Schilling's beautiful home, Mary explained that her father had died after a protracted illness. She and Sarah's sister, Anna Verne, were both babies and, because of the trauma of her father's illness, her mother had not been able to adequately nurse her. In Africa, no formula was available, so Mother volunteered to be Mary's wet nurse. "Had it not been for your mother... who knows what my mother would have done!" It was then that Sarah remembered the story her mother had told her some years before.

It was early dawn when the knock came at the door.

"Mrs. A., what is it?

"It's Andrew again," her eyes searched their faces for understanding. "Clara will take us to Nairobi, but it is the girls."

"Of course, I'll take care of the girls," said Kitty as an ominous feeling crept up her spine.

"He's having too much trouble breathing. They say his lungs are filling up with water again." She looked exhausted, and her forehead was furrowed with worry. "I don't know what I'm going to do about the baby."

Kitty remembered the same desperate look over a year ago, soon after they had arrived at Litein. Mrs. A. was already worn with the stress of Mr. A.'s illness. She had said, "My milk is drying up, and Mary cries for more but I just don't have enough."

Kitty had said, "I have plenty of milk after Anna Verne is done, and I can easily feed Mary too." Since then, she had fed both Mary and Anna Verne and felt a special bond with little Mary. She also loved the other girls, Lucile and Margaret. She enjoyed sewing for them and helping them learn. "Leave all of the girls. Everything will be fine. Now you go along, and we will be praying for you."

Bob and Kitty and the children watched as Clara and the Andersens drove away from the station and disappeared into the morning mist. Dewdrops hung heavily on the bushes. Light slanted through the trees and the equatorial sun rose abruptly. Their hearts were heavy as they turned back into the little house.

Bob knew he could step in to help, but things seemed desperate. Without operational funds from the U.S., many projects were at a standstill, and something had to be done. He thought again about seeing Mr. A. working on the truck that stubbornly refused to run. Everyone still hoped that the truck could be used for transport for hire, but no one was optimistic about Mr. A's recovery. The Andersens' son Earl had finished his college work and had returned. Perhaps if Bob could get the truck running, Earl could work driving the truck.

"Come on, girls. Let's get these babies cleaned up and ready to go outside for a walk."

"Me, too, Muddie?"

"Yes, you too, John Boy."

Mr. Andersen did have a short reprieve, but in just another few weeks, he was back in the hospital in Nairobi. Kitty had gone with Mrs. Andersen and the children this time.

> Now to get into the letter proper and real news. Our first is most recent and is of our great sorrow. Mr. Andersen on whose station we have lived for the past year has gone home to heaven. He had heart trouble and it was a question of time anyway. how long he would stay, but even yet it is hard to realize it. I was in Nairobi with Mrs. A. and was able to be of help to her in taking care of the little details and looking after the baby. Mr. Hotchkiss took her down and met all the bills including the casket and stayed with her at the hospital till the end. (John and Anna Verne were with Bob at Kericho.) There are four children. Earl (20 yrs) just returned from America. Lucile is 8, Margaret 5, and Mary not quite 2. It is so hard to see these kiddies left fatherless. Earl has been such a man and a tower of strength to his mother. He is very brave and a fine young fellow....

Excerpt from the May 26th letter

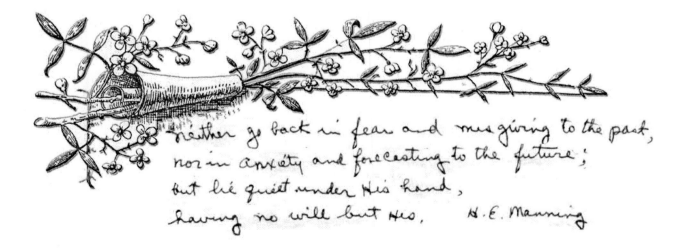

neither go back in fear and misgiving to the past, nor in anxiety and forecasting to the future; but lie quiet under His hand, having no will but His,   H. E. Manning

Dear Folks: May 26, 1934

Many things have transpired since we received your letter and many many since I wrote you. In fact, as you said, it takes so many days to get word back and forth that we can't be really explanatory. My biggest concern was that our church hold steady and not do anything that they would regret. If they will simply go ahead and keep their promise to give support this coming year all will be well for the present....

Well Mr. A's death makes a big change here and I'll have to go back a bit. I told you of Mr. Hotchkiss and his turning his schools over to the A.I.M. It healed a breach that has existed for nearly 30 years. It was Mr. A.'s dream that Mr. H. would have the superintendency of the entire work. But Mr. H.'s offer was made because of Mr. A. and he said just yesterday that in order for it to stand they must assure him that they are ready to occupy as of now or he requests that they turn everything over to him in which case we would affiliate and have what we were to have in the beginning. I do not look for this to happen unless the British take over their part of the American work of the A.I.M. in which case they will not have missionaries to put here. But the Lord has taken the whole thing out of our hands and we do not know what to expect from one day to the next. There is to be a conference here the 8th of June and these matters will be decided then. Now in order for Mr. H. to join the A.I.M. he had to promise to carry out their policy with the natives. Just what that means, I do not know....

Bob is home as I may have written you. His experiences would fill a book and just as soon as he can he will write many of them up. I hope he will be able to enclose a letter in this one as I know his folks are anxious for news from him again. But he did write them from the Congo he said. After he returned it looked like he had contracted intermittent or tick fever but since then he hasn't had any returns and the doctor thinks it is perhaps a bit more of malaria. If so he will take the Atebrine [sic] cure again....

We need your prayers badly about the truck that the finances may come in for it.

We are planning to return to Nairobi next week for a little vacation and camping trip. I had hoped to be able to have a photo taken of our family and perhaps we may. Anna Verne is talking a lot.... John cries to go on "safari" every time Bob goes....

We have been asked to leave this place to make room for new workers who will have to come and so we don't know for sure just where we will be, but we want to push the matter of the Vetende [sic] site so we may go down there and camp....

These are times that are dark and so uncertain that there isn't anything to write about. But the darkest time is just before the dawn and we are looking for that glow in the east.

Will write again next week but as this goes airmail there will be a space in between.

Much love, Catharine

"These are times that are dark.... But the darkest time is just before the dawn...."

Meantime in America, decisions were being made, word of which would not reach the field until another six weeks had gone by.

Meeting of the Missionary Board - April 30 & May 1, 1934

Brother Bishop reported on the situation in Africa, calling to attention the following matters:
1. Conditions in the Lumbwa Reserve covering the following points:
    a. Relationship of the Africa Inland Mission and our missionaries.
    b. The prospective opening of a new station by Brother Hotchkiss.
    c. The attitude of the Kenya Mission Council.
2. An application by our missionaries for a site in the Vatende and the moral support of the Kenya Mission Council given them largely thru the influence of the A.I.M. missionaries on the field.

It was moved and seconded that we send to Rev. Lee H. Downing, Field Director of the Africa Inland Mission, a letter of thanks expressing our deep appreciation of the loyal moral support which the A.I.M. missionary body has given to our missionaries since their arrival on the field. Motion carried.

It was moved and seconded that we also write a letter of thanks to Rev. A.M. Andersen of the Litein A.I.M. Mission Station for his valuable assistance to our missionaries in giving of his counsel, of granting to the Smiths and Miss Ford the privilege of living at his station and otherwise assisting them in every possible manner. Motion carried...

Board Minutes

"…it was hard to accept his death."

For as long as Bob and Kitty had known the Andersens, Mr. A.'s health had been poor. Bob and Kitty had learned to love him, admire his courage and persistence, and his counsel was treasured. Bob had learned not only from his words of advice but also from his example. But now he was gone, and it was hard to accept his death.

It is unlikely that Mr. Andersen ever received the letter of appreciation written by the board, as he died on May 22, 1934.

THE DARKEST TIME IS JUST BEFORE THE DAWN

A memorial that Kitty wrote for Mr. Andersen included the following:

"For miles around he was known as *Bwana Fundi*, literally 'Master Workman.' He was loved and respected by natives, Indians, settlers, government officials and fellow missionaries....

"How beautiful that his wish was fulfilled that he be called home while he was still in the harness. He was a living witness of a life wholly surrendered to the will of God. Again and again he was wont to say, 'It is all right because my Father knows.' The following excerpt from the life of Praying Hyde might well apply to his life. 'There is no power in the world so irrepressible as the power of personal holiness. A man's gifts may lack opportunity, his efforts be misunderstood and resisted, but the spiritual power of a consecrated will needs no opportunity and can enter where doors are shut. In this strange and tangled business of human life, there is no energy that so steadily does its work as the mysterious, unconscious, silent, unobtrusive, impenetrable influence which comes from a man who has done with self-seeking.'"

It was the day after Mr. A.'s funeral when Bob found himself kneeling at his graveside and praying. Bob had been honored to be a pallbearer, but the day had been heartbreaking. Earl, the older son, had just arrived. The three little girls clung to one another, bewildered by all the confusion and activity, the older ones crushed by the image of their father being lowered into the ground. Mrs. A. was stoical and coping once again, as she had for too many years, but still stricken with the finality of her husband's death. Bob prayed for each of the family then, "Dear God, you know my heart. I have been counseled and loved by this your servant. For that I am honored. If it would please you, Lord, help me to be such a servant also—let his mantle fall on me."

Several days later, he walked into Mr. A.'s shop. As always, he welcomed the fragrance of shavings and oil that greeted him at the door. There was something about a workshop that energized him. As he worked, he heard one of the nationals come in. "*Bwana Fundi*," he said. Bob whirled around to see to whom he was speaking, thinking perhaps the last several days had been a dream. It took him a moment to realize the African was addressing him and that he had just received a compliment that delighted him more than any he had received. Somehow in that moment, he felt a certainty that, at least in part, *Bwana Fundi's* mantle was falling on him.

"Mother was a missionary—not just the wife of a missionary. This made demands of her I began to understand only when I became one myself. She had some hard decisions to make concerning us children. And when she had to trust us to the care of others at boarding school nine months of every year, she loved us through letters. She was faithful in keeping contact. When we came home from school for vacations, the comforts of home were very inviting. They still live vividly in my memory—a bowl of oatmeal and hot cocoa at our pre-dawn arrival, the smell of polished cedar floors, a fire burning in the fireplace, a centerpiece of pansies on the dining room table, a welcoming bed dressed with fresh linens and Grandma's handmade quilt." Anna Verne

A later picture of the original building of Rift Valley Academy

Rift Valley Academy was the school, located 35 miles from Nairobi and overlooking the Great Rift Valley, where all of us missionary children attended in those days. The experience was both dreaded and loved. We boarded for three months then returned home for one month and then back again throughout the year. As six-year-olds, we were initiated into school life as "titchies" (the youngest students) by our big sister or brother (someone assigned to help us with making our beds and keeping our space clean and, if necessary, to hold on to us while our parents drove away). The first week there was always difficult, but soon thereafter, we all came to accept our plight and grew to be grateful for the experience. We have fond memories of our "dorm parents" Ma and Pa Lehrer, of our Saturday afternoon walks up into the hills above the school where we would swing out across ravines on monkey ropes or slide down fire breaks on our shoes and bottoms, climb trees, crawl around on rocks, becoming as dirty as a thoroughly happy child can get. We had chores to perform in the mornings before our outing. They included scrubbing out houses, emptying slop pails, doing dishes, laundry and generally keeping the place functioning—so we thought. In truth, Ma Lehrer and her African helper Shindo bore the brunt of the work. Many Saturday mornings we spent singing at the top of our lungs, to the tune of "I've Been Working on the Railroad." "I've been working on the pea pods, all the live long day.... Can't you hear Ma Lehrer shouting, 'Shindo, bake your bread'?"—as we shelled endless tubs of peas. The students were divided into two groups – the Livingstone and Stanley houses. We competed in many areas, especially scholastics and sports. Of the graduates of Rift Valley Academy, in those days, 90-95%* completed college and many of those went on to higher degrees of education.

---

* Phil Dow, *School in the Clouds*, William Carey Library, Pasadena, CA, 2004

David and Sarah remember the days of the Mau Mau insurgence when the school came under siege because of the national uprising. To protect us a ten-foot fence of barbed wire was built and out from that fifteen feet of sharpened bamboo stakes. African *askari* (policemen) lived under the porch of the building constantly on guard duty. We eventually were dismissed, and the school closed when the Lari Massacre just a few miles from the school took place. Many people were killed on that one night, and the school staff apparently came to terms with the seriousness of the problem. We remember well when the alarm rang (we had been instructed that should that happen, we were to get out of bed and lie against the stone wall of our rooms so that any arrows coming through the windows would go over us). This we did, but soon we were all herded into a central room where prayers were spoken. The next morning, our families were contacted to come and get us, and we were sent home. Some years later, we were told that two captured Mau Mau had given the same story independently. They said that they tried to attack the school but that there were bright beings at the four corners who seemed to be guarding the school and, therefore, they dared not attack.

Original RVA building—Courtesy of Mary Andersen Honer

Mrs. Andersen had long ago sent her first child, Earl, to R.V.A. Then when he was 14 years old, because the school principal was ill and there were not enough personnel to teach the high school years, had bid him goodbye as he left for America with 11 other boys known as the "Westervelt boys" to complete their schooling in Arkansas under the care of a Mr. and Mrs. Westervelt.

Still this new separation from her oldest girl so soon after the loss of her husband that Kitty mentions in her next letter must have been difficult for Mrs. Andersen and agonizing for Lucile. Yet as with every child, the necessity for this to happen, if one was a missionary child, was a matter of fact. It was simply acknowledged and accepted without debate.

Litein Sataion, Kericho
June 3, 1934

Dear Folks;

It is Sunday morning and as our Daddy and our John-boy have gone to take Mrs. Andersen and the children to Kijabi where they will leave Lucille in school, Anna Verne and "Mum-ma" as she calls me are alone. She is trying hard to help write this letter with the above results. She is such a fine big girlie you would hardly believe she is only 15 months, and she is talking quite a bit. She says "toto" (baby in Swahili) and "Ongebi" (let's go) in Kipsigis.

As I wrote you in the last letter, we expected to go to Nairobi last Monday. Miss Ford was going along, but Sunday night was taken sick, so we were detained. She was very ill and required care day and night, so we sent for her sister who is here now. She had at first internal hemorrhaging causing depleted blood but it has gone into pneumonia. However the doctor is quite pleased with her improvement and says it is only a light case. Just why it should come now we do no know, but the Lord knows best. Our next move is quite uncertain. We received a very disappointing letter from Bro. Bishop. Miss Ford thinks he has repressed all the information she sent from the General Board, even Mr. Chilson's letters. He treats conditions here like a kid's quarrel. I am learning more and more that we simply have nowhere to go but to the Lord. He alone can do something, and I am sure He is....

"He treats conditions here like a kid's quarrel.
I'm learning more and more that we simply have nowhere to go but to the Lord."

We received a lovely letter from Mr. Terry. I really could shut my eyes and feel I was sitting listening to him talk. It did so much to help cheer us up to know he still remembers us so faithfully. If our church now will only take our support as they promised....

I received the package of pieces. They are so lovely and some of them are large enough to make baby clothes. Just now we are expecting 11 babies. They are illegitimate children and would be killed as soon as born if the mission did not rescue them. I am going to write about them for the paper but will tell you what I can't write. In the tribal custom here they circumcise the girls as well as the boys. After the completion of the ceremony the girls go to the cattle boma and stay with the men until they become pregnant. Then this first baby is killed, they never let it cry and think it never lives so of course it isn't murdered. They only have to see if they can have children, else they won't be wanted. They are taught that as soon as the head is born they must kick it with all their might. Even when they come here and are watched carefully they will kill their baby if they can. But if they are made to nurse their baby for 2 months there is no more trouble and they are often saved and also the child by this means. The government appropriates $100.00 for the purpose, but of course that doesn't go too far. It means an orphanage and also a home for the mothers because they are no longer Kipsigis and no Kipsigis other than a Christian will marry them. There are surely some problems here in this tribe....

Must close, Kitty

Excerpt from June 3, 1934

113

THE DARKEST TIME IS JUST BEFORE THE DAWN

"...but there were even bigger chasms."

As much as she preferred to deny it, Kitty gradually saw what a huge gulf separated the people of Kenya from her people and way of life. She yearned to grasp a deeper understanding of what was in the African mind. She lived in one world while the Africans co-existed in another, yet the two could scarcely mesh. The biggest issues for her were those of cleanliness and health. Water was not readily available, and African hands touched everything from cleaning up babies' bottoms to wiping runny noses without being washed for days, as they had no idea that there was a connection between cleanliness and health. They took baths occasionally but rarely had soap. Their lifelong exposure to germs had produced an exceptional immunity, so it seemed to them that the cleaner white people were the sick ones. Fearing for their safety, Kitty tried to teach her children what to touch and not to touch and washed their hands frequently.

She was determined to do her part to try to overcome this gulf, but there were even bigger chasms. The natives' lives were ruled by customs, beliefs, and their constant insecurity. They were threatened by the *laibon* (witch doctors) of consequences if they didn't respond to the taboos these witch doctors laid on them. They frequently abandoned their huts partly because eventually the animal and human excrement would accumulate to the point they were unlivable and partly because new locations could

Kipsigis woman carrying burdens

fool enemy raiders. Their customs were particularly cruel to women who were the burden bearers (being responsible for moving any items related to the home), and did the gardening and cooking—this while carrying their children (sometimes one within, one tied on front and another tied to the back).

Kitty had read what Mr. Hotchkiss had written in his book *Sketches from the Dark Continent*. He was describing the Wakamba,* but the attitudes about women were similar to the Kipsigis tribe with whom they now worked.

Old women who performed initiation rites

---

* The total number of tribes in Kenya is debated. Most agree on about 76 tribes and 70% of those are lumped into five groups the Kikuyu, Luo, Luhya, Kamba and the Kalenjin. The Kipsigis tribe is part of the Kalenjin group; the Wakamba are part of the Kamba.

"Marriage is a mere matter of barter, and polygamy is universal. A man's social position and influence in the tribe depends largely upon the number of wives he has; consequently, his aim is to have as many as possible. This is because wives are an index of wealth, for a wife costs among the Wakamba from forty to sixty goats, a goat being the standard of value in a country where money is unknown. The man thinks just as much of his wife as he does of the goats he has paid for her, and no more. She is practically a slave, a beast of burden, reckoned as just so much *mali* (property).

"She it is who thatches the huts, cultivates the fields—her only farming implement a straight stick two and one-half feet long sharpened at the end; with this she laboriously digs up the ground. She goes long distances, chops down trees with little miniature axes, and carries the wood in great staggering loads to the villages."*

Men spent most of their time sitting around pots of hot toddies, sipping with long reeds and discussing a previous raid or an anticipated one. Their physical prowess was rarely noted except when they were hunting animals or more often raiding cattle from the neighboring tribe.

Kipsigis girl in initiation rites
Courtesy of Earl Andersen

But most horrifying to Kitty were parts of the women's initiation rites. They began early in November and lasted up to a year. A respected older woman of the tribe, who was chosen to care for the girls of the age of puberty, fed them and taught each one how to become an adult as well as a mother. The family center of worship, a clump of sticks outside the home called the *mabwita*, played a large part in the ceremony. New branches were placed in this *mabwita* at the homes of each of the girls who were going into the rites.

One day Kitty was looking out her window when she viewed "a most amazing sight." She had heard about them, but this was the first time she had seen one—a girl in ceremonial attire. The woman was covered with skins. Kitty knew that during their year of rites neither the girls nor the old women who were their instructors were allowed to cut their hair. It became long and matted with cow dung. The girls had been taught to be stoical during their circumcision. If they did cry out, they might have to marry an older man who had more wives. The old women of the tribe held the girls down, then with stones cut these young women, and in the process, took from them any joy they might experience from sexual relations, and also mutilated them beyond belief.

The procedure was done without consideration of sterility. Accordingly, the girls came to the mission dispensaries with tetanus, urinary retention and hemorrhage (some too late to save). These were the complications of the early stages, and in the late stages, women

---

* Willis R. Hotchkiss, *Sketches from the Dark Continent*, Cleveland, Ohio: The Friends Bible Institute and Training School, 1901, 22-23.

115

were so scarred from this procedure that they were left with only a tiny opening and needed surgical help to deliver their children.

As Kitty stood looking at her, she tried to imagine the pain the girls were suffering as they healed from their mutilation, and wondered what must it be like to live inside that smelly, hot tent of animal skins. The final phase of this custom, however, was even more horrifying to her. While these women were healing, older men would come to service themselves and try to make the women pregnant. Only if they conceived were they considered to be eligible for marriage. Otherwise they were rejected, remaining in the tribe as outcasts. The babies who were born of these unions were not believed to be humans. The young mothers were required to kill them immediately upon their birth. They would smother and strangle them or smash their heads. Kitty felt ill at the thought and her heart ached.

The government had made these procedures illegal and offered funds for girls to be housed and protected from the tribe. At Litein, this protection was being provided. The children who were saved, however, were named *Machi*(Not a person) by the tribe. Kitty was helping to care for the babies who resulted from these unions as well as helping the mothers who had decided to let their babies live. She held classes for the mothers, teaching them hygiene, sewing, childcare as well as reading and writing.

Mother found the treatment of women to be one of the most difficult issues. She prayed for understanding and worked diligently for solutions, and when she spoke of their plight, it was apparent how deeply this troubled her.

Mrs. Andersen continued to suffer from her loss but was showing herself to be strong. The support that Bob and Kitty were able to give her had drawn them all closer. On Wednesday evenings, the missionaries gathered for prayer, praise, singing and sharing. On one such night, Mrs. A had recalled her first encounter with the Smiths. "I was so unkind to the Smiths when they arrived. Those were terrible times for me. I told them they were not welcome. I just didn't think I could cope. The truth is," she turned and faced them, "I don't have any idea how I would have managed without you. You have been such a blessing to me."

Bob and Kitty let their tears flow freely without shame trying to imagine how difficult the time must have been for this courageous woman. Within a short time, she would move from Litein to Kijabi where she could work, have housing and be with her children who were still traumatized by the loss of their father, but she and Kitty remained fast friends. In years to come, Kitty worked closely with her son Earl to develop Kipsigis grammar lessons and complete the translation of the Kalenjin Bible.

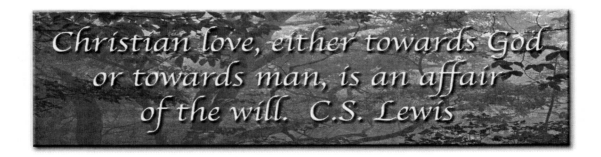

Christian love, either towards God or towards man, is an affair of the will. C.S. Lewis

Although our parents and the other missionaries we knew were some of the happiest people we have ever met, "tears" seemed to be a frequently mentioned word in their conversation. However, though their work was never easy, the stories they told revealed no self-pity at all. Instead, their tears seemed to be tears of gratitude for the miracles they witnessed continually—someone's newfound faith, a gift, or sacrifice from someone who supported them in their work. Accordingly, we often heard them say, "We listened with tears rolling down our cheeks."

CHAPTER 9
VATENDE—JULY 29, 1934—SEPTEMBER 2, 1934

To reach the port of heaven, we must sail sometimes with the wind and sometimes against it----
but we must sail, and not drift, nor be at anchor.
Oliver Wendell Holmes

The time had come for a change.

The work site in Sotik was still not secured. While they had high expectations, Mr. H.'s arrival had settled nothing with certainty. The attempts to affiliate with the AIM, although approved on at least two occasions on the field, had not been approved by their Home Council. Their position was that the Kipsigis area was adequately served, and while the missionaries in this area had graciously accepted their help for nearly two years, everything had changed with Mr. Andersen's death. His son had arrived and would be assuming his father's position, and another couple was coming under appointment of the AIM. Mrs. Andersen would be leaving to work at Kijabi. Kitty and Bob were also asked to leave the house that they occupied to accommodate the newcomers.

Continuation of April 30 & May 1, 1934 board meeting

The matter of future plans for our Africa work was considered at length, the main points in question being whether our workers should remain in the Lumbwa Reserve or take up work in the Vatende district.
In view of the following reasons:
1. Inasmuch as it would not be considered the ethical thing by the Kenya Mission Council for our missionaries to remain in the Lumbwa Reserve.
2. Since Brother Chilson recommends the location of our work in the Vatende.
3. Inasmuch as Miss Ford who represents the judgement of her father, shares the same view.
4. In view of the fact that Brother Hotchkiss' work is not recognized by the Kenya Mission Council;
5. Inasmuch as he has returned to this field and is again taking up missionary work; and
6. Since the A.I.M. Home Council has vetoed the proposition of our affiliation with them on the field; it was moved by Mrs. Vennard that we strongly advise our missionaries entering the Vatende field if the government grants their request for a site there. The motion was seconded by Miss Spann and carried.

The board's directives were known on the field by July of 1934.

There remained the nagging conflict between themselves and the Kirks. Everything would go well for a while, and then there would be another problem. Clara, Bob and Kitty called on all the reserves they knew and pondered over the incongruity of the lives they led and the message they tried to preach. At every turn, there seemed to be human failure, including theirs. What was the solution? For months, an idea had been germinating in their minds. By moving to an entirely new situation, new people, new location they could shed the baggage that attended this one. Enigmatically tied to this plan was the necessity to prevent any further debt, and both Bob and Kitty were totally committed to resolving its looming presence. The Kirks chose to remain in Kericho. Clara, Kitty and Bob would pursue the new path.

They had first begun to consider Vatende when Mr. Ford, Clara's father, a man of strong faith and an open ear to his African brothers' needs, spoke of a tribe close to the Tanganyika border called the Wakuria or Watende (the name used for the people).

"How did you hear about these folks?" Bob had queried with a note of anticipation.

"We have a station at Kisii, and the Vatende area is under the jurisdiction of the District Commissioner at Kisii. He spoke to us of this tribe. But the most compelling thing was a conversation I had with a man from Vatende who attended our school. He begged us to send his people some help." Mr. Ford's expression made it obvious that he wished he could have responded.

"It sounds like this may be a wide open field where we could work," Bob said eagerly.

"The gold miners are moving into the area. I know three mine operations there now. The coming of the gold mines has resulted in the roads from Kericho to Lolgorien being reworked and improved. They have even put in some new roads. I've spoken with the miners, and they say the Watende are an unspoiled tribe quite out of touch with the rest of the world. You know, I think it may be a perfect place for you to open a work." His kind eyes met Bob's approvingly.

Back in 1933, Bob and Mr. Ford had traveled to Kisii and spoken to the District Commissioner about entering Vatende. He had been cool and seemed intent on shrugging off their inquiries.

And so...time passed, and Bob continued to feel drawn to the Vatende country. In January of 1934, he and Clara spoke with the Chief Native Commissioner in Nairobi who instructed them to follow normal procedure, which of course they had already done. They decided to ask Mr. Andersen to accompany them on another trip to Kisii. Bob smiled as he recalled that trip made about five months before Mr. A.'s death. He had experience in dealing with the British officials. Where Bob was baffled with their lack of response and indirect approach, Mr. Andersen would likely handle them well. "Would you be willing to come with us to Kisii to speak with the D.C.?" he had asked.

Bob thought about how the Norwegian had lifted his eyes and looked penetratingly at Bob. "I vill do it, Bob. I tink dis is a goot ting." Mr. A. had been doing better at that time and his old spark was back.

And so the trip had been made. Before seeing the D.C., they had gone to Kaboti to visit members of the tribe. They seemed very interested in having the missionaries come, and encouraged by this, the missionaries went on to visit with Major Buxton, the new District Commissioner who was friendly and engaging. He agreed that he along with Mr. Montgomery, the Provincial Commissioner, would take the matter to the Local Native Council (LNC) the following week. Everyone had waited expectantly, but when no word came an inquiry was made, it turned out the District Commissioner had simply forgotten.

"My stars and little sawhorses! I can't believe it. I am so fed up with trying to cope with these government officials. The facts are forever different from the appearance of things. What are we going to do now?" Bob had lamented when he heard the news.

"In God's time," Mr. Andersen had simply said.

On February 20, 1934, Bob had written to Major Buxton once again to report that the Kenya Mission Council had approved their mission and to reinforce their interest in beginning a work in Vetende. He received a reply on February 27 from Mr. Montgomery, the Provincial Commissioner at Kisumu, that the matter would be taken to the LNC, but that there was no possibility of immediate occupation....

Bob realized he had paused a long time immersed in his memories. If they just spent some time in the area, perhaps that would convince the D.C. and the Watende that they were serious. His thoughts were interrupted by Kitty's voice.

"I was reading II Timothy 4 this morning. Perhaps this is what he was talking about. 'Be ready in season and out of season.' I just wonder when is God's season for us," Kitty said plaintively.

Bob was sitting at his desk. He reached into his file for the letter written in response to their first inquiries about Vatende. He handed it to Kitty to read.

Roughly speaking the tribe inhabits the triangle formed between the Kenya-Tanganyika (Tanzania) boundary, the shore of Lake Victoria and the Mara River, an area of about 2,000 square miles. The climate is pleasant; the country very hilly going from lake level (3,720 ft) to about 6,000 ft, the average height I should say is around 4,500 ft.

"It really sounds very interesting. Even though it is close to Lake Victoria, it is up in the hills and should be nice and cool. You know Clara is thrilled about the idea of going there. I guess it has been on her mind for quite some time. We will of course have to start language study for the third time," Kitty mused.

"Faye and Kirk have no interest in going. They are settled in Kericho, their needs are met, he has his jail ministry, and he continues to visit Mr. H.'s outstations. They have no reason to move."

"I really think it could work," she paused.   "We have prayed so hard for the Sotik plot, it breaks my heart to give that up. But we do have to do something." Kitty's frustration with their long vigil was quite apparent.

"We can take the truck and just enough things to camp for an extended time. We can go right to the area, meet the people and see for ourselves whether they want us," Bob said, almost cheerfully, and then with reservation, "It is going to be the same process as we have gone through for the Sotik site. First the D.C. has to approve it, then the L.N.C., then it would go to the land board, then to the Provincial Commissioner and then to the Chief Native Commissioner in Nairobi."

"This could take years, Bob," Kitty looked at him square in the eye.

Bob looked away and his voice was tender, "You're right, Kitty. You are so right."

Before the trip could be undertaken, Dad had gone to Nairobi to try to make arrangements for the remaining payments due on the truck's charcoal burner. But first, we will step back to another story that lays the foundation for what is to follow.

"...the most dangerous animal to hunt...."

There was nothing that thrilled Dad quite so much as hunting stories. He had several of his own including a hunt into the bamboo forests after bongo. He was successful, and the bongo's ivory-tipped horns from that hunt can still be seen in the museum in Nairobi as they were confiscated during WWII. But the truth is that apart from the hunts necessary for food, even in the later years, they could rarely afford the luxury of a hunt. Nonetheless, he had many friends who were game wardens, and we suspect he envied their adventures. The incident that is about to be described had happened nearly a year before in August of 1933 soon after Dad had made Mother an oven out of a *debi*.

"So you think the buffalo is the most dangerous animal to hunt in Kenya, Captain Oulton?" The old game warden's stories fascinated Bob.

"I could tell you any number of stories of buffalo that mauled hunters," his mustache and beard twitched as he thought. "Back in the '20s, a man called Colquhoun joined with his friend Hunter who had a farm

Kenya's most dangerous

in Subukia. The Cape buffalo herds had become a menace in the Aberdare Range, and the men decided to go for a hunt. Sure enough, they caught up with a herd of bulls at the edge of a forest. They opened fire, killing two and wounding two others. Following a trail of blood, they disappeared deep into the thicket where they realized they were surrounded by buffalo. With lightening speed, and before they could react, the buffalo were charging them and throwing them up in the air like rag dolls. Hunter was tossed and mauled so frequently that he begged to die. Colquhoun ran to try to distract the bull that was mauling Hunter, but he was charged by another and thrown high in the air, falling incredibly right on top of his rifle. Almost immediately, the bull that had thrown Colquhoun caught sight of him and again charged, and this time he was lucky enough to put a bullet through its brain. It fell lifeless on him. After he was freed, he and the Africans with them made a pole hammock to try to carry Hunter to help, but the man mercifully died on the way. Those buffs are crafty critters. If you don't kill them, they will circle around and serve you with retribution."

"What a story! Well, I don't expect to ever hunt buffalo. I do shoot for meat now and then. By the way, would you join Kitty and me for dinner tomorrow night?"

"My friend Mr. Curry will be with me tomorrow," Captain Oulton said with reservation.

"Fine, you bring him right along."

"Jolly good then. We'll be there."

Mr. Oulton arrived at the door wearing his helmet, an over shirt with many pockets, and khaki shorts with knee-length khaki socks and safari boots. It was typical wear for the British officials. *"Hodi! Hodi!"*

Kitty ran to the door – "*Karibu! Karibu!* You are welcome, Captain Oulton. How very nice to see you again."

"Mrs. Smith, this is Mr. Curry. Mr. Curry, Mrs. Smith, Bob Smith's wife."

Kitty and Mr. Curry shook hands.

Earlier Kitty had heated the flatiron on the stove and pressed her best dress. With attention to every detail, the table was set and made ready for the special evening ahead. The table looked beautiful with a centerpiece of fresh flowers, which she floated with greenery in a round, flat, glass dish.

"We are so glad you and Mr. Curry could join us for dinner."

"I can assure you that this chap is very happy not to have to endure my campfire cooking for once." The old game ranger eased himself into a chair. Kitty turned to Mr. Curry. " Please have a seat. My husband should be along shortly."

"Well, I'll be jiggered! You are already here." Bob burst through the door and extended his hand to Captain Oulton. "How's it going, old chap?"

"Splendid, just splendid, thank you! This is my friend Mr. Curry, Mr. Smith."

"A pleasure. Are you here on holiday or just business?" Bob smiled broadly.

"A little of both. I don't often get up to the tea country, and I am surely enjoying it."

"I remember when there was very little of it here," Mr. Oulton reflected. "I once met John Kerich the early tea planter for whom Kericho got its name. He was convinced this was the ideal place to grow tea, and of course he was right. It is already the tea capital of Kenya."

John Boy peeked around the door frame from the bedroom.

"But on to more important things. How is this little chap? What was that word I taught you last time I saw you?"

John Boy grinned. "Spectrascope! S P E C T R A S C O P E."

"How very clever of you. Has Mother been working on the spelling, old chap?" John nodded and lifted his chin proudly.

At first Kitty had worried that Anna Verne might be afraid of the beard, but Mr. Oulton had wanted to hold her, and now she was tugging at his whiskers and smiling her infectious smile, eyes twinkling.

"Charming youngsters!" he had said, as Kitty gathered up the baby and hurried John Boy off to bed. Customarily the children ate an early dinner and were put to bed before the adults ate.

"Say goodnight, children."

"Goodnight!"

Mr. Curry, Mr. Oulton and Bob stepped outside until the children were settled. It was easy conversation regarding hunting trips and new developments in Kenya.

"Mr. Oulton, I understand you knew ivory hunters, such as Karamoja Bell, Sutherland, Neuman. You must have had some experiences. How many years have you been here in Kenya?"

"It's going on twenty–five years now. I wouldn't give anything for the time. Bloody wonderful is what I'd call it."

Kitty set out the fresh bread she had made. "We'll have dinner now," she called out the door. They sat down around the tiny table. She had fixed a chicken dish with dumplings and fresh vegetables from their garden. She had picked a pineapple also and made an upside-down cake. It was a first.

"Mrs. Smith, your dinner is delightful!" Mr. Curry remarked.

"I did it in my new oven that Bob built me, but I do have to keep things up high in the space; otherwise they burn."

"How did you do that, old chap?"

"Well, I dug a hole in an earthen bank," Bob began. "Then I used a *debi* for the oven and surrounded it with brick and cement, leaving a space for smoke to escape from the firebox through the chimney above. I packed dirt back around the oven. The door is a lid from a packing barrel but it doesn't seal so well. I have a bit of work to do on that yet."

"I'll go get things cleaned up and then we can visit a little more," Kitty commented as they finished eating.

"Well, I'll just step out for a smoke, then," said Mr. Oulton, but seeing Kitty's expression added, "What, Mrs. Smith? You don't approve?"

"I apologize, I didn't think I was that transparent. I didn't mean to react, but the truth is, it took me by surprise. I didn't realize that you smoked. My belief is that as children of God we should not defile our bodies with anything that might have a bad effect on them. We are temples or vessels of the Spirit of God. Therefore, how can He approve?"

"That God should care how we take care of ourselves," he paused, "that's a new thought for me."

Kitty looked him squarely in the eye. "I do apologize. I didn't mean to make you uncomfortable." She began picking up the dishes. Bob wanted to change the subject, and Mr. Oulton seemed to have lost his desire to have a smoke.

"We've heard about your interest in some archeological findings in the pyramids that have some bearing on the tribes of Israel?" Bob said, addressing his question to Mr. Curry.

"Right! Actually an American named Charles Totten who is a military science and tactics teacher at Yale University has done some of the research that has fueled our Anglo-Israelism movement. Most of it has come out of the British Isles. We hold that the "lost ten tribes" of Israel, which dispersed after the Assyrians were defeated by Alexander the Great, migrated to Northern and Western Europe, where they established themselves, merged with the indigenous peoples, and eventually became the super powers of our current world. We believe the Anglo-Saxons are in fact God's chosen people."

"Why do you call them the 'ten lost tribes'?" Bob was astonished at what he was hearing.

"Well, the term 'Jew' as used currently applies only to the two tribes (Judah and Benjamin) and not to the 'House of Israel'—the ten tribes. So the return of Jews under Zerubbabel, Ezra, and Nehemiah to Palestine from their captivity was limited to the two tribes. The other ten ended up on the outskirts of Assyria and became known as the Sakeians. They migrated into Europe to become the Scythians and Saxons. Others emerged as Galics, etc. We believe the British monarchy is, in fact, from the line of David," Curry stated.

"It sounds quite remarkable." Bob's head was spinning.

"Our movement is growing," Curry continued. "Many in the Anglican Church have embraced these ideas."

"I guess I find it difficult to understand what difference it makes, even if these theories are proven true. My salvation has nothing to do with one race being superior to another. In fact, I would not be here trying to give the Christian message to the Africans if salvation was somehow related to race," Bob responded.

"The information is truly fascinating! We have surely enjoyed hearing about it," Kitty interjected.

"Well, we best be leaving." Mr. Oulton picked up his pith helmet as he stood up. Mr. Curry stood also. "We have a long journey ahead of us tomorrow. We will have some more talks about this. Look me up sometime when you are in Nairobi, and we will have a spot of tea. This has been a most enjoyable evening. Thank you both for your hospitality."

"You are most gracious. We have enjoyed your company also. We will most certainly look you up."

"Cheerio, then."

"Good bye!"

Little did Bob and Kitty realize that this night would become pivotal in determining their future.

By July of 1934, Bob was in Nairobi at his wit's end. The payments for the charcoal burner, the device purchased to make the truck run more economically, were overdue. He had waited in vain for salaries and other promised monies from the United States to arrive, and having exhausted every avenue he could think of, he was about to go to the bank for a loan. Kitty wrote about it:

> But to go back again. Bob had to take the truck to Nairobi for an inspection and as we had defaulted for the payments on the charcoal burner as funds had not arrived from home, he promised that he would not leave until they had come. He stayed for a month. Finally they said they could wait no longer and would have to file suit. That morning as Bob was going to the bank to see if he could possibly do anything, he met an old man who had visited Mr. Oulton, whom I wrote you about and who had been to our house for tea and for dinner. He stopped Bob to tell him to tell me that Mr. O had stopped smoking, and he was trying to (I had talked to him about the habit, or rather had stated my opinions when asked). He also asked Bob where he was going, and Bob told him and why. He said, "Oh you don't want to do that; let me give you what you need, and he gave him a check for Sh.600 Bob had told the manager of the company that morning that they had no prospects whatever humanly speaking but that they had made the matter a special subject of prayer and had the assurance that the Lord would supply the funds before night. When he took it to him, he said, "Here is our answer to prayer," and the manager was simply dumbfounded. Finally he said, "Well, that is a Christian's consolation, I guess."

"Here's our answer to prayer,' and the manager was simply dumbfounded."

And so when Bob arrived back at Litein, preparations were made to go to Vatende. Much of an afternoon was spent loading the truck with provisions and bags of charcoal. Mr. Hotchkiss, Clara and Kirk traveled by car via Kisii with the intent of speaking with the D.C. The Smiths went a shorter route, and all would meet at a designated spot, Nyabassi. Clara would remain with the Smiths, and Mr. H. and Kirk would return to the Kericho area.

125

Perhaps the most often told story of our parents' adventure follows. We children heard it more often than we can count and no one could tell it like our storyteller father.

"Every tin plate, pot and pan clattered to the ground."

Bob's own words are in italics: *When Isaiah Arap Misoi, Kitty, the children and I had set off on our trip to the Vatende area, we were slithering and sliding in our old international truck when—bang, our rear wheel slipped off the bridge, and we just about to fall into the river. We jacked up the rear-end and, with the help of passing natives, moved the truck back onto the bridge, and off we went again. Pretty soon the shambas (small farms) disappeared, and we were really "in the bush." Then the roads ended. Mr. Andersen had told me how to get there some years before. "You head toward that hill, go around it and keep on going until"….*

They had bumped and jerked and jostled endlessly over the trail. Mile after mile, hour after hour they struggled over increasingly rugged country. Long shadows stretched across the plains where animals in large numbers grazed. A few hills studded with huge rocks could be seen in the distance and in the great expanse before them; colors were brilliant and contrasts striking.

"Look at that, Kitty; it's like a whole zoo has been turned loose!" Bob said waving his arm enthusiastically and in so doing bumped his knuckles on the windshield. "Ouch!"

"I've never seen anything like it in all my life," she agreed as she braced against the next bump.

It had been raining through much of forenoon. Ahead more clouds were building, and in some places gray lines were streaking from the clouds to the earth.

"Great day! Look at that! More rain! We're not going to get much farther." They had arrived at a wooded area. The sun was headed toward the horizon, and the clouds were taking on a pink tinge. Even the hilltops had a rosy hue. Soon they were enveloped in the blazing glory of a tropical sunset. The whole sky was magically painted in hues of orange red, and some small areas of brilliant blue still remained among the clouds. Raindrops began hitting the windshield again. Soon it was pouring rain, and the International truck was slithering and sliding in every direction.

"We're going to have to give it up for the night." Bob said wearily.

"That is fine with me. The baby is tired and hungry. She and John Boy have about worn out their lungs screaming." Then turning to her son she said, "I imagine you would like to get out of the truck wouldn't you, John Boy?"

"Yes, Muddie," he said as he bounced up and down with anticipation.

A fine rain continued to fall as they pitched the tent. Bob built a fire under the bed of the truck so the rain wouldn't put it out. Kitty put the children in the 7x12 foot tent and set the beans on the fire to cook. Later she would make some gravy with the jerked beef they had brought and bake some biscuits in her Dutch oven. It would make a fine dinner. Bob had already lit the kerosene lantern and hung it in the tent. He saw Kitty bringing the food and quickly cautioned, "Let me sit down first and secure the table with my legs. It's so rickety that it will surely fall over if I don't. The rivets through the corners of the legs are hardly holding." He teased John Boy by releasing his hold on the table leg, letting the table free wheel, and reaching here and there for the next bite depending on where the tabletop had migrated.

John Boy laughed heartily.

"Bob, stop that! You're going to upset the whole table and then what a mess we will have to clean up," Kitty remarked as she grinned at him.

After dinner they propped the table against the wall of the tent and stacked all the washed pots and pans and tin dishes on it. The rain had finally stopped.

Kitty prepared the children for the night. It was good to get settled. Bob had stepped outside and built up the fire that he had moved from under the truck.

"My stars! Kitty, come look at this!" he called as he held the lantern high. They could see some creatures about the size of a jackrabbit. They were emerging from their burrows, a whole colony of them. Standing on their hind feet, their short forelegs held up, looking for all the world like miniature kangaroos.

"Aren't they something!"

"I think they are called springhares. I've never seen them before, but I've been told about them."

"What's that, Daddy?" John Boy pointed at the orange eyes of an animal lurking at the edge of the circle of light.

"It's a hyena," Bob said as he picked up a stick. He tossed the stick in the direction of the eyes, and they disappeared.

Not much later, they could feel their tiredness dissolving in the comfort of their bedrolls. It had been far too wet and rainy to bother to get out the cots and set them up, as was their usual practice. Suddenly the baby was making little grunting sounds. Before long it was quite apparent what was happening. Bob had no sooner lit the kerosene lantern than it flickered and went out. "Well, for Pete's sake! We're out of kerosene," he said as he shook the lantern.

"Oh, no!" Kitty moaned as she struggled to change the diaper by match light. Bob stumbled out of the tent to bury its contents and put it with the clothes to soak. The moon was appearing, and the rain had returned but was now just a light drizzle. It would be a beautiful night.

The children were already asleep as Bob and Kitty snuggled once more into their bedrolls. It had been exciting to plan this move and then pack up what they would need. Waiting and waiting for a plot to be granted had been excruciating but at last they were doing something positive! If there wasn't any work for them in Sotik, then perhaps at last they would find the place God wanted for them. Living with two children in the tent for an extended time would be a challenge, but none welcomed it more than they did. They could hear a lion roaring, but the sounds were becoming more distant with time. They drifted off to sleep, feeling at peace.

"Bob! What is that?" Kitty grabbed Bob's arm and sat up in bed. The floor of their tent was moving up and down. There was a swishing sound outside as if something large was walking through the wet grass. The ground was boggy from all the rain, and the rhythm of the rising and falling earth corresponded with the noise they heard.

Bob grabbed his .404 rifle, which was lying by his bedroll, and headed for the tent door. A trickle of water ran down his arm as he lifted the tent flap and stepped out into the brilliantly clear, tropical moonlight. The sounds were coming from the back of the tent, so he began to ease slowly around it. He later described it:

I surmised that a large rhino was approaching. Knowing that it might charge through our tent, killing us all, I slipped quietly from my cot, lifted my rifle, and edged through the flaps of our tent. Seeing nothing directly in front of me, I peeked around the corner, all the time gripping the trigger and expecting to see the large brute near at hand.

The baby still slept but John Boy sat up. "What is it Muddie?" he whimpered. Kitty took him in her arms and held him close.

"Shh! Daddy is finding out. It's going to be all right."

"I'm scared!"

"I know, sweetheart. I know. Mommy is, too."

Bob turned to look toward the rear of the tent; his heart was pounding.

But to my amazement, just twenty-three steps away stood fifteen elephants. They had been traveling single file, head to tail. Seeing our camp, they had stopped; but now, though I had been as quiet and cautious as I could be, they had undoubtedly seen me. Immediately, they lifted their trunks and trumpeted as is customary before elephants stampede.

He felt the hair stand up on the back of his neck. The rifle was heavy in his hands. He shifted his weight as he considered what to do.

My first thought was to fire, but good judgment checked me, for I knew that even if I were to fire every shot in the magazine, there would still be enough elephants left to utterly destroy our camp. Rather, I stepped back and, in doing so, unintentionally bumped the table on which were stacked our tin cooking and eating utensils. To my horror, the table tipped over, spilling the pans with a loud clatter.

The baby screamed, and Kitty set John down and picked her up.

Bob's heart sank. "Now you've done it!" he said out loud.

I thought for a moment that all was ended, but to my amazement the elephants trumpeted again, threw their trunks down, their heads back into line, and marched away in double-quick time. They were an angry herd as they retreated—pushing over trees, breaking limbs, and rolling rocks down the hillside.

He was jarred to his senses by the baby crying and John Boy calling, "Daddy, are you all right?"

He hurried back into the tent and hugged his family. "You'll never believe it. Fifteen elephants were heading right toward our tent, but when I bumped the table the sound of the pots and pans scared them away. Can you beat it?"

"Someone must have been praying for us," Kitty murmured as she quieted the baby.

John Boy hugged his daddy's neck. After a long while, he again relaxed, and his eyelids grew heavy. Bob and Kitty put the sleeping children back into their bedrolls.

Again the sounds of the night surrounded them. Kitty and Bob clung to each other, hardly able to speak, knowing they would never forget this night.

The next morning Bob stepped it off. It was twenty-three steps to where the elephants had stopped. There was a swath in the forest of large uprooted trees.

Not much later, Dad told us, he spoke with a white hunter (the name given to elephant hunters). We assume it was the same one whom Mother mentions in her letter.

Last week we heard on old rattletrap coming down the road and as we haven't seen a white person since Kirk and Bro. H. left we were anxious to know who it was. It proved to be an old hunter by the name of Mr. Dailey who was going to Webb's mine (our nearest neighbor 28 miles away) to see about some property he was going to sell them.

Well, he gave us a lovely basket of mangoes, my favorite fruit, and when he left he asked us if there was anything else he could do for us. We didn't have any gasoline to get the truck started (you start on gas and then switch over to the charcoal) so we asked to buy a gallon of gas. He gave us a gal. and refused any pay for it. As it comes to 80 cents a gallon and we had only about $2.00 in camp, that meant something to us.

"It proved to be an old hunter...."

"Mr. Dailey, what would you do if you were in the path of a herd of elephant? Is there anything a person can do?" Bob was looking intently at the old elephant hunter as they sat around the campfire sometime later.

"There's only one thing I know of that works consistently. In fact, I carry some tin plates with me when I'm hunting elephant. You beat the tin plates together. Elephant hate that sound, and it will stop them in their tracks."

"I hadn't known that that night, but God did, and He dumped all the tin in camp!" I said.

"Well, Smith, you did the only known thing that will frighten away elephants. Beat on a pan or piece of tin, and they will always run. Shoot at them, and they will charge!"

They came to know the rest of this elephant story several years later.

Back in Athens, Pennsylvania, Mrs. Ella Williams looked up at her windows. At this time of the day, the streaks in her windows showed up, and she just couldn't let it go another day. The time had come to drag out the stepladder, the bucket and the towels. Even though it was quite a chore, she liked things to sparkle. While she was working, she began to think about the Smiths, a young missionary couple. She had heard them speak and had decided to pledge financially and pray for them each day. She took this partnership seriously.

THE DARKEST TIME IS JUST BEFORE THE DAWN

But today was different. A sense of urgency and alarm came over her. She felt strongly that she should get down from the ladder and pray. "Just give me a few more minutes, Lord. I'll just finish up these last few windows."

It wasn't an audible voice, but it was unmistakable to her, "You should get down and pray now!"

She made a habit of obedience, so she climbed down and knelt by her ladder. "Dear Lord, I don't know what this feeling is about, but You know. Please protect the Smiths. Whatever is happening, please protect them."

As clearly as she had felt the burden come, she was aware it had lifted. When the windows were done, she looked at them and was pleased. She put her supplies away and found her calendar hanging on the wall. Each day had a place for notes, so she wrote down in detail what had happened. It had been such an impressive event that she was determined to remember to ask the Smiths when they returned.

In the years to follow, when the Kitty and Bob were being entertained in her home, she would go and get her calendar and say, "What in the world was happening to you on July 24, 1934?" They would consult their diaries and make adjustments for the nine-hour time difference. Bob wrote: *We were amazed to find that this lady was on her knees praying while the elephants stood outside our tent. She was 12,000 miles away from us but close enough to God to be used in our behalf.*

This is the account Mother wrote to our grandparents on July 29 of 1934:

I cannot tell you with what mingled emotions I set out from the only home we had known in Africa, even though only a little tin one, and started out into the blue with nothing but a tent and a truck. Mr. Hotchkiss came along with us to see the D.C. and help talk to the chief etc. The first night we were all together as the rain had begun and the truck got stuck. That night the children and I slept in Mr. H.'s car, Miss Ford in her tent, Mr. H. and Kirk in his tent and Bob and the native boy in the truck. The next day it was decided that it would be best for the us to go on to camp, so we divided provisions somewhat and started. We had not gone far when the truck in going on the small log bridge slid to the side and hung with the left hind wheel over the edge. We got out, completely unloaded the truck, jacked it up etc. and finally with the help of four men who happened along, got up on the bridge again. But that delayed us so we did not get to the camp that night. We had one of the tents so set it up and that in pouring rain. The children having ridden all day were tired and hungry and both howled the entire time. But finally we got there and settled for the night. Anna Verne was so tired she couldn't wake up to tell me and dirtied her bed, something she never does. When we tried to get a light we found our lantern was out of oil and no flash light or even candle. Bob lit matches till I fixed her somewhat. Then we settled again. Next we heard a hyena and as he kept coming nearer Bob got up and went out to see that he didn't disturb camp. That scared him away. Then we heard a lion but he was quite far distant so we weren't so concerned about him. Finally we heard something that sounded like the even tread of an army. Nearer and nearer it came until the ground fairly shook. Bob crept to the door of the tent and waited. I lay still and prayed. When it seemed the animal was about upon us, the tramp stopped and then it sounded like an engine blowing off the boiler. There were a few moments then of breathless anxiety when we did not know whether it would charge or go on. Twigs, limbs and trees were snapped or thrown down. Finally the tramp began again and the earth trembled and shook and finally the army passed on. And army it really proved to be. Bob came back in the tent and said, "That was a herd of 15 elephant" At once the verse flashed across my mind "The angel of the Lord encampeth round about them that fear Him and delivereth them."

"...we heard something that sounded like the even tread of an army."

130

Meantime Kirk, Clara and Mr. Hotchkiss had stopped at Kisii to get permission to camp in Vatende. The two parties converged at Nyabassi, their destination in the Vatende country. Here they found an abandoned camp with a mud-walled donkey shed already built. They stayed there for two days and then went on to Kibaroti where they hoped a plot would be granted to them. Mr. H. and Kirk started for home, and Bob began building a temporary two-room building and a place for Isaiah A. Misoi. Until these were completed they stayed in their tent.

July 29, 1934

Dear Homefolks:

I am writing with pencil because the ink is in the bottom of Bob's trunk and quite inaccessible at present. Here we are in a mud house for sure! We are now camping in the government camp in the Nyambassi [sic] country which is among the Vatende people where we are wanting to get our site. We had a very important trip down, and I must tell you about it.

We planned this trip some time ago so that we would be able to be here when the July meeting of the Native Land Board came off. You see, the way we get a site is this. First we go to the natives and make friends with the chief. Then we petition the government for a site, and the District Commissioner of that district takes it up in the native meeting. If they pass it, then it goes to the D.C.'s office and if he passes it, then it goes to the Provincial Commissioner, and if he passes it, then on to the Land Boards in the capital, and finally is granted. So you see, it is surely a lot of red tape. Our first attempt here was turned down as the D.C. was not sympathetic. He simply tabled it, and as he was going home on leave, it saved him a great deal of trouble. We now have a different one, but we do not know how friendly he is.... But the chief here is very friendly and so anxious for us to come that he even sent a special runner with a personal letter requesting that we be allowed to come. He has had his men cutting poles for us and grass for our temporary house, gave us permissions to camp and is doing everything to make us welcome. He's a comparatively young man and quite progressive....

"...among the Vatende people where we are wanting to get our site."

Bob, Kitty, Clara, John and Anna Verne

Looking for a new opening in Vatende

In the same way, let your light shine before men, that they may see your good deeds and praise your Father in heaven."
Matthew 5: 16

Typically Dad spoke to everyone he met and within a short time Mother and Dad were sharing their beliefs and life story. The way Dad put it was, "All along the way, where ever we went, I found God had been there first. He was working out His plan."

Here is another example of how God worked, but our folks had no idea what was happening.

"Kitty, remember the camp we passed coming here? Today I met the man who is there. He was having some car trouble, and I was able to get it running for him."

It was a story she had heard often. By now Bob must have worked on dozens of cars and trucks in Kenya. "Splendid, Bob. What is he doing there?"

"He is a surveyor, Mr. Wilkes, a very interesting chap! I invited him over for dinner tonight."

Kitty gasped, "Bob you didn't! You know we don't have a thing but *posho*. What are we going to feed him?"

"Well, my stars and little sawhorses! I totally forgot."

"Bob, how could you do this?" Kitty looked around wondering desperately what she might have that she had forgotten. They had not had anything to eat but *posho* for almost a week.

"I've got a few bullets. I'll go on out and try to get some guinea fowl," Bob said sheepishly, picking up his gun.

That evening supper was served with the two guinea fowl as the centerpiece, *posho* as the side. The absence of other food seemed to go unnoticed, and the guinea fowl tasted uncommonly good as they had been without meat to the point of becoming painfully hungry for it.

"What brings you folks to this area? I've seen no sign of a mission anywhere around here," their guest began.

"That's the whole point. We are looking for a site," Bob responded. "We hope to establish one where people have not heard about Christ. It's not an easy thing to get government approval, but we are hoping to achieve that here."

"You are spending your whole lives telling people about Christ? It strikes me as amazing! I consider myself a Christian, but it hasn't had much impact on my life. I can't imagine someone coming all the way across the world just for that reason." He rested his head on his hand as he contemplated.

Bob wanted to explain further. "God completely changed our lives when we accepted Him. Now it is a matter of walking each day, opening our hearts to the Spirit of God. God longs for a relationship with all of us. We want everyone, especially those who don't know, to have a chance to come to Him."

The surveyor seemed genuinely interested, so Bob continued, "A living faith is not a matter of reasoning, cleverness or a human achievement. We must be touched and educated by the Holy Spirit. The difference when someone is touched in this way is so profound that Paul calls this person "a new creation." In fact, he was so deeply moved by the reality of this complete transformation that he wrote in Galatians, "I myself am no longer live, but Christ lives in me!" Christ and His message of love to all people mean everything to us." Bob looked away at the horizon, remembering the dramatic change that had come to his life.

"How did you hear about Vatende?" Mr. Wilkes queried.

"From missionaries with whom we worked in the Kericho area."

"Ah, yes. I've been in Kericho. Nice place!"

"We have waited for two years for a site to be granted at Sotik, a place South of Kericho, and it has not materialized, so we came this way hoping there would be an opening for us here."

"Perhaps it was all a mistake," the surveyor mused. "Did you have the option to just give up and go home?"

"That might have been tempting, but the truth is, it was truly unthinkable," Kitty interjected. "No, God has brought us here for a reason. We didn't expect this would be easy, but it means everything to us, and we will continue to try to find His purpose for us. "

"You came believing that everyone needs to be told about Christ?" said the surveyor, astonished that these people seemed to mean what they were saying.

"Yes! We believe He called us here," Kitty continued. "God's love is for everyone, and He wants these people to know about Him!"

"You think that would make a difference?" He could scarcely hide his skepticism.

"Yes, we believe that through His love people's lives can be changed...even their very natures," Bob said with assurance.

"Natures. What do you mean by that?"

"Well, you have heard the story of Adam and Eve; it started with them. At first they had a beautiful daily fellowship with God. But eventually they longed for self-determination, independence and autonomy from God. When Adam and Eve stepped out of their relationship of nearness to God, it resulted in a dramatic change—detachment from God. That's where everything went haywire," Bob chuckled at himself for the use of the word.

"You mean they alienated themselves?" The surveyor was listening intently.

"Exactly! In this alienated state, man became completely self-centered. It became all about him, and he was cut off from God's truth, God's life and God's love." Bob paused.

"So without God, people are in this position?"

"Yes, we believe that alienation continues on in man in his self-relating, fallen state. But when we come to God, we have the opportunity of restoring that relationship and coming back into fellowship with Him."

"Very interesting. Go on."

"By accepting Christ, we accept that He has paid the penalty for our sin. But when we try to realign ourselves to Him, we find we still have within us the 'old self,' the self that wants to be for oneself rather than for God and for others. So to come into relationship with God, there has to be a fundamental change in us, the dying of the 'old self.'"

"I see. You are saying God can change a person's very nature."

"Yes, that's exactly it! Dying to self, in the New Testament sense, refers to the total and complete surrender of all of our thinking, feeling, and acting to Jesus Christ. The 'self' which needs to die is the 'old self,' that 'self' which has gladly listened to the tempter's lie, 'ye shall be as gods,' and seeks to be something for itself, not for God."

"You're losing me, old chap."

"Dying to 'self' means sweet, blessed surrender—not attempting to be something on our own steam, not trying to be something apart from God. Then we can be set free to be something in Him." Bob's long arms gestured toward the positions of "apart from God" and "for God."

"The most fundamental act of the Christian life is this act of submission in which I give God everything which, up to now, I have used to define myself: my talents (for example: mechanical ability or, in the case of my wife, her music or academic work—everything about us). I give God all those things without reservation, and maybe, maybe, if God wills, He gives them back to us to be used as means through which we can glorify Him in certain situations. But I no longer define my "self" in terms of them. In this new relationship with God, I welcome the Holy Spirit into my life and am educated and engaged by Him, and I strive for His holiness in my life. Paul talked about the person touched by the Holy Spirit as being a new creation. This belief that our natures need to be changed, which we call the doctrine of holiness, has caused us problems in this country. It seems your fellow countrymen think that people who believe in this doctrine are fanatics."

"Right you are. I've heard the same. Until now I would have thought you a strange lot also. But I see what you are getting at." He glanced at Kitty. She looked intense, and he was astonished to see a tear slide down her check.

She brushed it away and added. "Until I die to my own desires and become crucified with Christ, I cannot become like Him. Holiness is never just something that describes you and me as we are, in and for ourselves. Holiness describes Christ; He is the Holy One. We strive to be like Him. Any success is a result of His work in our lives: the claim He lays upon us. As we read the Bible, it is clear to us that God asks us to lead a holy life."

"Interesting. I understand now why you say your nature is changed, and God is everything to you." Without knowing why he was so deeply touched by all of this, he turned away.

Bob continued. "We are basically logical and pragmatic folks. I was brought up on a farm. I know how to live off the land, I was trained in engineering and could make a living at that, but since this change occurred, following God's call is more important to me. In spite of everything that has happened to us, we still feel He has a reason for our being here."

"This has been a fascinating evening. I have never heard anything like this before. Thank you for inviting me," the surveyor said, and he seemed to truly mean it.

Little did they know that within the year, this man would present himself to Canon Pittway of the Church Missionary Society and making reference to this evening would say, "I want the kind of commitment that those people have." He prayed with Canon Pittway, went back to England for training and served in the Northern Frontier District of Kenya with the Bible Churchmen's Missionary Society, the laymen's group of the Church of England.

> *I know the plans I have for you, says the Lord. They are plans for good and not for evil, to give you a future and a hope.*
> *Jeremiah 29:11*

Beautiful people! Such beautiful people!

The Watende (the people of Vatende) were there to meet them when they arrived and set up camp. The men, their bodies decorated with paint and jewelry, wore blankets knotted at the shoulder. The chief wore a small headdress with a peculiar knot on the top of it. Some of the boys wore nothing at all. They gazed unblinkingly at the white people murmuring softly to each other and occasionally waving away the flies that wanted to perch on their faces. When the stately women in their brightly colored beautiful necklaces, with little else on their upper bodies, and skin skirts saw Kitty and the children, they fell down and started walking on their knees toward them. The little children seemed poised to run away.

Watende men

"No! No! Please stand up. *Jambo! Jambo sana!*" Kitty gestured with her arms to help them understand.

Watende boys

They rose but stood transfixed, staring, and then with giggles and laughter, they bravely came closer, and reaching out long fingers touched the baby. They offered their babies to Kitty in exchange for the opportunity to hold hers. She reluctantly did so, but with great misgivings and yet the firm belief that in spite of the dangers of exposure to illness, somehow God would protect her child. Bob and Kitty spoke often of their first encounter with the Watende. "Beautiful people! Such beautiful people!"

Bob looked at the young chief. He was tall and sharp featured. The blanket hung open around his sleek well-muscled body, and underneath he wore nothing. He was excited and enthusiastic in his greeting. Bob conversed in his newly acquired and often sparse Swahili vocabulary, and although he could not understand everything, the response was clear, the chief wanted them to come. He would like a school and a church for his people.

It was good to be welcomed. The government camp had given them unexpected shelter. Everything was encouraging, and they excitedly discussed plans for buildings and school curriculum.   But first, the government would have to approve.

About twenty-eight miles away, a gold rush was occurring. Miners from all over the world were coming in large numbers. Close at their heels were Indian merchants who were setting up tiny shops with basic goods. From the miners, Bob had heard of a technique of creating roofing tiles that were light and durable, and he anxiously pursued the methods for making tile.

Vatende Country, August 5, 1934

Here it is Sunday morning again, and we are waiting the arrival of the Chief for service, so I will add some more to my letter. We have been having again and again the blessed assurance of the Lord's care and help. Miss Ford started school last Monday and I have never seen people so anxious to learn. Even the chief comes with his tiny piece of slate and a bit of a stone for pencil and works away with the rest. We are still in the government house at the native camp, but our little mud house of two rooms is about finished. It is plastered on the inside and is now drying out so we may be able to move in next week Wed. or Thursday. It has two tiny rooms 10x10 and a little porch 6x10. It is made of poles, the roof is grass, the walls mud, and Mother Earth, the floor, but it will be so nice to have two rooms and not be crowded in like we are now nor have to eat in the open. It gets quite windy and cold especially in the evening. The children have both bad colds especially John and it has seemingly affected his hearing so that at times we have difficulty in making him understand at all. He did have a terrible ear ache the second day of our journey here, but he had a real touch from the Lord and as I had to put both the children under the protection of the blood before we started I am keeping them there and trusting the Lord to protect and care for them. But we will be glad to get into the other house as Bob has made it warm and tight. We will have another mud house for a kitchen and Miss Ford has a frame house of poles with a grass roof under which she will put her tent. The grass is for protection from the sun.

You will laugh when I tell you what kind of curtains we will have. We have no glass for windows, so will make board ones to close when it rains. We will have mosquito net over the frame in the daytime, and then I made some unbleached muslin curtains. You remember the piece you had sewed around our Christmas package? I used that and some of the pretty pieces among them for ruffles around them. They are cute as can be and will serve as blinds as well....

"You will laugh when I tell you what kind of curtains we will have."

Drawing plans was a joy.

Kitty accepted the idea of another mud house, the dirt floor, the smell of a mixture of dry grass and mud. They were all becoming part of her life. She had been creative in her plans as they looked forward to moving in. She had been able to find supplies of eggs, bananas, tomatoes, white and sweet corn, potatoes and peas. She was also learning how to use the sago root. She could grind it into flour and add it to the real flour to make it go farther. It was of cornstarch consistency. Alternatively she could boil or fry it. Although she was a city girl, she felt she was adapting well to this life. She potty trained her children as soon as she could in order to keep some control of the washing. All the diapers had to be done by hand,

and for each washing, the water had to be carried by ox cart or other conveyance. Whenever she could learn something new, she was attentive. She remained determined to keep her family all looking as good as she could, but the challenge was mounting each day.

Catharine viewed her role in this venture as primarily supportive. Her own life was disciplined and orderly; her home would definitely be the same. It was to be a refuge for Bob and a haven for her children. It would be a special place where they could be reunited and be renewed. She was determined to make it beautiful and inviting, a protection against the ever-threatening dangers of this new land.

There was a strong belief that the tropical sun with very little exposure caused sunstroke. The famous Lord Delamare wore a helmet so huge that the brim extended well beyond his shoulders. He had twice suffered sunstroke. Accordingly, most early settlers and missionaries vigorously protected themselves against the sun. They did not venture from the houses without double felt lined hats or pith helmets.

Besides the sun, numerous other sinister threats abounded:

They had already had firsthand experience with malaria and its cure.

Snakes were present on paths or enjoying the cool of a porch or roof.

Wild beasts caused one to have to be ever vigilant and protected by knife or gun.

Ticks carried diseases such as the dreaded typhus.

Jiggas (chiggers) could penetrate one's skin usually burying themselves under the toenails where they laid eggs.

Amoebiasis caused by *Entomoeba histolytica* resulted in bloody diarrhea and occasionally in liver abscesses.

Trypanosomiasis (African sleeping sickness) is transmitted by the tsetse flies and was prevalent in the area. At first there is an inflammation at the site of the bite, then come fevers, chills, lymph node enlargement, shiny swelling of the hands and face and rashes. These come and go in episodes as new waves of parasites are produced in the body. Eventually they invade the brain, hence the name "sleeping sickness."

Ascaris lumbricoide (giant round worms*)* and *taeniasis* (tape worm) that entered the body by the digestive tract were very common in the African population and easily transmitted.

Around Lake Victoria, *schistosomiasis (bilharzia* as it is otherwise known), originating from the snails, would enter the skin of people swimming in these waters. The infestation would eventually cause bladder, intestinal, heart and brain problems.

But in spite of all this, as their experience grew, the "unknown" at least became less of a threat.

Although she accepted her situation, Kitty still dreamed of what it would be like, if only they could get a place of their own. Still there was joy in just thinking and making plans for the future.

August 19, 1934

Dear Home-folks:

We are still at our camp. Kirk and Faye came down on Friday arriving quite late. We have enjoyed their stay with us. They will be leaving again on Tuesday, and we are sending this mail back by them.

They brought our May salaries that had just come. We also received a letter from the Indian we owe for groceries that if we didn't settle in three days he was going to sue. Isn't that a pleasant outlook? But I don't think he will. We are doing our best to get out of debt but it surely is slow.

We all are quite well. I think John's hearing is improving and know it is simply a divine touch. And how I do thank the Lord for His goodness. I must tell you a cute thing that happened the other day. Bob and I were making out a little house plan. I heard a sort of subdued noise in the other room and went and peeked in. There lay Anna Verne and John in his bed, his arm around her. She had wakened and crawled out of her cart into bed with him. He was saying, "Do you feel good after your nap? I feel good. Muddie feels good and Daddy feels good and Aunt Clara feels good and you must feel good. Do you?" To which she replied, "Um" meaning "Yes". Then he said "Do you want me to read you a story?" and again "Um" so he got his book and showed her pictures and read stories for about half an hour.

We are now in our own Mud house. It has two rooms each 9x9'. It is so much warmer and snugger. The children are getting so they play quite nicely and don't take so much care. I spoke about our working on house plans....

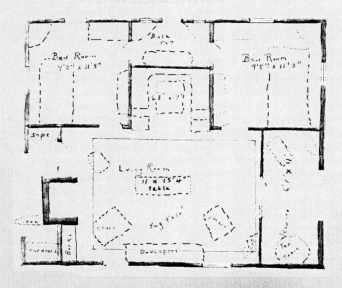

This house measures outside 24'x28'. The outside walls are 6", the inside 4". All windows are standard size except in the little bath where they are 1'x1 1/2', and in the dining alcove where they are 2'x4' and are high up on the wall. The doors are standard 3 1/2'x6 1/2' except into the bath from the bedroom where they are 2'x6' and the French doors in the front which are 2'x6 1/2' each. The walls are 9' high. Above the wall on the front and end (back) is built up to the roof with wood and small ventilation put in each end like this to keep it cool.

The roof is iron and the ceilings celotex. It is something like asbestos and is very cool and really sun proof. It is also much cheaper than wood. There are to be bookshelves on each side of the dining alcove on the living room side and china cupboards and silver wear drawers on the alcove side. These form the only front partition to it. Above is a large 6' arch. The alcove is made for a sort of breakfast set of table and benches. Next to the fireplace in the living room is a built-in bookcase. In the bedrooms are built-in wardrobes, and in the bath two small wash stands with shelves underneath for towels and wash clothes. On a little back veranda is a food safe and a cupboard, the kitchen being separate.

Well so much for the house. Baby sister just woke up, so I'll have to stop. She is such a sweet baby and as rolly-polly as a little pumpkin. She is still a laughing smiling baby. Her eyes crinkle up when she laughs... She just came up laughing hard as she could because she had managed to get her hat on backwards. You two grandmothers would about eat her up she's so sweet, and is so lovely to see John take care of her and love and comfort her if she gets hurt.

Do write soon all of you. Another splendid service today. Kirk preached. Great interest & attention.

Much love, Catharine

"Another splendid service...Kirk preached."

They had been living in the mud dwelling at Vatende for two weeks and were busy making plans for a future mission there when, much to their surprise, they were notified quite abruptly that they were to leave, as they did not have the right permission to be there. Bob had gone immediately to discuss the situation with the D.C. but found he was away, and the assistant D.C. told him that they had no choice but to leave. At some time in the past, the Mennonites in Shirati had invited them to come visit and, so being nearby, it seemed the appropriate time to do so.

Unfortunately the truck was now in use by Kirk, and they had no way to move their things. An Asian shopkeeper kindly offered to keep what they could not transport by car until their return. After returning from his trip, Bob was nearly out of gas, so after purchasing gasoline, they had between the three of them two shillings and one American dollar. For weeks, the only food they had eaten was *posho*. The semi-arid land didn't even allow the gathering of greens. The words, "The Lord will take care of us," were mentioned daily, but somehow the ring had gone out of them as their situation continued to deteriorate.

"Well, my stars! What have we here?" said Bob as he rounded a knoll. A large man was hunched over his fender peering into the motor of his *lorry* (truck). It looked as though he had been there for some time.

"Good day, sir. What seems to be the problem?" Bob had said.

In a heavy German accent, the man replied that he had not been able to get the truck going. Bob found the problem readily but told the man there were other things wrong with the truck. The man lived not far from Shirati and discovering that they were going that way, he invited Bob to come and work on his vehicle some more for pay.

When Bob returned to the car, he related the story to Kitty and Clara. They sat in silence absorbing it all. Here again was the answer, which always seemed to come. God was providing.

A heart rejoicing in God delights in all His will, and is surely provided with the most firm joy in all circumstances; for if nothing can come to pass beside or against His will, then that soul cannot be vexed which delights in Him, in all estates; not only when he shines bright on them, but when they are clouded. The flower which follows the sun does so even in dark and cloudy days; when it does not shine forth, yet it follows the hidden course and motion of it. So the soul that moves after God keeps that even course at His will in all circumstances, conditions, or events; is content, yea, even glad at His will. He hides His face;

R. Leighton

CHAPTER 10
SHIRATI, TANGANYIKA
SEPTEMBER 3, 1934—JANUARY 1, 1935

> *Sharatti [Sic], Tanganyika Sept. 3, 1934*
>
> *Dear Home Folks:*
>
> *I'm not quite sure how long it has been since I wrote you, but many things have happened since as you see from the date and place, Sept. finds us in Sharatti[sic] in Tanganyika. You can see from the map that it is on Lake Victoria and Tanganyika is a neighbor province of Kenya. There is quite a story to it. I better go back at the beginning. Before we came down from Litein to camp at Nyambasai [sic] we had word from the Mennonites who had opened a station on this side among the JeLuel [sic] tribe that they would be glad to meet us and talk over our plans for the future. We had planned to come over into this territory and work this side also so when we heard they were here we wrote them and told them our hopes etc. We received a most beautiful letter from them saying their only desire was that the people get the gospel, and if the Lord led us here first they would say "Amen." They also asked us to pay them a visit when we were able. As I said, we were just starting down to camp so couldn't go then, but wrote them that we would pay them a visit as soon as possible. I wrote you that we were in our camp. We had been there just two weeks when we received a letter from the District Commissioner that we had no permission to be there and that we were to move off at once.... We took a special trip to Kisii and the assistant D.C. told Bob the circumstances and advised us to leave, but to return when the D.C. got back and talk matters over with him. He was most kind and friendly and gave Bob some valuable hints....*

"September finds us in Sharatti [sic]...."

Located at 3,500 feet, Shirati, the Mennonite mission plot, commanded a beautiful view of Lake Victoria just three miles away. But unlike Litein or Vatende, it was extremely hot. The Elim Stauffers and the John Mosemanns had not been in the country very long, but they had readily obtained their site, set up their tents and begun to accumulate materials to build their mission station. They now were housed in temporary homes, and the Mosemans offered the Smiths their tent, which was considerably larger than their own. They also provided them with meals for ten days, and they accepted the help that Clara, Bob and Kitty could give. It seemed that staying at Shirati would be a perfect solution for their situation. It was not far from the German man who wanted Bob to work on his truck, and they could camp while waiting for word on the plot in Vatende. Clara could help with dispensary and school and could teach the Mennonites Swahili. Bob could help with building for which they had offered to pay him; however, because mission rules did not allow missionaries to work for personal profit, the funds that were earned both from the German man and those offered Bob by the Mennonites had to be turned over to the mission general fund and in the end were used to pay back the loan given Bob for the truck's charcoal burner.

When we got here we received a royal welcome. We had brought what provisions we had in camp and had thought we could get by somehow, but Mr. Stauffer insisted that we be their guests. They are all Pa. Dutch, by the way, and the ladies wear the little caps. They are such sweet, unaffected, wholely sanctified folks, it is a benediction to be here. Bob got to talking with them about their building plans and found they are simply, as they say, "saw and hammer" farmers, so he was able to give them some valuable information and help them somewhat revise their plans. As a result, they asked him to take Mr. Stauffer to Kericho and Lundiani[sic] and see about supplies, and on the way back stop at the D.C.'s at Kisii, and Mr. Stauffer is going to do all in his power to help get the site....

It has been a breath of heaven to be here. The spiritual atmosphere is so sweet, and they are just starting as we are, in fact haven't been here in Africa as long as we. So they are struggling with language too. Miss Ford interpreted for Mr. Mosemann last Sunday and has been helping with the dispensary work.

September 3rd letter continued

Elim and John were anxious to get their permanent house completed. Corrugated iron, which was widely used for roofing, had been purchased, and Bob was delighted to see the pile of the hard yellow lumber called *podocarpus* waiting to be used.

Dad told us of this lumber—"I'll tell you it was the most beautiful lumber you've ever seen in all your life. The pieces were 1" x 12" and some were 20' long. It was all rough sawn, but they had done a splendid job, and there was plenty for a fine building. It had been brought from Kisumu by boat on Lake Victoria."

"... the first vegetables we have had in months."

Upon their arrival at Shirati they had had one American dollar and 2 shillings between them. Their salaries were behind again four months. The Stauffers and Mosemanns had been generous with treating them as guests, unaware of Bob, Kitty and Clara's lack of funds to purchase food. But the time had come for them to again use their own supplies.

Mother recalled that her store of provisions was a good supply of corn meal, a package of macaroni, a little rice, sugar, tea and flour which she mixed with cassava root in order to stretch it, but these items quickly disappeared.

So... as the days went by, their family and Clara continued to eat their *posho*. Isaiah, the African helper who had come with them from Litein, had returned, as they were no longer able to pay his wages. Kitty, now responsible for all the meals, cooked on three stones arranged around a fire where she expertly balanced the cooking pot. She had become adept at keeping fires at the right temperature so that the food would not burn and then banking the coals at night so they would be live in the morning.

After making a trip with Elim Stauffer to Kericho and Londiani for more building supplies, Bob had worked on the German man's truck.

This was one of the many beautiful stamps from Kenya, Uganda and Tanganyika. Dhow—on Lake Victoria

In the midst of their struggle to survive was the urgency to continue with their efforts to get the Vatende site. With the earnings from the German man, Bob, choosing the cheapest means of transportation by dhow, traveled to Kisumu to speak with the Provincial Commissioner. The trip took two days and one night each direction. He learned that the outgoing P.C. had written the D.C. to proceed with granting the site in Vatende. Everyone was excited by the news.

Well Bob came back this noon with a strange story and two big baskets of vegetables and about five pounds of sugar. It had happened like this. He started to ask Bob if he wasn't out of supplies and Bob admitted he was. He named over certain things and Bob said, No we didn't have them. Then he said, "Vat you had dis morning for breakfast?" Bob said, "We had posho(that is mush and we have had it and nothing else for weeks)" "Vat!" said the German, "Nothing else? Auch! Do you tink I can eat and know does little kinder half nothing else?" So this is the result. And Bob says it isn't the end. Besides the German said not to think this was to go on the work on the truck. The Lord bless the old German! We have some other propositions that we don't know for sure about so will tell you later.

Here it is next day and there is so much to do. I may add a note before this goes, but I have to iron now so will close. Bob is working on the government sketch of the house plan and it is beautiful.

Kiddies are well.   Much love, Catharine

September 3rd letter continued

THE DARKEST TIME IS JUST BEFORE THE DAWN

Kitty welcomed the evenings. As the shadows advanced up the hillsides, the valley below them turned into a pool of darkness, and the refreshing cool of the evening overtook them. Dinner had been wonderful…the first vegetables they had had in months, thanks to the German man.

After dinner as the children were falling to sleep, Bob, Kitty and Clara would all sit by the campfire, watch the flicker of blue flames, and discuss the day's activities.

"Well, sir! I have had enough of riding on a native dhow. Lake Victoria is a big, big puddle of water and, boy oh boy, can she get rough! I was never so glad to see land." Bob waved his long arm in the direction of the lake that lay below them.

With the setting sun, the heat had abated. Bob and Kitty lingered and waited for the fire embers to fade when they would retreat to the warm protective cave-like refuge of their tent. Sometimes they could hear the squeak of a bat, the piercing call of an owl, or the distant laugh of a hyena.

Lying on the camp bed with the warm glow of the lantern, they were content and cozy. With the children asleep, Kitty had Bob all to herself, and if she could catch him before he nodded off (which didn't take long), she could learn of his progress, his delights and burdens. Although she, too, was tired, she liked to use this time to catch up on her correspondence.

Sherati[sic], Tanganyika
c/o Mennonite Mission
Sept. 18, 1934

Dear Home Folks:

Here we are still at Sherati[sic]. The terrific heat has somewhat abated, but the sun is still very hot. Bob has returned from his last trip to Kisumu by native dhow and was, in answer to prayer, not at all seasick in spite of a big storm near Kisumu and an unusually rough sea just above Sherati[sic]. His trip was also a successful one for which we are very thankful. He found that the new provincial commissioner is a very nice chap, friendly to missions and kind. He allowed him to read all the correspondence of the outgoing official, who we were delighted to find had written the District Officer to proceed at once. We are praying much about this because he may or he may not, just as he chooses. Bob's next move is to see him, and we are getting material in readiness for him to do so. The official told us, however, that even after it had passed the local native council, it would be at least 4 mo. before we could begin operations as that is as fast as it could possibly go through the government red tape. Then it would take a month to transport materials and a month at the least to get the first building up, so we are destined to camp for at least 6 more months. The Mennonites have invited us to stay here and have asked Bob to help them. I would like it very much in some ways, but I would rather get permission to camp where we were before as we could have services and do dispensary work even though we couldn't have school, and we could be working on the language. Six months of persistent work on it should give us somewhat of a knowledge of it. But our times are in His hands, and as He leads, we are trying to follow....

"…our times are in His hands, and as He leads we are trying to follow…."

Nor had the German man's kindness ended. Kitty again referred to it:

> When Bob came back from Kisumu we were down to our last 25 cents but a German near here had a truck he wanted fixed and Bob has been working on it for two days so that will bring us in some cash again just at the very time we need it. How faithful the Lord has been to us. I wish I could be as true to Him. I get so ashamed of my doubts. We went over to the Germans yesterday and took the youngsters in the A.M. They made so much fuss over them, stuffing them full of candy. It seemed so nice and were the first chocolates we had seen since Mrs. Williams' box last Christmas, though we had some hard candies and some caramels then.

September 18th letter continued

Moreover Mother and Dad told us that the German provided them with lamb, fish, jam, bread, and honey. One day he left corned beef and cabbage at their tent.

Dad said, "Perhaps it was because we were so hungry but that corned beef was the best I've ever tasted."

On another occasion when they asked to purchase more vegetables, he sent along all the vegetables but returned their money as well.

Among the things Bob had brought from America were a 19-inch saw and the engine to run it. He had gotten this from Kericho, and it was proving a boon to his building. Bob had never really known any Mennonite people very well before. These folk had a quiet and unassuming way about them, but their dedication and resolve were clear. He and Kitty found a special fellowship and kinship with them in ways they hadn't anticipated, and yet their meeting place was closed on occasion to Bob, Kitty and Clara since they were not members of the Mennonite Church.

Dad spoke often of his time with the Mennonites and their relationships. Whenever they visited each other they were asked to speak in their respective churches, and as adults, we remember Mother and Dad visiting them in this country after their retirement. Dad told us of a conversation he had with Elim Stauffer.

One day Bob noticed Elim Stauffer standing watching him work. He had his hands on his hips and he said brightly, "How is it going, Brother Bob?" He was wearing overalls and, in spite of the heat, a long sleeved white shirt (the traditional Mennonite dress) but his hat was a pith helmet. Even his wife wore a pith helmet over her dainty head cover.

"It's going well, Brother Elim," he called over the sound of the saw. Bob looked affectionately at his godly friend, and then shutting off the saw, he walked over and looked him straight in the eye. "If I'm truly your brother, and I believe I am, why aren't we allowed to take communion with you in your worship?"

Elim Stauffer's face reflected his surprise. He paused a long while and then looked up again at Bob. "You know, you have got a point! You are indeed my brother, and you should not be prevented. I can't do anything about it at the moment, but I think I will take it up with the home conference when I return to the States." (This he did, and in the years ahead, the practice of closed communion in this part of the Mennonite church was abandoned.)

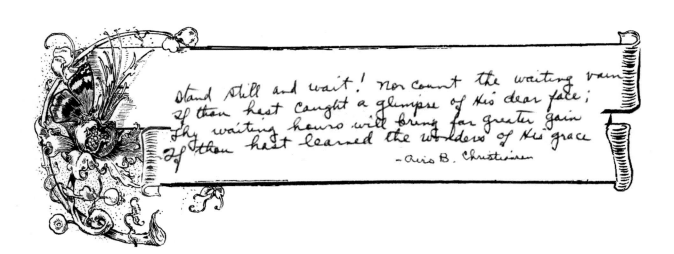

Stand still and wait! Nor count the waiting vain
If thou hast caught a glimpse of His dear face;
Thy waiting hours will bring far greater gain
If thou hast learned the wonders of His grace

—Avis B. Christiansen

Dear Homefolks: Sherati[sic] via Musoma c/o Mennonite Mission
                                                                          Oct 8, 1934

We just returned [to Shirati] from our trip up country [Kericho]....

The enclosed letter explains our current circumstances. [We do not have the letter to which she refers but we do know that in the second week of September, Dad had gone to Kisumu by dhow to speak with the P.C. and returned with hope, but on September 24th, the D.C. had written to the acting P.C. in Kisumu and reported that he had been to Nyabassi, and the people perferred the Catholics establish work there.] I really believe the Lord is letting everything go beyond human help so that He can work a real miracle! As things now stand we are really sunk but He has said, "In quietness and in confidence shall be your strength." We are still holding on for the miracle.

We had a lovely time with Faye and Kirk this visit, such fellowship and understanding, and it really did our hearts good. I really believe the Lord is answering prayer.

We are back here now for a couple of months. The L.N.C. [Local Native Council] is in November about the middle and that is why this is coming via air. [This meeting would be crucial and their last hope for the Vatende plot as the native people would make their desires known officially.]

We are now over 4 months behind on salary, but the Lord is still providing....

Clara needs a furlough badly. She is so tired out with the burden and responsibility of everything and needs a change. I would like to see her go home in the spring....

We are a bit more comfy since returning. I have mosquito net on the windows and some old curtains I fixed for curtains. We have about two feet at one end and three feet the other way to turn around in....

John just wakened. He is such a cute one when he first wakes up. He crawled over and cuddled up beside me and said, "Mother, I will hold your pen for you if you want me to and I won't take off the top a bit...."

Bob hopes to finish the work on the truck this P.M. We are invited to the Mennonites for dinner tomorrow, as it is Aunt Clara's birthday. After today, then Bob will be working here on the mission helping them put up their first permanent house. We are all well and happy.

I am dipping into Swahili again and am studying the gospel of John. Bob preached his first Swahili sermon two weeks ago tomorrow. They asked him for again tomorrow but he asked for more time. He did real well....

Love to all, Catharine

"We had a lovely time with Faye and Kirk this visit...it really did our hearts good."

Bob didn't believe he was eloquent. In fact he knew he wasn't. When he tried to give a message, he struggled for the right words to say what he felt so strongly. But he could speak to people, one on one, anyone, anywhere, and he loved them deeply. "Now there's a real man" or "I'll tell you, I love that man," he would so often say. But if there was a job to be done, he was energized by it, and he was thoroughly enjoying his work here at Shirati.

THE DARKEST TIME IS JUST BEFORE THE DAWN

September had slipped into October, then November. The shortage of food loomed daily.

C/o Mennonite Mission Sherati[sic], via Musoma, Tanganyika, Oct 1934

Dear Home Folks:

...These days I long for His return more than I ever did. I think we are going through hard places, and then I get ashamed when I wonder how it is with you folks at home. I am sure you don't tell me of your hard places. I often think of Papa and how he works on day after day, and day after day. And the powers of darkness are arrayed against him though perhaps not in just the same way they are against us. And then I know some of the tests that have come to Mother because we are so much alike, and I have my black days when it seems no use even to pray. So we share our joys and our sorrows and mutual burdens bear, because we are all Pilgrims and Sojourners in a strange land. But we see a better country, even a heavenly, a city without foundation whose builder and maker is God.

I have thought many times as I have sat and watched the sunset here how I wish you could see it. Dad loves the beautiful, so he would surely get a feast for his eyes. Last night there was another remarkable one. Clara says her mother used to say sunsets like that were so beautiful they hurt, perhaps because she knew they wouldn't last long. That is one thing about an African sunset – they last only a short time. At six P.M. the sun goes to rest, and at 6:30 it is quite dark. But some nights are so moonlit it seems like daytime.

The work here is progressing nicely. Bob has a saw rigged up and did all the sawing of rafters, beams, purloins etc. last week. They are now laying the foundation (above ground) up to the level of the floor. Bob thinks by the day after tomorrow, they will be ready to pour the floor. They will have cement floors here also because of the ants and because of the cost of lumber. Their houses will be screened throughout and part of the front veranda because of mosquitoes. They are very bad here, the worst of any place I have yet been in Africa. But as yet, I have not seen any anapholes[sic], or malaria mosquitoes. Then because it is so very warm here, they will not have any glass in their windows, simply bars or a network of metal beside the screen. That is to insure safety from thieves and wild animals....

"Bob has a saw rigged up and did all the sawing of rafters, beams, purloins etc. last week."

Shirati, Tanganyika
Nov. 6 1934

Dear Folks:

I trust you will forgive pencil as my pen is dry and I am sitting writing, while the children go to sleep, so can't get it filled right away. I sent a note in Bob's letter to his folks last Sunday. I am not sure whether it will go through any faster than this or not, but thought I'd write again to keep you informed along. We are expecting again this mail to hear from Kirk and Faye that some money has arrived for us. Our situation has been relieved somewhat in that Bob is helping here now, and we are getting our living out of it. So we have food. I have never before been so close to facing real hunger. I can imagine parents getting desperate for their children and actually stealing. I have a greater sympathy for the honorably poor than ever before....

"I can imagine parents getting desperate...and...stealing."

150

Much needed rain was delaying the building and because of this delay and the impending meeting of the Local Native Council, Clara, Bob and the Mosemanns had decided to return to Vatende to try to establish whether what the D.C. at Kisii had said was correct as it contradicted their impression of the Vatende people's desire to have them come to work there. This crucial meeting was to be held on the fourteenth of November. Clara had written to the home office asking that the week of the seventh to the fourteenth be made a week of prayer for the Vatende site. Communication had been sent out to all the supporters to join in this prayer. At Shirati, Kitty, Bob, and Clara met with the Mennonite missionaries between the hours of eight to nine each evening of that week to pray for God's will in this matter.

Shirati, Tanganyika
Nov. 6 1934

...Tomorrow begins the week of prayer for the site. I suspect you already have the airmail that Clara sent home.... I love to think of the volume of prayer that is going up on both sides of the world for this thing. Surely God will hear and override the powers of darkness....

I must tell you about our haystack, or so we have named it. It is our new dining room, but it is made with the roof almost touching the ground and it is covered with grass so that the effect from the outside is of a big haystack. But the room inside is quite cozy and oh! so much cooler to work in than the tent was. So I am more than grateful.

Well, I'll try and finish up this evening. It is Wednesday, and again the kiddies are safely in bed. It is raining outside quite a storm, but we are in the dry so that is something else to be thankful for. And I was just counting up some of our other blessings yesterday, and I found that if our salaries were paid up to date, we could get nearly out of debt. So these months of poverty have at least done one thing for us, and that is helped us to save what is coming to us, since we decided to run no more bills. Of course, there is the question when will we get it? I guess only the Lord knows as we have looked in vain until we have almost stopped looking.

Well, they finished pouring the floor of the new house today. It is all nicely covered with sheet iron so the rain tonight won't hurt it, and it will give us some much-needed water. The biggest drawback to this station is lack of water. There is very little rainfall besides, so the large storage tanks are not as useful here as most places. However, when they get all the buildings finished, they expect to put up about two tanks on each building it may be enough to last them through the entire dry season. Please excuse the terrible writing. My lantern is very poor light tonight and is flickering besides....

Here it is the next day and I am finishing up with ink...Bob is out again on the job. He works so hard and is so tired when he comes in. Do pray much for him, for even when you get this letter, it may be we will be beginning our own building, and he will rush that as hard as he possibly can....

I must close now...If I have a few minutes I'll write on the back of this as it is against my principles to let a letter go with any space on it.

Love to all,
Catharine

"I love to think of the volume of prayer going up on both sides of the world about this thing."

Blessed be nothing!

On the tapes Dad tells of this trip to Vatende.

It was pouring rain as we set off for Nyabassi. We got stuck again and again, but eventually we arrived at our former campsite where we had been for six weeks. What do you suppose we saw just as we were coming into camp? Two impala! Now there is some good meat. We had not had meat for over a month because I had not been able to use my gun in Tanganyika. We simply had no money so I could not afford another license, but back in Kenya I could hunt again. It was already dark, but we got it all dressed out and decided to hang it from the rafters in the hut to keep it from being eaten during the night. The door of the hut had disappeared in our absence, so we blocked the entrance with branches and sticks. Clara and Mrs. Mosemann were in the back room and John Mosemann with his flashlight and I with my rifle were in the front, and off we went to sleep. Sometime in the middle of the night something whacked our cots. John got his flashlight on just in time to see a leopard disappearing out the door with our impala. What a loss that was! In future years, I was much wiser.

The morning rays of sunshine were a welcome relief to them all. Not only did they receive a warm reception from the chief, but his scribe, a man trained in Catholic schools, had said they prayed for the Smiths and Clara to return. They also gave gifts of four chickens along with reassurance from the chief that he would do all in his power to get permission for them to locate in his area.

On their return they had of necessity camped beside the swollen big river. A gold miner, also camped there, needed repairs on his car that Bob was able and willing to do.

"I certainly hope this stream recedes by morning." Mr. Mosemann had counted on being home by now.

"I hope so, too," said Bob, "but I shouldn't like to guarantee it."

In the morning, clouds clung to the distant hills and dipped into their crevices. The plains below were shrouded by mist, but the rapidly rising heat was causing the clouds to vanish one by one. Through the day, they watched the water impatiently. By late afternoon, they saw a man walking across the stream, and much to their surprise, the water was up only to his ankles. They felt sure that the water had receded sufficiently for them to cross, and they did so without difficulty. Thirty-five miles from Shirati they were crossing a smaller stream. Porters went first with the heavier belongings on their heads. The car then

heaped with the remaining suitcases, chickens, passengers, and supplies began to venture into the stream. The stones beneath jostled everything one way and then the other. Mid stream the rising water splashed onto the motor, killing it. Bob jumped out of the car and ran to the front to crank it up again. The car restarted but the tires would only spin.

In minutes the small stream was a torrent.

152

There was no rain in sight but it was falling somewhere in the hills. Suddenly, out of nowhere, came a roaring torrent—a wall of water four feet high. The car was surrounded and water was reaching window level. The Mosemanns could not swim, and the water terrified them as it rapidly filled the car. Bob quickly carried Mrs. Mosemann on his shoulders, slipping just as they arrived at the shore plunging them both into the water. He had attached a rope to the car; this he secured to a tree on the bank. He encouraged Mr. Mosemann to pull himself across the water using the rope.

Clara, the ever-adept missionary girl, was busy swimming back and forth trying to rescue and keep dry bedrolls, belongings and chickens from within the car. Eventually the car was completely submerged, so she dived down, swan into the car, and gave what she could retrieve to Bob who was standing waist deep on top of the car throwing things to the Mosemanns on the shore. It had all happened so suddenly.

Bob stood staring at the carnage, steam rising from his shoulders. The swollen waters had appeared out of nowhere. The treasured chickens, that the Watende had given them, were dead in spite of all their efforts.

"Clara, for crying out loud! Where are your suitcases? I just realized they aren't here."

"They are gone. I guess they must have fallen off the top on the way here. I think we rescued everything from the car, so we must have lost them somewhere else. I'm afraid everything I own was in them."

"But you haven't said a word about it." Bob gazed at her. She'd lost everything.

She shrugged, "I guess all I can say is—Blessed be nothing!"

As the stream receded

Bob laughed, but he was trying to wrap his mind around the statement, and somehow he fully understood that material things were of little importance to Clara. She had riches elsewhere.

The Mosemanns were already spreading the blankets and clothing out to dry on the surrounding bushes and domed boulders. Clara busied herself building a fire. The evening was fast approaching, but things never the less were drying quickly in the sweltering heat. Africans who had viewed the spectacle gathered in large numbers. Pushing, stamping, chanting and pulling, they could not dislodge the car from the creek bed. Then, amazingly in this isolated place, a truck appeared.

Clara remarked, "That truck was not sent for but was sent!"

The friendly driver agreed to help, so Bob swam down and attached a rope to the submerged front axle and then with people surrounding the car and pushing and many *Harambee! Harambee! Saukuma sawa, sawa!'s* (the Swahili chant meaning *All work together—push very, very hard!—which* in Kenya always accompanied such collaborative effort) the mud-covered car was moved to solid ground. What a mess it was! Before it would run again, water would have to be removed from the gas and oil. Bob looked around for a useable container and then carefully drained the oil into the hubcap. He squatted by the fire and gingerly balanced this on the surrounding rocks over the fire. As the oil heated, the water escaped as steam but what remained looked like mud and was not sufficient to fill the crankcase. Inquiring of the nationals Bob learned that there was no motor oil available in the area, but an Asian did have a machine that used oil. It turned out to be a milk separator. The truck driver willingly went after the oil and soon

153

returned with it. Although it was not motor oil, they hoped it would work when combined with the goo they had extracted. The gasoline was carefully separated from the water as it rose to the top bit by bit, and when they had finished, they found they still had five of the precious seven gallons remaining. By the evening of the third day, everything was dried, and by nine o'clock, they were on their way. Behind them, what had been a raging torrent was now a mere trickle again; ahead the land was vast and dusty, spotted with thorn trees and barely traversable. In spite of all their effort to separate the water from the gas, about every six miles the car would sputter and stop. Bob again and again dismantled the carburetor, blew out the water, dried it out and reassembled it. At daybreak, exhausted they arrived at Shirati.

Shirati, via Musoma %Mennonite Mission, Nov. 18, 1934

...I started before to lead up to the experiences the folks had over the week-end of Nov 11, 12, 13. We felt it would be a splendid thing for them to see the chief and his men again because we knew how much a little encouragement might help them to press their case in the L.N.C. (Local Native Council where the petition first has to pass and where the D.C. has full power). They made the trip up just fine. Mr. and Mrs. Mosemann of this missions went so that Clara could go. I did not feel at this time of the year it would be wise to take the children and so it proved. They saw the Chief and found them anxious for us but afraid of the D.C. They had services with them and a splendid time, and started back that same day. They got to within 35 miles of here and came to a stream they couldn't cross so camped there all night. Next morning the river steadily went down until the P.M. they thought they'd start across. By the time they were packed and down to the river it had started to rain above them and the river started up again. So making loads of all the heavier things they sent across first on heads of porters. Then they started in the car. In midstream they stuck and the natives couldn't budge it. Neither Mr. nor Mrs. M. could swim so Bob took her on his back and they stretched a rope for him. By that time the water was up half way in the car and Bob stood on top and threw things ashore. They saved everything in the car. But they had put in 7 gals of gas and some oil just before and they knew this would be ruined. In just one hour just the top of the car was visible. They sent in a runner to get food, oil, gas etc. thinking they would have to be there for days. But the next morning the water went down sufficiently to drag the car out and the Lord sent along a truck to help and that on an almost unfrequented road. Then they began work on the car, the ladies inside and the men on the engine. Everything was mud caked and water soaked. They worked and dried stuff and put it together again and oh! yes I forgot the remarkable thing. The gas was practically all there. The oil was somewhat spoiled but not so much of it had gone. They got some from the native truck driver, and another remarkable thing – he wouldn't take any pay for all his help. A native usually not only takes pay but demands an exorbitant price when he helps someone out. They got into the car stepped on the starter and it went right off. When they got back and I looked at the inside I simply couldn't believe that it had seen water in the inside at all. It surely was wonderful how the Lord preserved everthing and helped and kept them We were surely glad when they rolled in home here.

We are still holding on to the Lord in prayer about the site but have had precious victory about it. Wondering how you are feeling in your praying.... *Much love, C*

"We felt it would be a splendid thing for them to see the chief and his men again...."

"Be a man!" Bob had heard his dad say it again and again when he was a child. He expected their sons to embrace duty, to face the future as the present, to turn toward their light as they saw it and to be a man among men. Tough and rigid, he worked the boys "like slaves," some of them would tell you. Sometimes during harvest, they were up all night, having put in full long days of work. Bob believed his "Heavenly Father" expected at least the same. Accordingly, he carefully planned all the steps of construction on the Mennonite home.

Awakening abruptly and fully at five o'clock each morning, he emerged from the tent. It was usually still dark, so he would light the kerosene lantern and be on his way. Since very few others were up and about, he reveled in the peace that was followed by the melody of waking voices, all with hope and laughter, the night done, the morning emerging in the beautiful sunrise. In his mind, the words kept coming back: *"Look out onto the fields, which are white unto harvest."*

To him the Scripture meant there was work to be done. Not a single touch and then abandonment, but continuous involvement, hour-by-hour, day after day.

Kitty meantime cooked the meals for her family and Clara, cared for her children, did the washing and cleaning and continued language study.

But in Shirati, Tanzania, the heat seemed to press down and squeeze out their energy. The evenings were treasured, as when at last the sun went gone down things cooled rapidly. Some parts of their lives were so ephemeral that they hardly qualified as stories. At other times, it was more like an endless dream of sultry, drawn-out days, of fighting bugs, of waiting for jobs to be done. They wondered if there would ever be a time when Bob would be building their own home on their mission station, a time when plans could be realized, a time when of all of this would make sense.

> Shirati c/o Mennonite Mission
> Nov. 18, 1934
>
> Dear Folks,
>   These are full and busy days. I come in each evening quite tired enough to sleep. I find little time for correspondence or even time to think. This will soon be over, a breathing spell, and then I hope things will be going in earnest on our own station. I think we've all had enough of this hot location for a while. Vatende, in proper houses, is ideal climatically. We are praying and trusting and are going on, by God's grace. I must close. Thankful for all your loving prayers and helpful efforts. Be sure to give my love to Mrs. Wms. Say hello to Bro. Terry, and tell him I still await his reply to my letter.
>
>   Your Bob

"I come in each evening quite tired enough to sleep."

Kitty stepped out of the tent into the moonlit night. She could make out the shapes of all of the temporary houses on the modest Mennonite mission as well as the much larger frame of the building Bob was cutting the lumber for and noticed that the frame was nearly completed. The cool of the night was a relief but she didn't stay long, knowing the threat of mosquitoes and the malaria they carried.

What a blessing it would be to get to Vatende! The word was constantly on their minds and their lips. They anxiously planned what they hoped would be a bright future. Then as November ended, they received a letter from the Provincial Commissioner that would once more turn their dreams upside down.

Most likely the building at Shirati

155

Dear Folks;   Dec. 2, 1934

Just a short letter this time to keep you posted as to our whereabouts and a few things of interest. We send mail off today but we do not get any more until next Thursday... If all goes well we will be leaving here for Kericho in less than three weeks. The house here is up to the roof and the back post on the porch poured. The front ones they expect to get on rafters joists etc. for the iron roofing. There is still a great deal of work to be done but Bob thinks it will be ready for them to move into by three weeks. The finishing they can do at their own leisure.

We have had a hard week in some respects and a glorious one in others. In the last mail we got a letter from the head official of our Province, the one who has been so kind and given us all sorts of encouragement. He said he had been to see our District official and he is convinced that our people want the Catholics and therefore our petition for a site would not even be considered. Well, you can imagine that that was quite a blow to us, especially as we had put so much hope in this man. Well, we all came together that evening for a conference and prayer and we found that the Lord had been talking to us all along similar lines. Then Bob began to exhort us, and if ever the Lord spoke through him he did then, and how heart searching! ....

Somehow the vision came to us that all the eyes of the colony, the eyes of folks at home, the missions of Kenya and Tanganyika, the gov. officials concerned etc. were looking toward this thing. If we went down in defeat, it wasn't us but the Lord and He gave us all the faith to believe for the impossible. Then we were reading in Streams in the Desert. Look at the readings for Nov. from the 15th on and especially the one on "With God nothing is impossible." Since then we have had wonderful victory in spite of tests and absolutely no sight. This is having faith and I never knew anything like it before. We have felt that we have His mind and His will and dared to command Him and we have that feeling of expectancy as if we are on tiptoe for something.

All of this has been under tremendous pressure of work and physical strain. It seems all of our bodies have been attacked in one way or another....

Well now to more personal news. We are quite worn with the heat here and will be glad to get to a higher altitude. The children have had no signs of malaria and I am praying they may be kept from infection while we are still here. They are talking every day about going to Kericho and Anna Verne is wide-eyed while John tells her all the mysteries of the box and how it is coming on a big boat from America. [This was Grandmother B's Christmas box.]

...Not long ago, Anna Verne ran in from her play and said, "Muddie, let's pray now." I said, "Alright, you may pray." So down on her knees she went and said, "Dee Lord, we thank dee, dee Lord, we thank dee, dee Lord we thank dee. Amen." Then she said, "Now you pray, Muddie." So I got down and as truly 'A child shall lead them" learned a lesson in saying just, "Dear Lord, we thank thee...."

"He said...our petition for a site would not even be considered."

156

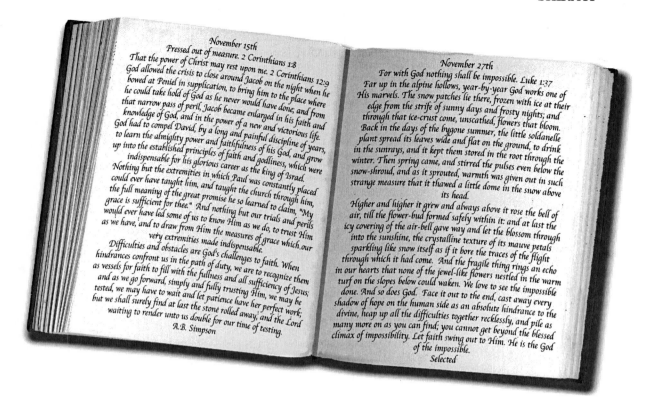

November 15th
Pressed out of measure. 2 Corinthians 1:8
That the power of Christ may rest upon me. 2 Corinthians 12:9
God allowed the crisis to close around Jacob on the night when he bowed at Peniel in supplication, to bring him to the place where he could take hold of God as he never would have done; and from that narrow pass of peril, Jacob became enlarged in his faith and knowledge of God, and in the power of a new and victorious life. God had to compel David, by a long and painful discipline of years, to learn the almighty power and faithfulness of his God, and grow up into the established principles of faith and godliness, which were indispensable for his glorious career as the king of Israel. Nothing but the extremities in which Paul was constantly placed could ever have taught him, and taught the church through him, the full meaning of the great promise he so learned to claim, "My grace is sufficient for thee." And nothing but our trials and perils would ever have led some of us to know Him as we do, to trust Him as we have, and to draw from Him the measures of grace which our very extremities made indispensable.
Difficulties and obstacles are God's challenges to faith. When hindrances confront us in the path of duty, we are to recognize them as vessels for faith to fill with the fullness and all sufficiency of Jesus; and as we go forward, simply and fully trusting Him, we may be tested, we may have to wait and let patience have her perfect work; but we shall surely find at last the stone rolled away, and the Lord waiting to render unto us double for our time of testing.
A.B. Simpson

November 27th
For with God nothing shall be impossible. Luke 1:37
Far up in the alpine hollows, year-by-year God works one of His marvels. The snow patches lie there, frozen with ice at their edge from the strife of sunny days and frosty nights; and through that ice-crust come, unscathed, flowers that bloom. Back in the days of the bygone summer, the little soldanelle plant spread its leaves wide and flat on the ground, to drink in the sunrays, and it kept them stored in the root through the winter. Then spring came, and stirred the pulses even below the snow-shroud, and as it sprouted, warmth was given out in such strange measure that it thawed a little dome in the snow above its head.
Higher and higher it grew and always above it rose the bell of air, till the flower-bud formed safely within it: and at last the icy covering of the air-bell gave way and let the blossom through into the sunshine, the crystalline texture of its mauve petals sparkling like snow itself as if it bore the traces of the flight through which it had come. And the fragile thing rings an echo in our hearts that none of the jewel-like flowers nestled in the warm turf on the slopes below could waken. We love to see the impossible done. And so does God. Face it out to the end, cast away every shadow of hope on the human side as an absolute hindrance to the divine, heap up all the difficulties together recklessly, and pile as many more on as you can find; you cannot get beyond the blessed climax of impossibility. Let faith swing out to Him. He is the God of the impossible.
Selected

"Then we were reading in Streams in the Desert."

Accepting God's closed doors

When the Fishes were interviewing our parents for the book *The Place of Songs,* they described in detail the last days at Shirati, the time at the SDA mission, and then their trip back to Kericho. These experiences had a profound effect on them and upon the attitudes and respect they would have for other Christians whose traditions of faith manifest themselves differently from their own, all the while they remained true to their own beliefs. Along with the Africa Inland Mission family, their close relationship with the Mennonites, the Seventh Day Adventists and the Friends missionaries continued over all of the ensuing years and even after they came to this country.

By the end of 1934, the Smith family and Clara Ford had lived in tents at Shirati for six months. As the day wore on and evening approached, a dark green gloom enveloped the tent. Its walls rippled with the wind, and provided a welcome barrier against the elements. The lantern cast a warm glow and created shadows as they moved about the tent. Once again they were dealing with the harsh reality of rejection.

Bob, exhausted from his heavy day, slept through the baby's crying, while Kitty kept watch over her children. She sponged their heads with cool water and moved them to her bed while she replaced their perspiration soaked bedclothes. The fever alternated with deep shaking chills. She covered them and cradled them during these periods. Occasionally she herself could drift off to sleep, but she was immediately responsive to any noise that came from either of them. It had been five days now since she had truly slept, and she was feeling the strain. She noticed that her lips were becoming sore and slightly swollen, and even the insides of her ears were unusually tender. Their clothes hung loosely on them all; they had all lost weight.

"What are we coming to?" she thought to herself, as she looked at her children in their shabby clothing. But somehow now that her children were so sick, vital issues of cleanliness, even her sense of style and dignity simply did not seem important any more. She prayed for them to be well. As she prayed, day broke abruptly. A blade of sunlight slipped under the tent flap. Soon the sun was shining brightly, and the canvas walls that through the night were a welcome barrier were now becoming hot. The musty smell that filled the tent encouraged Kitty to take her children and seek relief in the open air.

Bob's work on the Mennonite home was coming to an end, rafters were up, and the roofing materials were on hand. He worked tirelessly, grateful for the opportunity, not only to be of help but also to be able to use the money he received to pay on the mounting debt that so rankled both him and Kitty. Even though there was promise of salaries arriving, they had not materialized. The idea of freedom of debt stood constantly in the back of Bob's mind. Accordingly, he was gently urged on by the promise of pay for his labor.

Since the days had been extremely hot, Bob first blamed the external heat for the way he was feeling, but soon his muscles began stiffening, and a wave of chills swept over him. By now the symptoms of malaria had become so familiar that no doctor was needed to confirm the diagnosis. While he should complete the job, he and his sick family had reached the end of their tolerance. He needed to move them to care and safety, and he contemplated how he could accomplish both.

The dust of Mr. Matthew's truck was a welcome sight as it approached. The Seventh Day Adventists had a mission in the town of Gendia in the Kisii area, close to the Mennonites. All of the missionaries had become acquainted, stopping by to visit each other whenever in the area. On this day, as always, tea was served and pleasantries exchanged. Kitty was absent, and when asked why, Bob told of the children's illness. "Kitty is not looking so well herself," he added.

"I saw her earlier and suggested perhaps she could go to Gendia with you, Mr. Matthews. She needs some medical care," said Mrs. Mosemann.

Mr. Matthews was quite willing. And so it was that Kitty finished packing and bade their dear friends, the Mosemanns and the Stauffers, good-bye. But it was not without concern that she hugged Bob. "Honey, you are burning up. I don't like you being up on that roof when you're sick like this."

"It's malaria, I'm sure. I have only three days of work left. I'll finish cleaning up here and return the tent. I'll be all right. You and the kiddies go along. You need some rest, and this is God's provision for you, I'm sure. I'll be there ere long."

John Boy didn't want to let go of his daddy's neck. "We'll see Daddy soon," Kitty reassured him.

And off they went...away from Shirati.

"The name Shirati means prostitute, I have been told," Kitty said, wondering why she had just thought of that.

"You're right," replied Mr. Matthews.

It did not seem too far. Kitty had been busy minding the children as Mr. Matthews chatted pleasantly and all braced themselves against the bumpy road. She felt exhausted, and it was hard to think straight. What a welcome relief when they rounded the last corner and Kitty saw the house—a real house. The children were delighted to see a pet dick-dick in the yard.

The Matthews showed Catharine to a room with a proper bed. "Now you never mind. I will take care of the babies tonight. It will be like having my own back. I miss them so much. Wash up and climb in bed and I'll bring you something to eat," Mrs. Matthews ordered kindly.

The food, prepared for her, tasted good. Her mouth, however, was tender and her tongue felt raw. She gratefully sank back into the bed. Things seemed to be swimming, and the next thing she knew, it was morning.

Dick-dick, Kenya's smallest antelope

"The children!" she thought jumping out of bed. She dressed hurriedly and went to the living room. There they both were, dressed and playing happily. Mrs. Matthews was looking lovingly at them.

"It is so wonderful to have children in the house again. They both slept well. I think they are nearly over their malaria. You know, our boys are away in school. How are you feeling, my dear?"

"I have not slept like that for so long I can't remember. I feel much better. Thank you so much for caring for my babies." She gave them each a hug.

"You are ever so welcome. You needed it. But you still are not well, and you need the attention of a doctor."

"You are kind and I do so much appreciate it." Kitty unsuccessfully fought back the tears.

"Let me get you some breakfast. We have some nice fresh bananas."

"That would be wonderful." Kitty looked out of the window. She could hear the doves cooing. Little weaverbirds were busy flying in and out of the nests as they wove them. She felt glued to the seat as if in a beautiful dream, drinking in the pleasure of being at rest. It wasn't long until she had dozed off again. This time when she awoke, she was very warm and drenched with perspiration. She felt light headed and slightly nauseated. Mrs. Matthews was startled by Kitty's appearance when she re-entered the room.

"Catharine, I think you need to get back to bed. You are not looking well. I'm going to take your temperature."

Kitty did not resist. She gladly returned to the room. Her temperature was 101°.

"We are going to try to get in touch with Bob and let him know you need to get to a doctor."

"Thank you again for everything," she murmured as she slipped back into a deep sleep.

Weaverbird nest

A message was sent to Bob, making clear that Catharine's conditions was not good and further medical help would be required. The next day, he arrived at the Adventist Mission. Kitty had begun to improve, but everyone felt that she needed to get further medical care. The Smiths gratefully bade their new friends goodbye. Bob and Kitty reflected upon the fact that not long ago they had been heart broken by the news that Bob's parents had become Seventh Day Adventists. Now with the reality of the love and devotion of these new found friends, that feeling had disappeared and been replaced with the warmth of a true kinship in Christ.

"…a kind British family."

The plains ahead opened into a magical vista teaming with animals in every direction one looked. In abundance were zebra with their stunning contrast of the black and white, comically frolicking gnu, kongoni (Coke's Hartebeest), tawny colored eland with their drooping dewlaps and striped withers,

Thompson's gazelle

Thompson's gazelle with black, white and brown sides and constantly flicking little black tails. Surprisingly they all fed there together, not excited by a pride of lion sunning themselves nearby.

"Watch this, John Boy!" Bob said as he tore off the road driving up beside an impala herd walking along in single file. He beat repetitively on the car door, and with each recurrent sound, the sleek little antelope simultaneously leaped higher and higher in graceful arches. It was breathtaking. Kitty laughed as the baby she held clapped her little hands in glee.

They were still surrounded by animals when the car sputtered and died.

"Well, can you beat that?" Bob climbed out of the car and lifted the bonnet. It seemed he was forever fixing a car or a truck gone wrong. And how they could go wrong! By this time in Africa, he had heard many stories of motorists who had managed to get themselves into diabolical trouble and somehow find their way out. He loved such a challenge.

Early vehicle chassis were nothing if not simple and robust. The whole machine had such casual tolerances almost anything would substitute for the right part. Springs broke easily on the rough roads, especially when the vehicle was over loaded. Repairing a spring, on the other hand, was a tough knuckle-busting job. It was quite a trick to get the semi-curved leaves lined up and staying put until they could be pressed together and the bolt fastened. Car springs were the "leaf type" (i.e. long flat pieces of steel held together by a center bolt and little brackets). The main leaf had curled ends, with a U-shaped shackle to hold that end of the spring either to the axle housing or to the body. If the main leaf broke, one had a problem…no way to hold the spring in place to do its work. If any other leaves cracked or broke, one could limp home with a decided list to port or starboard. Bob had heard of replacing broken springs with tree limbs or healing a spring leaf by wrapping it with freshly skinned zebra strips, allowing the hide to dry; as the hide contracted, the spring became useable again.

Zebra

He had also discovered the effects of the equatorial sunlight, which ruined tires almost as fast as stones punctured them. An extended journey required a trunk load of patches, with a repair kit, an extra tube, a tire pump, tire irons for demounting and a gaiter (a special patch to reinforce a gash in the sidewall). Maintaining a car in Africa became a mixture of ingenuity, imagination and careful planning.

He had heard of a coffee farmer from Limuru who had met a steaming very old model T Ford on the road. The previous day, they'd ripped a hole in their sump, and all the oil had drained out. They had removed the sump, packed the hole with kapok from the seat cushion, and then hammered the buckled metal straight, effectively sealing the crack with the kapok plug.

Impala

They then shot a zebra, stripped the fat off it and boiled it up in a *sufuria* (a round metal utility basin). They poured the hot fat through a mosquito net into the engine, and traveled around six miles before dark. In the morning, they put a primus stove (a portable kerosene cooking stove) under the sump, and when the zebra fat was good and hot again, they set off.

Bob, already learning the tricks of helping a motorcar find its "tortured way" in this inhospitable place, followed his usual routine of "looking under the bonnet," then "cranking her up," and finally "getting down and under." In spite of all that, he still was not satisfied that he had found the problem. The fine dust had covered every grease-lined part, and by the time he emerged, he was a mess. He had a partially filled *debi (*gasoline container*)* and for once they were not lacking the precious substance.

"Now what?" Bob remembered thinking as he looked at his listless wife and then out across the plains. No house or building of any kind was in sight. John Boy had found a stick and was entertaining himself by using it to push ants off course and then watch as they circled and returned to their programmatic journey. Then, suddenly in the distance, Bob saw a cloud of dust. It wasn't moving erratically like a dust devil but was making its way in their direction. If it was a car, Bob knew it would stop. Motorists under no circumstances would pass another on the road without offering assistance. Bob circled his car once more checking the tires and trying to dust himself off.

Eland

"I think it's something in the fuel line, but I can't do a thing about it here," Bob explained. "My wife is ill, and we are desperate to get her to a doctor. May I offer you our gasoline for a tow?" Bob pled with the driver of the car.

The strangers took one look at Kitty and the children, and never hesitated. A towrope was produced, and soon they were on their way. The Smiths were about to experience the generous warmth of a kind British family.

Dear Folks: *Kericho Kenya, B.E.A. Jan 2, 1935*

...We had a very eventful time trying to get here for Christmas. I guess I wrote you that the children both took malaria at Shirati. They had terrible cases of it their fever going to 105 degrees and staying there for two days. I was up with them night and day for a solid week. At the end of that time the S.D.A. missionary from up the highlands came through and offered to take us up to his place until Bob finished and came through to take us on. We were delighted to go, and found them the loveliest people and very Godly. They took us right into their hearts and gave the children especially their love. They have two boys of their own who are in England in school and they are lonely without them. So they stepped into the empty place. Well the long strain told on me and first I had a bad case of flu. Then I had a peculiar case where my ears, mouth, nose etc. were covered with great white ulcers. They sent for Bob who came at once and then the Lord surely undertook for me. We left there to get to the doctor's as soon as possible. When we were in the middle of the game reserve the car broke down completely and what to do we did not know. A man and wife came by and because of my condition towed us to the nearest shamba, a distance of 40 miles. There they sent a car down for us and took us in for the night giving us a nice warm supper and good beds and the next a.m. took us on to Litein a distance of 35 miles. There we got on in to Kericho to the Doc. He said the months of hardship and privation had been too much and I had broken down in general. Also I have been having chronic malaria and a bad case of anemia. So I am having a grand rest. I must say I am very weak and get spells of having my arms like lead as you used to but I am sleeping very well and the doctor is delighted with my progress. There is nothing organic and no need to worry. I shall take another course of Atebrin [sic] as soon as the doc has built me up some...

Excerpts from Jan. 2, 1935 letter

Clara had left Shirati earlier with a family going to Kericho. From there she had gone to be with her father at Musoma. When Kitty and Bob arrived at Kericho, they were welcomed into the Kirkpatricks' home for a few days while Kitty saw Dr. Dixon. Comments were tempered by the uncertainty of Catharine's condition, and miraculously there was little conflict. They shared the details of their time apart and discussed Clara's expected furlough. And they learned of Faye's pregnancy with delivery expected in February or March. They relished the harmony they were experiencing.

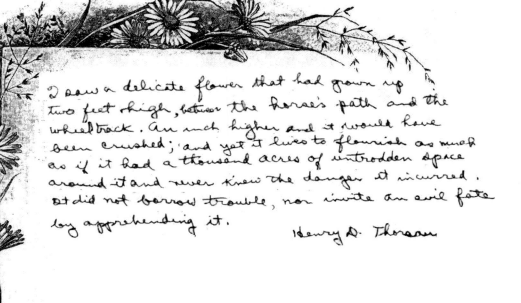

I saw a delicate flower that had grown up
two feet high, between the horse's path and the
wheel track. An inch higher and it would have
been crushed; and yet it lives to flourish as much
as if it had a thousand acres of untrodden space
around it and never knew the danger it incurred.
It did not borrow trouble, nor invite an evil fate
by apprehending it.

Henry D. Thoreau

CHAPTER 11

KERICHO—JANUARY 2, 1935—NOVEMBER 1, 1935

"...the familiar creak and crack of the wattle...."

Sometime in January they left the Kirkpatricks' home in Kericho, at Mr. H.'s invitation, to live at Chaigaik next to his home in a small hut. It was now about two and one-half years since they had arrived in Africa, and other than during the first five months, tin and mud huts or tents had been their homes. Kitty had made curtains for windows when she had material for them, hung pictures on the wall where she could and always the place became transformed into a warm, inviting home. Her first experience with a mud hut had been harsh; how terrified she was of the snakes and insects that inhabited the grass roof. Now once again, she would be living in a mud house, hearing the familiar creak and crack of the wattle as it warmed in the hot sun, but how much nicer this was than the tents where she had lived for the last six months.

"I'm going to have to leave...."

Kitty had finished her morning chores, and the children were happily romping in the sunshine. She stood at the door of her grass hut and gazed across at Mr. H.'s little house. Through the window she could see him moving about and decided that this was the time to try to cheer him up. He seemed so subdued lately.

She knew she could keep an eye on the children from his window. "It's tea time, Bro. H. Look, I brought you some flowers."

"Right you are, Catharine, it is tea time. There should be a vase for the flowers in the kitchen. Will you fix them for me?"

She was used to his kitchen since they took their meals with him. She turned on the kerosene stove and set the pot to boil. From where she stood, she could see his desk piled with tablets and papers. "What are you going to call your new book?"

"Well, it's about the changes that have taken place in Kenya since I first came. I think it will be *Then and Now in Kenya Colony.* Mr. H. was tall and slim. His eyes were piercing and his gaze intense. His lined face reflected the long life's journey he had made, but his jaw was set and determined.

"Is the writing hard? You seem so burdened lately. I wish I could cheer you up."

Bro. H. sighed, "Well, Catharine, no, it's not the book. That is largely done. It is that I'm going to have to leave and go to America."

Kitty gasped. She wasn't ready for that reply. "You are leaving so soon! But what are we going to do about the work and the site? We can't lose you now!" The idea of losing his assurance and leadership was daunting. Only recently had they dared to believe that his site would be approved and turned over to them and their dream of beginning the work would finally materialize. She stared at him dumbfounded.

Bro. H. noticed Kitty's distress and quickly added. "I have no choice. It's my son; he needs me." Kitty searched his face.

"Here I am thousands of miles away in a foreign land, and my son is losing his way. I simply have to go to him. There is no other way." His eyes were brimming with tears as he poured out the whole story.

"I'm so sorry." Kitty lifted the pot of boiling water and poured it over the tea leaves. When the tea had steeped, she poured it through the strainer into the milk already added to the cup, causing it to bubble perfectly. She knew she could make a perfect cup of tea. She carried it to her old friend, tears also brimming in her own eyes. Again she said, "I'm so sorry. When will you be leaving?

"I don't know, Catharine, and I am not ready to tell this to the others here."

"You need not worry. I will not mention it to anyone here." Kitty listened as Mr. H. shared his concerns while they sipped tea together.

"There, that tea was wonderful, Catharine. It was good to unburden my heart, and I think you see the importance of this trip."

"I do indeed, and I will be praying for you as you bear this burden." She left him sitting there with his head bowed, quietly closed the door and walked out to where the children were playing in the warm sunshine. She wondered what would become of her own family as the years passed. Would she ever have a real home in this land? Surely the time would come. Surely!

> *Our plans are still very indefinite. ...Mr. H. is going to come home. Not as one might think for his bride, but to make a home for David. He absolutely needs him...Bro. H. is heartbroken. He poured it all out to me as if he must tell someone. I am so glad he did trust me...His great heart-ache is in leaving the work and he fears he'll not get back to it....*

Excerpt from Jan. 2, 1935

On March 19, 1934, Mr. Hotchkiss had written to the Provincial Commissioner at Kisumu applying for the site at Sotik in the name of the Lumbwa Industrial Mission. On January 25, 1935 the Local Native Council granted the site. In late January 1935, Mr. Hotchkiss went to Kijabe and made the proposal outlined in Kitty's letter. Although the AIM had agreed with Mr. Hotchkiss's plan, and the government had verbally promised the site, approval from the Kenya Land Board was required but as yet there were no legal documents in hand. Confronted with continuing uncertainty as a *fait accompli*, the Smiths rallied to the task of vigorous preparation for a move to Sotik with the strong belief that the papers would somehow materialize.

Kericho, Kenya B.E.A.
Feb. 10, 1935

...Now to answer your letter. As you have already heard, I am much better. We have left Kirkpatricks' and have gone out to Bro. H.'s place and are living in a tiny grass hut 10'x20'. It is larger than anything we have had for the past 6 mo. so it seems quite nice. We have rats etc., but we have learned that that is a small matter. We all eat together in Mr. H.'s house, and he seems quite happy about it. He announced his intention of returning to America, so you need not keep it a secret any longer, but he has told no one but me his real reason for having to go. While at Kijabi, he made the proposition to the A.I.M. that he turn over his schools in these two districts to them, seven in all, and they in turn give him their two schools in Sotik, and then he turn everything in Sotik to the N.H.A. He now has the site we applied for twice and didn't get and wants to give that to us. The A.I.M. have agreed and are welcoming us with open arms, quite different from their past attitude, and it is truly a miracle of the Lord. So Dad, your vision you wrote us so long ago is actually coming true. Had it not been for the changed attitude of the A.I.M., we could never have gone in as it would have spoiled any contract we might hope to have with the other missions in the future. So in perhaps a month, we will begin building down there....

Excerpt Feb. 10, 1935

We loved Dad's constant sense of humor. He rarely could restrain it, so when he arrived a party always began. Laughing almost constantly, he gained the African name Ng'erechi (The Laughing One.) Mother would act upset when his antics got him into trouble, but she always, in fact, adored her "sunny" Bob's humor. Although we never heard this conversation, we heard the story and many such conversations.

"Bob, you didn't."

"I'm afraid I did. Kirk's camera was lying there so handy, and I thought to myself what a great joke it would be for him to find a picture of himself taking a bath in the cow trough. I had no idea it would be Clara who developed the film," he said as he laughed almost uncontrollably. Kirk had used the same film for Clara's passport photo, and since she needed it, she had taken it in to be developed."

"Clara was pretty upset, wasn't she?" Kitty said shaking her head.

"Well, the merchant warned her that she probably wouldn't want to look at the pictures herself. She needed to, though, to get her passport pictures out of the bunch." He laughed again. It wasn't so bad, though. It was from a distance, and he was turned away from the camera."

"Bob, it's not funny. You should be ashamed of yourself." Kitty knew her words would never make a difference. It was just part of his nature to play pranks, and when the next chance came along, he would probably be at it again.

Dear Folks,

I'm as busy as a one-armed paperhanger with the hives and I consider it a rank injustice for your daughter to insist that I take time to try to write behind where she has written when there is scarcely a behind to write on without writing on the front. The Lord has been leading and teaching us many things. One thing especially has been impressed upon us, and putting it in African setting, it sounds like this:

De higher up de monkey climb,
De mo' he show his tail.
De gal what switch in her Sunday clo'es
Jes' show she a fool, ez de good Lawd knows.
Git along chile! Git along chile!
De boy dat's proud, den his pride gwine fail—
De higher up de monkey climb,
De more he show his tail.

De higher up de monkey climb,
De more he show his tail.
De purson what carry his head too fas'
Got to stump his toe on a flea at las'
Git along chile! Git along chile!
'Taint always safe on de toppest rail---
De higher up de monkey climb,
De more he show his tail.

       Nancy Turner

My dearly beloved accepted through matrimony, and supported until now, does not approve of my choice of literature. She feels that it tends toward vulgarity. This was not at all in the mind of the author as I have told her. If it was, she was a naughty girl. Anyway I think she said, "Pride goeth before a fall." I'm not keen on fallin' so I'll keep off the up'est rail.

  Yours for evermore!

"My dearly beloved...does not approve of my choice of literature."

"Remember your Papa always said, 'The Lord enjoys a good joke,'" he rejoined.

"Well he didn't mean it like that!" she said, but she had to turn away from him to keep from grinning. "The truth is that, were it not for your sense of humor, things would get pretty thick around here."

"I'm glad you can see it that way."

"Well, I can but I would never admit it in regard to this incident, my dear. You need to be more careful," she said seriously.

"I search my soul all the time to see if my attitudes are at fault. I know God is at work in me and is helping me. I didn't mean for this to go so far," Bob said, and he meant it.

We children all remember the rains. We can imagine how it must have been.

The rains began in earnest; a cold wind shook the trees, and then huge raindrops came down as cold as ice. The wind sounded as if it would tear the roof off of the tiny grass hut. Lightening turned the sky into a painful dazzling white. Soon a wall of water seemed to be pouring off the roof, turning the ground into a swirling mass of chocolate. In the unheated hut, Kitty and the children huddled together shivering. The thunder crashed and reverberated. Kitty held her baby close as she shivered in her arms. She draped a blanket around John and they clung to each other. Finally the water wall thinned and disappeared, but the cold moistness hung in the air. It was several days since the rains had begun, and with each passing day, the cold penetrated more in a way Kitty had not experienced for some time.

"Bob, we just must get some heat. I'm afraid the kiddies are going to get sick again. We can escape to Mr. H.'s house but we can't be there all the time."

"We'll work out something, Kitty. I think I can make a little heater for you."

Feb. 25, 1934 (*Error this was likely 1935*)

Dear Mother:

We are sending you a birthday letter written on Anna Verne's birthday and supposed to reach you by yours or on John's birthday....

You spoke of the devil being on our track. I have never had such a time. I remember your struggles with understanding now. I get the awfullest feelings and sometimes would like to stomp and scream and tear things. I think the old nick knows my nerves are on a frazzle and attacks me there. But it has never been harder to pray. I sometimes think a big victory is just ahead, and the devil knows it.

I mentioned the Sotik affair. Mr. H has not yet received the government papers, but all the other details have been attended to so that as soon as he does, he can make the transfer to us. We are here now in a little grass hut just about 30 ft. from his door. We all eat together at his place, and we live and sleep here. It is 10'x20'. Beginning at the front and going back we have a tiny book shelf, table (steamer trunk under) a tea table, our bed, (back) wash stand, double decker of the children, (under steamer truck), cedar chest, chest of drawers, large trunk, door. There are two straight and one rocking chair. It has been terribly cold here as the rains are on, but Bob lined the house with grass mats and put a rough stone fireplace in the front and so we can stand it now. In fact, it is quite comfy if we keep our sweaters on.

Miss Ford isn't sure just when she will be sailing. She hasn't yet been able to get bookings. Everything seems very full. But I am sending some things home, which I have marked. I've tried to stretch them as far as possible and hope no one feels slighted. Some of the things that seem the least really cost the most.

The children are well, and Bob is hard at it sawing logs. We had quite a victory about that matter as we received notice that the mill must go back at once, and it meant a dead loss as Kirk had done the logging but no sawing. But Mr. H. was able to get an extension of time, and they are sawing as fast as they have water. Mr. H. is furnishing the logs and the water power. He does not know yet when he is leaving. He hasn't the money at present. Clara Ford will come first, I expect. She will tell you many things. Just be sure and keep confidence. All goes well here by spells. Must close for this time.

Love and many more happy birthdays. Catharine

"*Sotik...Mr. H. has not received the government papers....*"

"We'll...miss you."

They stood on the train platform. Bob had prayed and Kitty, as was her custom on each occasion of a journey, had quoted the "Travelers' Psalm" (Psalm 121) in its entirety—"I will lift up mine eyes unto the hills from whence cometh my help...The Lord bless thy going out and thy coming in from this time forth...."

"God's speed, Clara. We'll surely miss you." Clara's health was not good, and medical care would be sought in the U.S.

The engine belched, and a plume of sparks like a coil of fireflies rose into the air and was swallowed up by the dark African night. The train slowly pulled away, and they lost sight of Clara. They paused, thinking what it would be like to be heading home to America.

"Come on, Daddy, let's go," John, tugged at his daddy's trousers.

Kericho, Kenya B.E.A. Mar. 13, 1935

Dear Homefolks:

I am going to write this little note to you and send it with Bob's to his folks to save postage.....

I wrote Anna all about our trip to Nairobi to see Clara off. She sailed on the Usarama, Monday, Mar. 11th about noon. She sails from England on the Berengoria which lands in New York Apr. 16th. I am not sure how or when she will come through Ohio, but I think it would be nice if you would send a letter to the boat inviting her. She expressed a desire to go out on the farm for a rest, but I guess that would be after Board meeting which is to be the last of Apr. So she may want to go straight through from N.Y. to Winchester, Ind. where it is to be held. It is quite important for her to be there as she will have many things to tell the board. I am sending some little things to you. Hope they arrive O.K. and are liked by all. Wish I had been able to send more....

I am anxious for you to have a good talk with Miss Clara. I am sure she will help you to understand many things. She really hasn't an enviable job at home as she will have to be pretty plain with the board about many things. I hope she has courage and wisdom from the Lord and am trusting she will.

Mr. H. saw the D.C. today, and he said that the meeting of the Kenya Land Board is to be in April, and that is the reason he has not heard from his application and site in Sotik, but there is no doubt about it whatever or so Mr. H. thinks. He just received his bill for the survey, and it came to $400.00; that is on his farm here, not on the Sotik site. He is really heartsick about it as that is an outrageous price. He doesn't know when he will get home with a bill like that hanging over his head. He is looking very worn and tired these days, In fact he is showing his age quite a bit....

We are quite expectant these days. Faye has still not had her event....

John says "I want a love to Grandma." And Anna Verne echoes.   C

"...the meeting of the Land Board is...in April...."

Dad regarded Grandmother B. as his spiritual adviser and over the years wrote her several letters in which he bared his heart. The conflict with the fellow workers was not discussed openly with us. We knew that there were problems, but they were never understood, and we suspect our parents never intended that we should know. In fact, we did not hear any missionary with whom they worked discussed in a negative way. It just didn't happen. We do know that Mother and Dad had an enduring bond with these missionaries in spite of or perhaps because of what they had been through together. As our mother and father unburden their hearts in these letters to their parents, we see that their conflict was a major spiritual issue that was constantly dealt with in their prayer lives.

Kericho, Kenya, March 17, 1935

Dear Mother Biesecker,

I felt that I wanted to take you off to the side and have a good old chat with you again. When I feel as I do tonight, I can write. So often I'm too tired, and though I should do so, I have not sufficient energy to write or express my thoughts. I've neglected you sadly of late and must repent. Would like to be able to step out of the house in the face of an old "Northwester." I miss the cold. But I suppose you would welcome some of Kenya's heat.

When this reaches you, you will be planting garden or thinking of it. Miss Ford will have arrived and told you all that there is to tell about the situation here. We are so happy you will get to hear "the straight" of it all. We have great confidence in Clara and feel sure she will not over emphasize or under emphasize our situation. We are going steadily on with a settled certainty that God's best for these black souls is the gospel of full salvation. When God sees best, we will push forward unhindered, I'm sure. We're doing our best to prepare for coming active days. Just today, I started work on window frames for our houses on the station. Work doesn't bother me. My physical weakness is no great burden. What weighs the heaviest is that seeming partition between us here. The burden for souls cannot draw us on in study and effort as it would if this impediment were removed. Why does God permit it? We cannot say. Nevertheless we are determined, and He who called us is faithful. We shall feel the power of His blessing on the work here! But it must rest on His servants. I cannot feel that it is a lack of yieldedness on our parts, Catharine and me. If it means more light and revelation for us, we want it and pray for it. It seems a physical impossibility for us to continue on as we are. We have had two openings in the way of appeal for us to come to other missions for definite work. But we feel called of God to the N.H.A. work, and shall remain true until He closes the door and thrusts us out through the instrumentality of our own Board into other work. We are called to Africa of the Lord, and we shall minister here under another Board if God sees fit. But we are resting it all on Him. These things are a telling burden.... But we have a heritage in Christ, which supercedes all earthly aspirations.

Kitty has such a good, happy spirit these days. Our married life is all I ever expected it would be. How God has helped us over some difficult experiences and bound us nearer together. The kiddies are happy and quite strong. Enjoying their Christmas puppy. Bro. H. is still with us. He is certainly proving himself to be God's gentleman. My light is going out, so I will quit.

Bob

"...we have a heritage in Christ, which supercedes all earthly aspirations...."

"…she once again was radiant."

We can imagine this conversation between Faye and Mother.

"What a doll baby!" Kitty held the tiny frame to her and touched the soft skin. She was perfect in every way. Her tiny eyes blinked against the light.

"She is the image of you, Faye! And look at you; you look splendid! You are amazing. Are you sure you have everything you need?"

Kitty looked at her friend. Since they had arrived in Africa, Faye had gradually changed. Life no longer seemed to bubble up in her. The experience had taken its toll, but today she once again was radiant. Kitty hugged the baby once more and held her out to Faye.

"Are you sure you are all right?" Kitty asked again.

"I'm doing fine. Thank you for the blankets you made her, Catharine."

"I have in mind to make her two little dresses with the material I've saved. You rest now, and we'll be on our way. Bye, bye, little Marilyn Beth."

Kericho, Kenya, B.E.A. April 7, 1934 (error: must have been '35)

Dear Folks:

…I expect you have seen Clara by now. We were not sure of the boat as she said she might miss the Berengana but we hope she didn't. She may have gone straight through from N.Y. to the mountains as she very much wanted to get there, but you will see her after that no doubt….

Marilyn Beth came to Kirkpatricks last Wednesday a.m. at 4:45 – April 3rd. She is the very image of Faye. Both are doing so well. Faye looks like she could get up today. The baby weighed 7 1/2 lbs. She had one stitch….

Mr. and Mrs. Mosemann were here for a while when they came to Kenya to get their car. They had been in Shirati so long they needed a rest badly, so stayed here a while under the doctor's care. After they returned, Mrs. Stauffer was taken sick quite suddenly and had her baby which was dead. They thought it was between 6 & 7 months. I really don't think a woman could carry a baby through full term in that climate. Mary said I must tell if there are any "secrets" here at any time. I'm thankful there is nothing yet. Bob and I both feel that until we get settled, another baby is quite out of the question. We do not believe as many do that such things are exactly in our hands, except that we are careful of certain times. So far, the Lord has been very good to us. However, I do want more babies, if I am permitted later to have them. We all felt so sorry about the Stauffers as they love children so much and were so happy over this one….

The Mathews, S.D.A.s with whom we stayed on our way from Shirati, will drop in on Thurs. of this week for a little while. We surely will be glad to see them as we count them among our dearest friends….

Bob is sawing every day now and has most of the lumber ready for the first house. If the permit goes through….

So glad Dad is his old faithful self. What would we do without him? He surely is an example of courage.

Much love to all, Catharine

"…we count them among our dearest friends."

...I am sitting now by the fire. We went in to Kericho to the service at Dr. Dixon's house. A young missionary from Nakuru was supposed to be there but didn't arrive in time, so Mr. Hotchkiss had the service; it was a splendid one. Now we have our supper, some vegetables, soup and pineapple. The fireplace has some big logs in it and is lovely and warm with a beautiful fire. I expect you need no fire there now. Perhaps you are sighing for cooler days.

We are expecting a letter from the government very soon now about Sotik. Mr. H. has seen the D.C. twice & he has written especially about it. Things surely do move slowly. Tomorrow is the big celebration for the 25th anniversary of King George's reign. There are fire works etc. like our July 4th and a service like our Thanksgiving. There is to be a big party for the children at the Kericho Club and Anna Verne and John are invited. They received regular invitations from the Assistant Officer's wife.

Must close with love, C

"We are expecting a letter…very soon now about Sotik."

May 20, 1935

Dear Daddie and Mother,
Daddies letter came a few days back and along with it was one from the Hartford Office. It was the photo static copy of the completed loan of $ 140.00 and a copy of the power of attorney. I can assure you that it was a shock to us when we read the letter and found that instead of relief from our financial burden we found it increased. We not only have the premiums to pay but interest as well as the principle. This was not as we had expected for we would have been relieved of premiums, monthly payments to Asbury. True we would not have the protection of the insurance. If we were able to see how we could manage it we would not feel to badly over the prospect. Our situation is worse than if we owed Asbury and were paying them $5.00 per month. Nevertheless we could manage all the financial troubles and give you folks a lift if we did not cherish our call as we do. Just yesterday I received word from the manager of a large transport company that he wanted me to drive his new 15 ton truck which he is importing. He would give me a possible 700/ Shillings per month or about $175.00. This would amount to about 2200 dollars per year. Nevertheless we are determined to stick to our call and prove the faithfulness of God in meeting our need. We've had two offers from other missions since coming here to Africa but have felt that even though we are so thwarted by the enemy we shall be faithful to our vision....

   Kitty is back from her visit to Kisumu with the Baileys.... I suppose Clara has been with you and you know all about our evil natures. Well, each day here brings new and interesting developments, most amusing at times. The answer from Nairobi is all that keeps us from starting at once in Sotik. Mr. H. and I were down last Friday for a day with them. They are anxiously awaiting our coming. John just spoke up and said, "I'm as hot as a snow horse!" Just where he gets his ideas we cannot say but he is certainly all boy, steamed up for straight ahead.

Blessings on you all.   Your Sonny,   Bob

"Nevertheless, we are determined to stick to our call and prove the faithfulness of God...."

Mother and Dad's decision to buy life insurance was one they had often regretted. The premiums reduced their income by $12.40 each month, and they had apparently asked Father B. to discontinue Dad's policy. Instead, he took out a loan from the insurance company to pay the Asbury bill. We know that Mother and her sister Anna helped pay for their younger sister's education, and the bill mentioned in this letter no doubt refers to Mary's bill. The inability to communicate except by letters, which took such a protracted time to make their rounds, was a constant source of frustration. We often heard the phrase "the letters crossed in the mail" used, meaning the same subject being discussed was coming from each direction at the same time, but it would be another twelve weeks until their response would be received. In the meantime, messages could be misinterpreted. Whether Grandfather misinterpreted or simply did not heed their instruction is not clear. In the end, Dad's policy was cancelled, but they managed to continue Mother's until it matured, and then a monthly payment came to her from that. Each of us children was the benefactor at some point during our schooling. Finally, when we were all through schooling, she kept it for herself.

May 20, 1935

Dear Folks:

I'll add just a line. Had a good time at Baileys'. Made 6 dresses for her & 5 for her little girl, a pr. of pajamas for him and some underwear, a couple of mosquito nets and cut out the clothes for the new baby coming in July. How is that for 10 days?

We are going into Kericho today for Bob to get a shot. He has been having infections in his hands and Doc. says it is poor blood due to so much malaria. He is feeling pretty tough, but I am really glad for the enforced rest. He won't take any any other way. His letter sounds brief and a bit terse, but it is because it hurts his hands so to write.

No word yet about Sotik. The D.C. has written the second time.

Must close. Will write more later.

Lots of love, Catharine

I think in spite of everything, Bob is still glad he has his $2,000 policy intact.

"No word yet about Sotik."

Then at last the miracle happened! The site was approved, and they held in their hands the 33-year lease for the plot at Sotik—two years and seven months after they had set foot in the country. Immediately a telegram was sent to the home office. Not much had to be said.

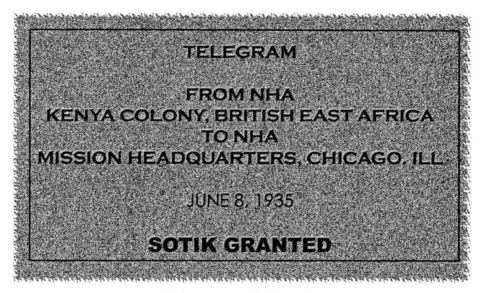

TELEGRAM

FROM NHA
KENYA COLONY, BRITISH EAST AFRICA
TO NHA
MISSION HEADQUARTERS, CHICAGO, ILL.

JUNE 8, 1935

SOTIK GRANTED

Telegram sent to the home office

Kericho, Kenya, B.E.A.
June 9, 1935

Dearest Mother & all,

I have decided to write so it is easier to read this time and write smaller but only on one side of the paper.

You have already had the news about the site. There is no doubt now but that we can go ahead, and at last we will have a permanent house. The plot must be surveyed and building materials hauled down there, and then we can begin to build. It will probably not be until Aug. or Sept. that we will actually get into the house, but at least we have something to look forward to. I imagine they will wait and send Miss Day back with Clara.

Let me say before I go further that Dad's letter came and the explanation of the loans etc., and it is more comprehensible to us now, so we feel better about it, and that it will all work out for the best. I can hardly imagine about the house etc., but as you say, it may be the Lord's way. Since Uncle Jack's is gone and Aunt Tilly is poorly, it might even mean going there for her last days. I have been thinking many things, and one is the sale of the farm there and the sale of our house etc. would bring enough for you to come to us. (Mr. H. has promised us a piece of land on his place next to himself, and we could put up a little cottage for you & dad, Anna could take the position in Kijabi and you could all live nicely.) This will be the safest spot as well as the healthiest in a very short time , I believe. Bob and I have thought a lot about this lately. Who knows but the Lord may have a hand in it....

Mail just in, and Dad's letter to Bob surely rejoices our hearts. It is the way out and the best. Dad does have the business head o.k. Bob will sign at once. It is nearly church time here, so I must get ready. We just warded off a raid of army ants. I never saw so many in my life, literally millions. I am surely glad they didn't get inside or we would have had to leave our house for the day and perhaps the night as well. There goes the church gong. Will finish later.

11:30 - had a good service. Mr. Jenzen preached and then Mr. Hotchkiss. I can understand practically everything either say, but I couldn't do it myself. Anna Verne is now singing the chorus of one of the songs we sang. "Tell it to Jesus" but she is singing "Imwajin Jesu" which means "You tell Jesus." Hers is a real sweet little voice, but she can't carry a tune perfectly yet.

Earl Andersen is back from his vacation so he is coming once a week to help us in Kipsigis. We are soon going to try and take the first exam. It covers the first 10 lessons. We had the little test the other day. I got only 80 but the other marks were 63 and 53 so I didn't feel so bad, though I should have had much more except for a couple of very foolish mistakes. We meet on Wed. and Sat. for lessons. Kipsigis is really very hard, and it has never been properly reduced to grammar.

In order to save money and paper, in a previous letter Kitty had written on thin airmail paper on both sides. She also wrote in the margins so that every space was used. But since the ink showed through, it made the letters hard to read, as is apparent in the above letter.

We just stopped for dinner and on returning to our house find it taken over by the ants, so we do have to leave. The children are now going to sleep on Mr. Hotchkiss's bed and I'm sitting on the foot and writing. It isn't much use to try and fight against them. If you get them driven out from one side they get you at another and they work so fast it is next to impossible to keep up with them.

We are surely rejoicing about the site, as you can imagine. The only fly in the ointment is the fact that there are more things to disagree about now. If there was just once when there wasn't dissention it would be a relief. Well, there must be a way if we could but find it!

One thing about the ants as we said before we'll have a "de-bugged" house when they get through and if any snakes happen to be around they won't stay long. We'll have to beg bed in Kericho tonight.

I guess I'll lie down a bit. I am so anxious about you all and want news from you so badly....

So glad Clara was with you. I know you enjoyed her and she you. And don't you really have a better understanding about things? I have been so anxious that you should have some one to talk to instead of having to depend upon writing. Mr. Hotchkiss is not specific in his descriptions etc. as a woman can be, anyway, and of course he really had no way of knowing just how things would be with us when he himself wasn't here.

Must close.   Catharine & all.

"... and on returning to our house find it taken over by ants, so we do have to leave."

Dear Homefolks: Kericho, Kenya, B.E.A. June 25th 1935

I am sending a note with Bob's as it can still go for the same. Isn't it strange that at the very time we have prospects of at least having a home here, you may be losing yours there? Yet, I can't really believe there isn't some way out. I have looked at it from every angle and am convinced something is going to result for the best.

You are rejoicing with us about the site, I know. Bob just took a load of lumber down on Monday and thought he might get back today, but the rains are still heavy, and it may easily be that he has been detained. So we are expecting him tomorrow. It is hard for us to be shut in so much. Especially the children mind it, as there's no place to play. I surely will enjoy a house with some room in it. I guess I told you we are going to put up the garage and shop first. It is a building 16'x32' so it will have a little more room in it than this has, and there will be a little veranda that will later be the car entrance so they can play outside some.

We received an airmail from Clara last Sunday mailed June 2nd. It arrived here the 23rd, so that was exactly 3 weeks. That is pretty good. She hadn't much to say except the Board meeting.

We expect to hear from you in the next mail that comes tomorrow, so I'll wait and perhaps add more then. We are all very well. I still get quite nervous but it is due to circumstances, I think, and close quarters. I guess I told you in the last letter that Kirk's attitude has somewhat improved again.

Mr. H. expects to sail July 24th. He is going via South Africa and will take nearly 2 months at it. He is going on a merchant ship that carries only a few passengers all one class. Accommodations are very nice, I believe, and food excellent, and he has never been to South Africa so wants to visit around on his way. He surely isn't enthusiastic about going. I feel sorry for him, really, he is so blue. But he is now hoping to get back, perhaps in two years when David is taken care of.

I wonder if Rhea is home yet. She should be on her way now.

                                            Much love, Catharine

...I'll close this in order to get it off via air.

"Isn't it strange that, at the very time we have prospects of at least having a home here, you may be losing yours there?"

Apparently Grandfather somehow held on to his home at 52 Columbus Ave., Delaware, Ohio, an address familiar to all of us children, as this was our refuge at one time or another when we arrived in the foreign country—America.

July 21, 1935

...Mr. Hotchkiss has gone. It was a very hard parting, and we miss him terribly. We had a lovely farewell picnic for him here. His train left Lumbwa for Nairobi at 7:00 P.M., so they had to leave here at 5:30. At about 4:15 we gathered our under the trees in front of his house, 11 adults, and 4 children at a small table of their won. We had high tea and a picnic supper all in one. Everyone enjoyed it so much. Then we said the traveler's psalm, sang "Blest Be the Tie," and prayed.

Work progresses quite nicely for the Sotik building. We are getting two more native boys from Kaimosi if possible to help with making windows and doors and planing and tongue and grooving flooring. It is building of the most primitive type here, from rough sawed boards, you know. Bob put in the foundation for Kirk's little bungalow and is going to pour the side walls while Kirk tours the rest of the schools in Sotik, and keeps an eye on progress there. As soon as that is finished he will return and finish his cottage and Bob will go to Sotik....

L to R Front row— Hannah with Donald and Faye Kirkpatrick
Back row— Mr. Hotchkiss and the Smith family
Courtesy of Richard Adkins

In America, the board meeting that Clara was to attend in June, according to Mother's letter, did not occur until July. The minutes prior to this time referred only to letters from Clara, Kirk and Bob being reviewed.

Afternoon Session, July 16, 1935

The meeting was called to order at 1:35 P.M. with Rev. C.W. Ruth in the chair. Those present were: Rev. C. W. Ruth, Mr. Ludwig Andersen, Mrs. Iva D. Vennard. MissAnna L. Spann, Rev. James Bishop, George Warner, and Clara G. Ford.

After the singing of "What a Friend we Have in Jesus," Mrs. Vennard led us to the throne of grace in prayer. After the singing of the chorus. "Let the Beauty of Jesus be Seen in Me," matters connected with our Africa work were taken up.

The President mentioned the granting of the Sotik mission site as an occassion for special praise.

A thorough discussion of the general Africa situation followed.

In view of the fact that the furloughs of Brother and Sister Smith and Brother and Sister Kirkpartrick in Africa would naturally come due at the same time, it was moved and seconded that we grant the Kirkpatricks their furlough in January. Motion carried.

In July the minutes indicate Clara was present at the meeting, and the Africa situation discussed.

178

Kericho Kenya, B.E.A.
Sept. 3, 1935

Dear Folks:

...I expect also that you have seen Bro Hotchkiss by now. We got a letter from him from Durban and again from Cape Town. He is now in Trinidad, I expect, and will arrive in U.S.A. about the 20th. He likes the boat and is enjoying the trip and has had a chance to have a great time with a young Jew who was placed in the cabin with him....

Bob didn't go on this hunting trip as we had no money and also because he didn't want to spend the time. But my greatest concern is our debt and it seems we can't get out or keep from going in more. How glad I will be when we get to Sotik! Here it is Sept. and the building hasn't been begun there yet. The materials are all ready, but Bob has been tied here finishing up Kirk's house. [The Kirkpatricks had purchased land from Mr. H. and on this they built a home before returning to the U.S.] That was another reason why he didn't want to go away now, he wants so much to get down there. It has become a real conviction with us that we must get down there. There are so many things to do! Kirk & Faye have to leave their house in Kericho Oct. 1st. So we will go to Sotik and if they can't get their house ready they can move in here. I am so tired of camping! How thankful I will be for the garage to move into!

We ordered some fruit trees this A.M. some apples, peaches, pears and plums. We are not sure how they will grow, but have ordered one each. They are $.75 each. They are all from a nursery whose altitude is similar to Sotik so ought to grow well. It will mean so much to us to have our own fruit. We want to get some oranges and lemons started also, but we have to get them from another place. Then the next thing is to get in some garden. I want to get in lots of potatoes both white and sweet, some corn, and the smaller vegetables, tomatoes, cabbage, carrots, turnips, beets etc. Everything grows very well there. I am also going to have some chickens down there, and if we think, advisable, a cow or two. We will have to have native cows probably, as they are immune from diseases that the grade cows get such as rinderpest and tick fever and east coast fever...

War is still imminent, but the actual fighting will be too far away to affect us. Prices however, do, and very much.

Just rooted John and Anna Verne out of a mud hole. John says, "We're catching fish." It looks like Grandpa Biesecker might have a fishing companion when we get home....

Much love to all, Catharine

"We've ordered some fruit trees...chickens...if advisable, a cow or two."

CHAPTER 12
TENWEK—NOVEMBER 1935

"...they headed for Sotik and pitched their tent."

In the months that preceded the site's final approval, Bob had worked diligently getting logs sawed to the right lengths, windows built, and all materials purchased in readiness to promptly build the initial building

at Tenwek. Several workmen trained at the Friends mission had agreed to come with them to help on the project.

Excitement was mounting, and it was difficult to wait until the roads were built and loads could be moved by oxen or by truck. But five more months passed before they saw their way clear to pack up and head for Tenwek.

The Sotik area was an endless series of rolling hills cut through by gorge-like valleys through which rivers such as the Nyangores meandered. At the base of the Tenwek plot, this river tumbled noisily over a 200-foot granite cliff, creating a beautiful fall. A flume starting at the top of the fall brought water past a large cave which undermined the rock, where it was rumored a giant black mamba lived, to the base where a tiny hut housed a huge grindstone. Dripping into the hollow center of the stone from a bin above was a stream of corn. Ground corn extruded from the lower edges of the stone. Donkeys heavily laden with sacks of corn made their way down zigzagged trails to the mill and back again, carrying away the treasured corn meal, the staple of the native diet. This plot of land was named Tenwek after the native name for the falls that could be translated to mean "The Place of Songs." It was 10 acres and encompassed the western slope of one of the hillsides and looked out over a breathtaking view of the surrounding

These two pictures of the Tenwek falls hung over the fireplace of our home.

hills, deep green and verdant, then fading to purple in the distance with clouds billowing high from the horizon into the brilliant blue sky.

181

The altitude was close to 6,800 feet, and the temperature varied very little throughout the year, but evenings and mornings were cool, making a fireplace very welcome. Nights were cold, while mid-day the temperature was about 80°, and with the equatorial sun directly overhead, there were no shadows. Although typical seasonal changes were absent, there were changes in rainfall. Predictably in October to December, the "short rains" would begin and from March to May, the "long rains" occurred. Consequently during that time, the vegetation was usually lush, but during the dry season people often ran out of food, and famine was a pressing problem.

There was a very primitive road to the post office known as Sotik, but from there on, a simple pathway lead to the Tenwek plot, which would become the future mission. In preparation for their arrival, Bob, with the assistance of native workmen, had widened the path, chopping through the thicket with *pangas* (large machete-like tools). Then with hoes and shovels, the branches and creepers were cleared, along with stones and an occasional boulder, to create a primitive road of red soil. He had learned from Mr. Hoyt at the Friends Mission a method of piling wood on large embedded boulders, burning the wood until the boulder was red hot and then pouring water over the stones, thus disintegrating them.

Workmen

Dad met at the beginning of each day with the workman and spoke to them about spiritual topics. He told us that as he built the road, he talked about the One who said, "I am the way, the truth and the life."

"I used to say—He came here to this earth to lay out a way for us to go. Just like we are doing as we build this road, He built a road—a way of life and truth that we can follow, a way to get from one place to another in our lives and living. He said, 'If you make my message the rule of your life, you will then know the truth about life and you will be free.' It is the very best way of life—to know Jesus." This daily devotional time became an intrinsic part of every endeavor and activity whether construction, schools, churches, dispensaries or hospitals on the mission field, and is continued to this day.

"This road is splendid, Bob," said Kitty as she and the children rode with him on the final run, after he had brought down load after load of supplies. The road suddenly ended after making a long graceful curve along the slope of the hill.

"Here we are!" Everyone tumbled out of the truck. The sun warmed their shoulders as they stood trying to grasp the reality of what would be their future home. A close-knit layer of grass carpeted the hillsides

Oxen arrive with more goods

where they were not covered with brush. Across the hills, meandering pathways circumvented any obstruction they met. From where they stood, they looked across at a view more splendid and vast than they could take in—hill after hill of lush bright emerald fading to azure in the distance, studded with occasional grass-covered huts. They stood for a long time in silence, feeling dwarfed by the expanse of the place and drinking in the warmth of the welcome they felt. They wanted to taste the deliciousness of this moment

for as long as possible and smell the fragrance of a new day that was dawning for them.

"Hear that sound, Kitty?"

"I do indeed. Is that the falls?"

"That it is, and someday we will harness it and bring electricity to the station," Bob exuded.

"For now, my love, how about just pitching the tent?" Bob smiled at his practical, no nonsense wife.

"You're right," he observed. He looked at the well-worn tent. "When we got it, they said it was guaranteed not to rip, ravel or run down at the heels. But look at it. Did you ever see anything like it in all your life?"

Men working on building projects

By the time they set up their cots and unrolled their bedrolls, there was very little room left in the tent, but they were cozy and content. They slept soundly and as each day of activity passed, they continued to feel more energized. "My stars, Kitty. Every time I look at you, you're grinning."

"I know, I'm just so happy, but you are too. Look at you!" Kitty beamed at her husband.

"I can't help it! It seems we've waited for this since Hector was a pup!"

"I know. But here we are at last, and I am truly happy!"

"Me, too," John chimed in and little Anna Verne's eyes sparkled as she smiled widely.

In the days that followed, Bob returned to Chaigiak (just north of Kericho), Kericho (north approximately sixty miles), and Litein (about twenty miles from Sotik) repeatedly for truckloads of supplies. He bought a span of oxen that were called into service when the rain made the roads impassable to the truck. Soon the rains began predictably, starting right at noon and pouring throughout the early afternoon.

On the tapes, Mother told of one remarkable day. It is recreated here as best it can be.

"How very kind...."

The tent leaked diabolically, and Kitty tried hard to catch the drips in all the receptacles she could find, but soon they filled, splashing over onto everything. She quickly emptied them—running from one to the next, but in the end she had to give up, and consequently the night was a soggy one. The morning sun dried all that was laid out on the grass to dry but that afternoon came the rain, and the same thing happened all over again. Bob was stuck in Litein, unable to get through because of the muddy roads.

In the morning sunshine, Kitty was once again spreading things on the bushes and grass when she noticed a group of men coming up the path toward her. At first she felt a pang of fear, but that quickly subsided as she recognized Johana, their friend, among them.

Kitty waited, as women did not greet men until first addressed.

Johana extended his hand in greeting. "*Chamege?* (Do you love yourself?)"

"*Ee, agot okwek?* (Yes, and yourselves?)"

"*Ee.* (Yes.) " She paused, "*Omachi ne?* (What is it you want?)"

"*Kagebwan amun kimachi kitech kong'ung!* (We have come to build your house.)"

"Johana, did *Bwana* Smith ask you to do this for us?"

"No, *Memsahib.* We saw your shelter is not working, so we decided to make you a dry house."

Kitty's eyes filled with tears. She thought of the mud houses she had lived in with great reluctance. This one would be very different. It was built with love.

"How very kind of you!" she said when she could compose herself.

Kitty watched in awe as a framework of wattle poles was laced together with twine vines. The men then dug a hole, poured in water and manure, and went about kneading it with their feet until it became a thick soupy mixture with which they plastered the poles. The roof was then woven in sticks, and finally the grass thatching was added.

Bob would soon be back she hoped. What a surprise he would have!

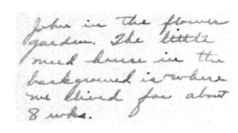

Kitty wrote on the back of this picture.

Anna Verne said of Mother, "She was, in truth, a teacher. I learned from her to speak proper English, to read the classics and other good literature, to love the music of great artists, and to be selective in my entertainment choices. She taught me also the beauty of our surroundings—the birds, the trees, flowers, and especially the clouds. It was natural to hear her say, "Oh, just look at those beautiful clouds!" She created beauty by making the house we lived in a comfortable and secure home. She taught me to sew, knit, tat, and crochet. She encouraged singing and playing musical instruments. We were surrounded by positive influences for enrichment."

Although the constant rain was a nuisance, Kitty appreciated the resulting vegetation. The hillsides were covered with wild flowers, including a black-throated yellow flower that she called a "black eyed Susan." She had learned to identify *keldichek,* a wild green leafy vegetable used by the Africans in stews and soups. She often hunted for it with her children and added it to her soup, hoping for the benefit of its iron and vitamin content. In the early mornings, the air was fresh and the sun warm. This was a special time of the day to be outside. Loving detail and beauty so she would often comment on the sheer unexpected loveliness of a dewdrop highlighted by a beam of light, brilliant in its rainbow of colors or spider webs jeweled by condensation. She and the children found wild gooseberries hidden in their paper-thin shells. These they would take home to eat but the hard yellow kaffir apples were good only for John Boy to throw like tiny balls. A stalk-like yellow flower with a black base, when beat against one's hand, gave an aroma of freshly popped corn.

The popcorn plant

"What is popcorn, Mother?" John had asked when Kitty made the observation. Kitty looked at John surprised to realize he hadn't ever heard of it. She took joy in explaining the mystery of the popping corn and promised to make some for the children when they came back to America.

"...the men smiled at Bob's humor...."

Morning was also the best time of the day for Bob. No rooster had crowed yet nor had the eastern sky shown any sign of the sun when Bob's inner alarm clock sounded. On the equator, dawn occurred abruptly. He was out of bed and into his work clothes, using a flashlight as needed. He had several jobs to organize or accomplish before the workmen arrived for their work assignment at 7:00 AM. He found this time alone just what he needed to ask for God's guidance for the day.

THE DARKEST TIME IS JUST BEFORE THE DAWN

As the dawn arrived, Bob looked out across the gently rolling, grass—covered hills enveloped in the morning mist. Even in the early morning, clouds were billowing up, cloud upon cloud against the deep, deep blue background. The sun was breaking through, warm and invigorating. He could hear the roar of the falls in the valley below him—the falls he had dreamed would someday be harnessed for the station's electrical power.

Following a brief devotional and prayer with the workmen, they dispersed from the circle to the construction site. Some were digging a deep hole for an outhouse. Some gathered wood; a few went to the river for water, hauling it back by ox cart. Bob briefly returned to the hut to wash and shave with the water Kitty had warmed for him. He would spend a short time with his kiddies, eat breakfast and have family devotions before getting back out on the job. He endlessly gave directions and worked alongside the men who, though they may have never seen anything similar to what he described, diligently labored with him to make his dream a reality. The steep hillside was not conducive to building, and long ago as he looked at the future plot, Bob had planned the terracing project. To begin with, four terraces, each 200-300 feet in length and 70-100 feet deep, needed to be created. It was a monumental task, but it would have an enduring effect, and so he would find a way to make it happen. Without wheelbarrows, the dirt was moved forward the 70-80 feet from its cut margin out to the border, which created the new edge and a flattened surface. What would have taken a few days with a bulldozer took many weeks. It was all done by hand. Hoes were used to chop away the hillside, and *sufarias* (basin-like metal pans) to carry the dirt forward, flattening the area. There were no tampers other than the bare feet of the workers. Between each of the terraces there would be a set of stairs. The structures he built would all be on solid ground; the fill dirt would be used for planting. Kitty had many plans in that regard and had been collecting plants and starting clippings for quite some time.

> I must tell you something about our new site. It is a beautiful place. We are surrounded by hills. You would love it. At the left is the valley to the river and falls and on the other side a high mountain. Tonight after the rains it was encircled by a rainbow. In front is a series of hills with native huts dotting them and patches of dark green trees and lighter green of the cultivated parts. To the right is the grand view of series on series of hills losing themselves in the distance of the horizon. Our station proper is on an incline and we have terraced it with four main levels. The garage and shop is on the first, the two dwelling houses on the second and the church, school, dispensary and others will be on the lower. It has been and will yet be a great deal of work, but will be beautiful when finished. I have been busy planting. Flowers, cuttings, fruit trees, etc and a nice garden. Everything is doing nicely and the soil seems splendid. Everything is just temporary now, but as we get places we will put them all in permanently. We are so happy to be here and even a leaky house doesn't dampen or down our spirits.

Kitty's later description of Tenwek

Mother was always interrupting Dad's day with tea. Faithfully at 10:00 A.M. and 4:00 P.M., she would arrive with it wherever he happened to be working.

"Here is some tea, Bob," Kitty called as she and the children arrived. "I have a big pot of *chai* and cups for the workmen also. Where shall I put it?"

Bob pointed at a nearby stump at the same time shouting to all the men in the area. "*Kuja happa*! (Come here!) *Kagochabok chaik*! (The tea is ready!)" He was mixing two languages (Swahili and Kipsigis), and the men smiled at Bob's humor as they gratefully gathered for a break.

"Thanks, Kitty."

"It's the only way I can get you to stop for a minute or two." Kitty had a concerned look. "I think you are in the sun too much."

Bob adjusted his helmet. He wished he could pitch it "to kingdom come," but such a thing would be unthinkable knowing the menace of the tropical sun.

The poinsettia now almost six feet tall

During a visit many years later, Sarah paused to look at the poinsettias, which stood taller than she. As she looked around the station, she could see many of the buildings her father had built during those early years. She and her family had returned to help at Tenwek hospital. Her husband, a radiologist, had been reading x-rays, and she was seeing neurology patients through the morning, but now it was time for a lunch break under the trees. She thought of her mother carefully planting those poinsettias along with the many roses and flower gardens. She remembered how the flowers and garden were watered. The family washed in a tin tub or sponge bathed in a basin. For as long as she could remember there was no such thing as a bathtub or bathroom. The outhouse served as toilet. Bath water, which had been brought up from the river by oxen, was heated on the stove. Baths were taken—the children all using the same water, then hand laundry was done in the same water, then Mother washed the floor with it, and what was left watered the flowers or garden. But now at Tenwek, running water was available in each building and the place surely had become a place of beauty!

Pineapple grew in the garden as noted in the next letter.

*Chief Arap Baliach and Chief Arap Tengecha
referred to in Kitty's letter*

Dear Home Folks: Tenwek, Sotik Post, via Kericho, Kenya, B.E.A.
                                                          Nov. 3 1935

Your letter written when you were all at home arrived here the last week in October. So they made good time in spite of war conditions. I think the mail still comes through the Mediterranean, as the Suez Canal has not been closed.

I was so glad to hear from you all and, of course, my heart contracted a bit with longing to have been with you....

I am writing to the whole family and ask you to send the letter from one to the other as fast as possible so it gets around before the news is too stale.... I can't quite remember what I wrote you before. Did I tell you about our fruit trees? We bought some and had a bunch given us, so now we have prospects of some day having the following: apples, pears, peaches, quinces, oranges, lemons, loquats, granadillas, cactus fruit and pineapples. So far all the trees are living. Whether all will bear fruit or not, we will have to wait and see. My garden plot is about ready. We are going to put a rough fence around it, as we have had sad experiences with goats and donkeys so far. I had a pineapple almost ready to eat, and the goats got it, and some kale was coming beautifully, and the donkeys got it. So in the future, we won't take any risks. We have small branches forming protections around all our fruit trees and berry bushes. When we bought our trees, we ordered two maples and two poplar trees, and they are coming beautifully. It surely makes us feel like home to have them. I have been given loads of rose slips, too, and all are coming fine. I transplanted the roses from Mr. Hotchkiss' place and a couple of poinsettias, and they are all doing well so far.... So don't you think this will be a place of beauty in time?...

...various delays: first window frames, then cement, then a plane, now corrugated iron, nails and window glass. It isn't here as if one could phone an order to the mill or the hardware and have things here in half an hour. It is days of waiting, sometimes weeks. But as I said, it is a great patience cultivator. I find even so mine needs more cultivation. I haven't learned to wait gracefully.

The men came today from all the out schools and started the foundation for the Church. They furnished the labor and the rock. We will furnish other materials. They are very anxious to have a nice one. It is to be Hotchkiss Memorial Chapel, you know. One of the chiefs was here Prayer Day when they were discussing it, and he said "Bwana, you make the nicest church you know how, and we'll all help." He is the oldest chief in the district and has surely stood by us these days, in fact from the beginning. His name is Arap Beliach (Bell ya'ch).

We are very happy these days in spite of heavy work and new problems. The Lord is blessing us daily and setting His seal upon the work. I begin a sewing class next week. The women are very anxious to start, as they can save so much if they can make their own and their children's clothes.

Well, must close with love to all and wishes for a very Merry Christmas and Happy New Year.

    Much love, Catharine

Forgot to tell you something funny. John was helping water the plants and fell with his water, spilling it all over himself. He came in not knowing what to expect, and explained his accident. I was looking at the damage and Anna Verne came up. So he thought it a good time to get some sympathy, so he said, "Just look here, Anna Verne, what happened to your little brother!"

"I transplanted the roses from Mr. Hotchkiss' place and a couple poinsettias...."

"If the canal is closed...will we ever get home?"

> Mother mentions the war concerns in her letter. The Italians were humiliated in the late 1800s when they tried to colonize Ethiopia. It was disastrous and eventually a large number of Ethiopians, about 100,000, defeated about 25,000 Italian troops. Once again Ethiopia was in the news. Although short wave radios were eventually available, Dad and Mother did not have access to one during their first term. Somehow the information still got through as isolated as they were. It is likely their conversation went something like this.

"I so wish we had a radio. What are you hearing in the towns about affairs in the world now, Bob?"

"Well you know that Ethiopia makes up most of Kenya's northern border. Mussolini invaded Ethiopia last year. He actually used chemical weapons. Now Hailie Selassie, the Ethiopian emperor that Mussolini ran out, is protesting to the League of Nations. Anthony Eden, the British minister to the League, is going to bat for him and trying to negotiate with Mussolini. The league has let Hailie Selassie down badly." Bob paused.

"Remember how we heard that FDR visited Ethiopia and the Suez Canal last year? The British are pretty sore that he won't take sides against Mussolini or for that matter Hitler. When Hindenburg died, Hitler became the supreme commander of the armed forces. That was August of '34 and rumor has it that things are going from bad to worse. It is going very hard for the Jews in Germany. Remember the old German who gave us food when we were in Shirati? I'm told he was a Nazi and went back to Germany to fight for the Fuehrer. He was killed."

"Yes, I think we heard that from the Mosemanns when they were visiting. It breaks my heart. It's amazing that God would use someone like that to help us when we were in need." Kitty was absorbed.

"I'm with you, Kitty. But who knows what was in his heart. The whole world seems to be in a mess. Britain's power is faltering, and it looks like a world war is coming. There is talk that the Suez Canal will be closed."

Kitty was silent for a long time.

"What are you thinking?" Bob eyed her, feeling troubled at her look.

"If the canal closes and we are at war, will we ever be able to get home?"

"These things are in God's hands; we can't worry about it."

"You are right! What about materials for building, Bob? I heard you say something about nails."

"They are in short supply now, and I haven't been able to get any. We have to build using doweling in place of nails. It will take an awfully long time to complete the two-story home just for that reason. But the main part of the family house will be made of blocks. We have found a place we can get stone, and we will just chip them into the stone blocks."

The garage house—meant to become a garage but always remained a house

"Doesn't that also take interminably long?"

"We'll just have to do whatever it takes."

"I love you, Bob, and I just hate to see you working so hard."

"Think nothing of it, Kitty. You know I love it." He grinned.

"Yes, I do know." And she smiled because she also knew that whatever she said would not change a thing.

Tenwik, Sotik Via Kericho, Kenya
B.E.A. Nov. 24th, 1935

Dear Folks:

...Now for some news about us. We are in the garage house at last! Got in last Tuesday the 19th. As Bobbie B. says, "The best laid plans of mice and men---etc." We were working hard in it putting in the temporary things to make it a house instead of a shop and had given up getting in last week, when last Sat. P.M. we got a call from Kirk asking Bob to come up and bring the native carpenters. So he promised to go on Wed. and Monday and Tuesday worked himself to death to get us in before he left. I decided not to go, as the trip in the truck is quite hard especially where the roads are bad. Well, we got in. Bob had the partition in the living room and he built the closet and a partition in the bed room, put the window in the kitchen, moved the stove, put up the stove pipe, made a door for the front room and stripped the temporary doors, boarded up the windows that weren't finished, put a temporary front in the garage and poured part of the fireplace. Besides this he had to have a business meeting with the native teachers. And then a native came seeking the Lord and they had prayers with him till he came through to victory. So they were full days. I have done most of the settling since Bob left and now we are quite cozy. He will bring more of our goods down when he comes back this time and we will get pretty settled in.

It is lovely to have more than one room. Really I don't know what to make of so much space. I actually have a pantry about half as big as ours at home. And I have a clothes closet the same size. We had tho't of having a bath, but decided to put Bob's desk in it instead, as he really needs a place where he can be quiet and write. I'll enclose a floor plan of the house and then show how we have the furniture placed. You pass it on first to Smiths and then to the rest of our family so I won't have to make another one. We didn't bring down our big rug but I shall for the sake of the children. It will be so much warmer and they like to play on the floor.

Bob had expected to get back yesterday, but didn't. So of course, I don't know what may have happened. That is one thing we have to learn to do in this country is just wait. There are no means of communication, that is, no rapid ones. The phone call we got from Kirk was sent via three relays from Kericho and finally arrived at some Indian dukas about 6 miles away. They sent a runner to us and we drove over in the truck to get the message. Then it was very much "bungled." The first sentence read, "Can you come up before we move the shade?" We didn't know what it could mean unless it was "Can you come up before the date we move?"

"As Bobbie B. says, 'The best laid plans of mice and men —etc.'"

There were no telephones, but telegraphed messages could be sent to a *duka* (shop) about 10 miles away where the Indian shop owner received the message, wrote it out, and then sent it on by a runner to the mission stations. In the Olympic games, one often hears the Kenya names beginning with "Kip." These are men of the Kipsigis tribe—exceptional runners. The "runners" mentioned in Mother's letters were employed to carry written messages, often bypassing the telegraph system since messages that arrived through that system were often unintelligible.

Mother and Dad both had nice singing voices and as children we loved the lullabies and songs that they would sing to us. This one sounded especially nice, a theme song for meetings during one of their furloughs.

Pray On

By Oswald Smith

DUET

Pray on, O soul of mine, pray on! This night of sin will soon be gone,
The break of day will come ere long. Till then, my soul, pray on!

Pray on, O soul of mine, pray on! The Lord will keep thee true and strong
And answer all of thy pray'rs ere long. With joy my soul pray on!

Pray on, O soul of mine, pray on! The days are short 'til Christ shall come.
There are still lost sheep that must be won. With zeal, my soul, pray on!

A duet often sung by Kitty and Bob, the last verse written by them.

CHAPTER 13

TENWEK—DECEMBER 1935

"I'm so sorry, rafiki *(friend)."*

> Dad's love for Johana was apparent to all of us. As children we saw them as almost constant companions. Dad spoke often of their conversations and experiences. Anna Verne and her husband, along with David and his wife, witnessed the reunion of Dad and Johana. It was 1974 when, after their retirement, Bob and Kitty returned to visit the work in Kenya. Years had gone by, and the men now were 70 & 87. There were tears of joy as the two men embraced and memories came flooding back. "I've saved you a plot of ground right beside my house where you can build yours," said Johana.
>
> "Johana, how I would love that! If only it were possible," Dad said, and he meant it.

Bob and Johana meeting again after 26 years.

Bob remembered the day Mr. Hotchkiss had first introduced them. Even from the beginning, there had been a special bond.

"Bob, come here. There is someone I want you to meet." His face glowed with anticipation. "Johana Arap Ng'etich. Johana, this is *Bwana* Smith."

"*Jambo!*" Johana looked directly into Bob's eyes.

"Oh, yes! Mr. Hotchkiss has spoken often of you. It is an honor," Bob shook his hand vigorously.

Little did they know what dear and fast friends they would become.

Now a few years later, Bob stood outside the family's tiny house at Tenwek, cupped his hands around his mouth and called. "Oh, Johana *Wee.*" Johanna lived on the hill across the river. It was within shouting distance. Bob could see a figure emerge from his house and begin making his way down the winding path in his direction. They had called each other this way since the beginning and would for years to come. When one wanted the other, he simply called, and the other would reply. They would drop what they were doing and meet to discuss problems or exchange important information. They had spent hours communicating in this way.

Johana spoke Kiswahili[*], the trade language, well. Bob had learned it rather than the tribal language because he spent so much time outside of the tribe in his travels. Especially the younger men more

---

[*] Swahili language—Kiswahili—developed primarily from a mixture of Arabic and local Bantu languages, though it also included elements of Persian, Portuguese, Hindi, and English. It is now Kenya's official language, spoken as a second language by the majority of Kenyans (their first language is generally that of their tribe). www.bluegecko.org/kenya

universally knew Kiswahili. Women and older men rarely knew that language. Accordingly, Johana became a valuable interpreter. Although he and Bob always conversed in Swahili, they greeted each other in Kipsigis. *"Chamege* (Do you love yourself?)" *"Ee, agot inye* (Yes, and what about you?)"

Johana had learned Kiswahili in his many travels. As a teenager he had been the gun bearer for W.D.M. Karamoja Bell, a famous ivory hunter, and he enjoyed telling about his experiences.

"*Bwana* Bell was a man who was very particular about how an animal was shot. He would say that a small bullet in the right place is effective while a big one in a poor spot is worthless. One day I was at camp alone. Everyone else was nearby hunting the elephant. Suddenly the elephant burst into the camp. I picked up *Bwana* Bell's gun, and doing exactly as I had seen *Bwana* Bell do, I shot the elephant. The gun knocked me down, but the others arrived almost immediately and were surprised to see the dead animal right in the camp."

Outstation

Johana's age wasn't known, but he was judged to be about seventeen years Bob's senior. More than that, Johana first converted to the Muslim faith, and had then become a Christian before Bob had. He had suffered much for his faith, and Bob respected him deeply. This day they were going to a council meeting made up of elders (actually pastors, but in the absence of formal training called elders) in the fledgling churches that had been planted. At each of these "outstations" was a church as well as a school, and it was the duty of the elder to teach children to read and write, preach, hold a weekly catechism class for candidates for baptism and serve as a liaison between the people and the missionaries. There were twelve such elders in those days, some of whom were converts under Willis Hotchkiss's ministry. These twelve became the nucleus of the emerging church.

Bob watched the group of men as they slowly gathered, oblivious of time constraints. Each carried a spear, a walking stick and a *rungu* (club). They would form a circle, and the one who had a problem or concern would stand, raise his spear and drive it into the ground. The subject for discussion was then introduced by this man, i.e. "When a Christian has his cows stolen and he knows who has done it, how is he supposed to respond?" (Tribal custom would have him kill the man.) Another would then rise to speak, driving his spear into the ground forcefully, but speaking of separate though related issues. There was never, from that point on, any direct mention of the problem, as each in turn spoke of related issues. This sometimes took hours. Bob sat listening and not speaking, as he did not know Kipsigis well enough to speak it. He observed Johana's body language—a bowed head and drooped shoulders, a bright anticipatory gaze, a set jaw. As they walked home, he would hear the whole conversation from Johana. Somehow, by this convoluted method, a problem was viewed from all angles, the Christian ways were compared to old tribal ways, and in the end everyone had seemed to come to an understanding of what was God's way.

One day as they were walking home, Johana said, " I want to take you to a special place." His face was drawn with emotion.

"What is it, Johana?"

Rungu

"This is the place I buried my first wife and my child. They both died in childbirth. It was a day of great difficulty for me."

Bob knew how much a wife who could conceive meant in this tribe. He also knew that Johanna's new wife had been unable to bear children. He looked at the spot that meant so much to his dear friend. Johana had bowed his head, his jaw tightened.

'I'm so sorry, *rafiki* (friend)." Bob had never borne such great sorrow. He wondered what was in the heart of his dear friend as they walked on silently, and felt honored to have been shown this sacred spot.

The group of twelve elders* with whom Dad met on a regular basis to discuss problems in their churches (as described in the previous section) was meeting once again. Each was assigned a church that was established in the "outstations" around the mission. Dad met with them monthly on the Thursday before Prayer Day on Friday, also a monthly occurrence. Elijah A. Busien was one such elder. On the tapes Dad tells the following story:

"Bob! What is the matter?" Kitty noticed Bob's troubled expression.

"I have just heard of Chief Arap Katam's death. Kitty, remember what I told you about the church elders' meetings? Well, just before we came together as a group the last week, Zephaniah said to me, "*Bwana*, come with me here and ask Elijah to take off his shirt."

I said, "Zephaniah, why would I ask Elijah to take off his shirt?"

"Just ask him to do it, and you will understand."

So I went to where they were gathered and I said, "Elijah, I have been told to ask you to remove your shirt."

"Oh, "*Bwana*, I do not want to do that."

"Elijah, please do it." And so he did. "What do you suppose I saw? Across his back were wounds—some were healing, some were new and bleeding, some were old and scarring."

"Elijah, what has happened to you?"

And so Elijah told the story. "I have not been assigned to any church recently, but God told me I should go to Area 14. It has been closed to the gospel, and Chief Arap Katam who is so opposed to Christianity rules there. The tribal retainer (the man who enforced the chief's wishes) was at my first meeting. He allowed me to speak but when I was done, he beat me. He said, 'The chief does not want you to come

---

* The names of these twelve with their Kipsigis meaning were: Johana A. Ng'etich (*born at the time for the cows to go to graze*), Nuhu A. Maina(*a name of a generation of people beginning in the late 1920s*), Paul A. Kapketwany (*parents of the wife were at the birth - generally means they have a close relationship with in-laws*), Isaiah A. Cheboing'oing' (*father has stayed in Maasai - wants to remember some of the things that happened when he was in Maasai land so gave the child this name*), Lazaro A. Chebongoror (*someone who is rough in doing things or in his thinking and finds himself in trouble. This person may have been the father's father and so they name the child this to remember the father's father*), Dishon A. Kesembe (*give me a knife to go and cut the tops of my millet. At the time of birth they were reminded of the time when someone forgot to bring back the knife*), Zephaniah A. Maina (*a name of a generation of people beginning in the late 1920s*), Reuben A. Kibet (*boy born during mid-day*), Elijah A. Busien (*black and white or not many colors*), and Erasto A. Sio (*born outside in the center of certain plants. These plants cause much itching*). Courtesy of Ezekiel A Kerich

same time next week. The tribal retainer said that he would beat me again if I came back to speak. I did come and spoke, and he again beat me. That has happened four times."

I said to him, "Elijah, Why haven't you told me of this?"

Elijah said, "No *Bwana*. The Bible says we must suffer for Christ."

Kitty eyes filled with tears as Bob told her the story, "Bob, what did you do?"

"Remember when the Day of Prayer meeting started last Friday, I told the congregation, 'There is a chief in Location 14 who doesn't want the gospel to get to his people. But he has no authority to keep the gospel away. Let's pray that God will do something with Arap Katam—change his mind, change his heart.' So they all prayed earnestly. Now this runner just arrived with the news of the chief's death. The runner said, 'Did you kill him?' I said nothing except, 'No, we did not kill him.' Then after a pause, '*Shauri ya mungu!* (It is an affair of God).'"

When Dad told this story about his dear friend, he was often moved to tears. "Elijah was a man who loved God and his people deeply," he said, "but he suffered and was treated roughly.... What he did for Location 14, nobody knows. He gave his blood. Bless his heart!" In fact, in Location 14, Merigi became an outstation, and others such as Samituk and Chemaner followed, and many people came to know the Lord.

Mother had begun to teach a Bible School which would eventually become a two-year course. Her students were primarily the elders whom we have referenced in the above story. She told us the following story about Petero A. Sigira. Mother had mentioned the date 700 A.D. in conversation with him.

What is the meaning of A.D.?" Petero looked at her with anticipation.

"Why, it means the years after the birth of Christ. B.C. means the years before Christ."

"Do you mean that it has been one thousand, nine hundred and thirty-seven years since Christ was here on earth?"

"*EE* (Yes), Petero, it is indeed so many, many years since He was here."

"How long have you known about Him?" he went on to inquire.

"All of my life I have known of Him," she replied.

"Did your parents know about Jesus?"

"Yes."

"And their parents?"

"Yes."

"Then why are my people only now hearing about Him?" He paused, "My father never heard of Him."

They both stood in silence trying to take it in.

Dear Homefolks:

Mother's last letter surely filled me with a great longing....

Tenwek, Sotik Post
via Kericho, Kenya
B.E.A.
Dec 1935

I guess I told you we had received word from the Board that Kirk was to come home in January for deputation work. He doesn't want to go and seems to be trying hard to work it so we'll go and I admit there is a strong desire humanly speaking to be the ones to go first. But for the sake of the work, it would be better for him to go first. So we are happy to stay. Even so I'd love to join that circle around the home fireplace...

Well, Mother dear, I hope your dream may be realized in the Lord's best way and Daddie may catch the disease too and become an enthusiast.

At last our dreams are beginning to be fulfilled....

This Sunday we had planned on visiting the nearest out school when the native preacher arrived again saying that the church was coming over here as they thought it too far for me to walk. And sure enough here they all came until we had close to a hundred. Johana preached a good sermon on Luke 12:1-13. In the process he asked the question as to why we are forgiven a sin against the Son but not against the Holy Spirit. One boy answered like this. "A sin against the Holy Spirit is one which a Christian commits. He has known the way and has had the Spirit in his heart. Then if he goes back he can never say there is no such thing without a sin against the Holy Spirit." Wasn't that a Spirit guided answer? The boy himself is untutored except by the Spirit....

We had a sad experience. Kirk was to bring down the doggie "Kidogo". He came fine until they were almost here and then jumped out suddenly and the truck ran over him. When he didn't arrive it had to be explained and I thought for a while John would not be comforted. Finally he asked if he was with Jesus and I said I thought he was and then he was comforted because he said Jesus would make him well and he'd have a good time in heaven. Now what would you have done? Anyway there are going to be animals in the new heaven and new earth and so maybe they have a heaven...

The way isn't rosy, that is, there are great needs but we feel at last as if what we do will count.

We are quite well. Bob has had a bad cold but is getting over it. I have occasional twinges. We killed a huge puff adder yesterday, so we have to take the Lord daily for the children's and our own protection. They have killed five here already. Keep praying for us as we know you do and we do for you.

Love,
Catharine

"At last our dreams are beginning to be fulfilled."

"I didn't know you had it in you."

Kitty stood with the gun still in her hands. Her knees felt a little weak as she paused and thought what might have been.

It was a warm afternoon, and she had moved Anna Verne out onto the porch for her nap. She had been sleeping peacefully. Kitty peeked out to see how she was when she saw the snake crawling up the screen looking for a way onto the porch. Instinctively she grabbed the gun and ran out the back door and around to the front. The snake had climbed down and was slithering across the grass. She took careful aim and fired. The snake lay dead at her feet, but the Africans who quickly gathered were telling her, "You must kill the other one, too. You must find it and kill it." (Although other snakes had been killed, this was Kitty's first time to have killed one herself.)

"Will you help me? I don't know where to look." But before she could consider it further, she heard someone shouting.

"It's here! It is here!" He was pointing into a nearby tree. Kitty took careful aim once again with success.

"Great day, Kitty! You are quite the shot. I didn't know you had it in you," Bob had said that evening. He was always amazed at what his "city girl" found the capacity to do.

"You don't know a lot of things about me, Bob!" she said grinning.

> Tenwik, Sotik
> Dec. 11, 1935
>
> ...We laid the foundation for the family house this morning. We had thought it was going to be so big but it is a little place after all. However it is going to be nice. Bob is putting in the foundation for both houses at the same time so they can become well settled before the walls go on. He also wants to get rid of the stove that is piled here. Of course you know we don't put in basements here so we don't have to excavate for foundations. We simply dig down about 4 ft. for the outside walls, 2 or 3 ft for inside walls all a foot wide. The walls will be 4 in. thick and plastered inside and out. That is if we use cement. If we build of stone they will be 7 in. thick. We are not sure yet which it will be. Whichever is cheaper will decide...

"Whichever is cheaper will decide...."

The first residence built after the garage house

Be not afraid ...
for I am with thee
to deliver thee,
saith the Lord".

Jeremiah 1:8

CHAPTER 14—TENWEK
JANUARY & FEBRUARY 1936

In addition to the sewing classes, Mother began spinning and weaving classes soon after they arrived at Tenwek. She was unable to dye the wool but could make patterns by using wool from black and white sheep.

Kitty had learned to make soap, sheer sheep, clean and card wool, then spin yarn and weave wool into blankets, and now she was teaching these crafts to the girls in the girls' school along with reading, writing, and childcare.

The first sewing class

An example of the blankets produced in Kitty's class

Later spinning class

"Why do you ask?"

Kitty and the children were alone again while Bob was getting supplies for the never-ending building projects that consumed much of his time. It was not as difficult these days since her time was filled with teaching the girls in their first little school. Bob had built a dormitory to house the six girls. The mission was protecting them from the tribe who would kill their babies if they had a chance. These were girls who had gone through local customs but had been persuaded not to kill their babies at birth. Kitty was teaching them about childcare, beginning some elementary education, teaching them to sew, to make soap, spin yarn and weave wool into blankets. She told them the story of Jesus also, who came to give a full and abundant life to both them and their new little babies.

It was late. Kitty's own babies were asleep when a frantic knock at the door sent Kitty running to open it. "*Memsahib*, it is *chemosit!*" The terrified girl was clutching her baby and trembling. "Please help us. He is coming back tomorrow to kill us if we don't do something."

201

THE DARKEST TIME IS JUST BEFORE THE DAWN

Kitty gathered both the girl and her baby in her arms to comfort them. She then picked up the .30-06 that Bob had left with her. It was on safety now. There were no bullets in the chamber, but once she had loaded the chamber she had no idea how to unload it. She decided she would need to shoot every bullet in the magazine in order to keep the gun safe. "Show me where *chemosit* went."

African Jewels—Courtesy of "Call to Prayer"

By then she was at the girls' school, and all of the girls were gathered around her. They all pointed to the thick brush that surrounded the mission station. "Did you see this thing or just hear him?" Kitty was afraid it was a prankster trying to frighten the girls. She had no idea what a *chemosit* was.

"We saw him. We saw him. He looked in the window. We saw his big head looking at us." They were all talking at once. "He looks to see which one of us he will kill tomorrow. He will kill us and eat our brains—nothing else. Please, please help us."

Kitty was determined she would help. She called down into the brush. "I'm going to shoot. If you are down there, go away because I will shoot." She turned to the girls. "Now, you say it in case he did not understand me."

They all shouted loudly. Kitty shot all five rounds down into the brush. The looks of relief that came over the girl's faces were unmistakable. "Are you alright now?" Kitty wondered what was in their hearts as they faced all the terrors of their young lives. They seemed threatened from every side. This, too, may have been only a prank to torment them further.

Kitty and her children

They returned to their dormitory with their babies and Kitty to her house and her own children. She quickly checked them. It was hard to believe they could still be sleeping. She breathed a prayer of thanks for God's help.

"By the way, what is a *chemosit*?" she asked Bob several days later when he had arrived home. They had been so busy talking about all of the adventures he had been through that she had not mentioned hers. "I know that is what a left-handed person is sometimes called, but this was something more."

"Why, I think it is a huge hyena-like animal. I have heard about them. The Europeans call them Nandi bears. They are supposed to be mostly up in the Kakamega Forest and Kapsabet. No one seems to know exactly what these creatures are. Kirk and I may have seen one once on the road. It was dark, and we were not sure what we were seeing—only that it was enormous and looked like a hyena."

"You know, it just occurred to me, *chemosit* means the child of a monkey; monkeys are supposed to be left-handed."

Bob was puzzled." Why do you ask?"

Kitty related the incident. "By the way, how do you unload the .30-06 once you have shot a bullet? I had to shoot all the bullets for fear the gun would go off again if I didn't."

"Oh, no Kitty, you didn't," Bob groaned. Bullets were costly and precious. He paused for a moment as he processed the story. "You did do the safe thing and I'm glad you did. I just wish I didn't have to leave you and the children alone so much."

"God takes care of us. I can feel it," Kitty said…and she truly meant it!

When Sarah and her husband were visiting in Kenya, they were invited to the home of Daniel A. Salaat who had been one of Mother's students. During the evening, we asked Daniel many questions regarding how his life was now, as compared to before the missionaries came. He spoke to us about the famines, how his sisters had been sold to the neighboring Kisii tribe in exchange for food and how that all changed with the knowledge of how to raise food more efficiently and how to store it—lessons that had been taught by the missionaries. We asked if he happened to know what a Nandi bear was. He got a schoolbook down from his bookcase and showed us a picture that was included in a story about Nandi bears. Much to our astonishment, the picture was of a small sasquatch. Dad's description of a hyena-like creature seems to be more consistent with other reports.*

---

* Nevertheless, there may yet exist in Africa a creature which, if not of the bear family, at least answers to the description of a bear. Along the River Tana in east-central Kenya, there exists some animal called *duba* by the natives; Bernard Heuvelmans suggests that this word derives from one of two Arabic words: either *dubb* (bear) or *dubbah* (hyena). Most commonly, the predator is known simply as the Nandi Bear, after a Kenyan tribe.

Geoffrey Williams, who was a member of the Nandi Expedition in the early years of this century, recorded in the *Journal of the East Africa and Uganda Natural History Society* an encounter he had on the Uasin Gishu plateau.

...I was travelling with a cousin on the Uasingishu just after the Nandi expedition, and, of course, long before there was any settlement up there. We had been camped...near the Mataye and were marching towards the Sirgoit Rock when we saw the beast...I saw a large animal sitting up on its haunches no more than 30 yards away. Its attitude was just that of a bear at the 'Zoo' asking for buns, and I should say it must have been nearly 5 feet high...it dropped forward and shambled away towards the Sirgoit with what my cousin always describes as a sort of sideways canter...

I snatched my rifle and took a snapshot at it as it was disappearing among the rocks, and, though I missed it, it stopped and turned its head round to look at us...In size it was, I should say, larger than the bear that lives in the pit at the 'Zoo' and it was quite as heavily built. The fore quarters were very thickly furred, as were all four legs, but the hind quarters were comparatively speaking smooth or bare...the head was long and pointed and exactly like that of a bear ... I have not a very clear recollection of the ears beyond the fact that they were small, and the tail, if any, was very small and practically unnoticeable. The colour was dark..

In 1919, a farmer named Cara Buxton related the following story:

A short time ago a 'Gadett' visited the district. This name is given to the animal by the Lumbwa and signifies the 'brain-eater.' Its first appearance was on my farm, where the sheep were missing. We finally found all ten, seven dead and three still alive. In no case were the bodies touched, but the brains were torn out.

During the next ten days fifty-seven goats and sheep were destroyed in the same way; of these thirteen were found alive... Finally it was tracked to a ravine and killed by the Lumbwa with their spears. It turned out to be a very large hyaena of the ordinary spotted variety. It had evidently turned brain-eater through some type of madness.

Many reports, especially Buxton's, clearly argue for identification of the animal as a hyena, possibly an undiscovered species. The temperament of the animal seems to fit that of hyenas almost perfectly; bloodthirsty and savage, at times timid, and mainly nocturnal. www.fortunecity.com/roswell/siren/552/af_nandi.html

Tenwik, Sotik, Kenya B.E.A., Jan 5th 1936

Dear Mother and all;

Christmas is past and now it is my pleasant duty to sit down and thank you all for the lovely gifts. I wish I could write each one personally who had a part, but as that is impossible I'll write notes and enclose to you that you may give one to each of those who had a part. (She goes in to detail to recognize each person who sent items and tell why they are so much appreciated.)

All in all you can see we had a wonderful Christmas. Bob remarked that our kiddies fared better than many in the homeland and I really believe that is true....

We are also so pleased about the money coming in for the houses.... We also had word of a gift from a class in Chillicothe for screens for our house. That is one of the loveliest things yet, for you can imagine what it is like without any screens. At night it isn't so bad except in the bed-rooms if we have a light as all sorts of bugs etc. come in, but in the daytime the flies are terrible. So far we haven't seen any mosquitoes. But there is malaria in the district though not here. It seems the "Luo" who are very good to work roads and are used by government for this purpose, are bringing malaria in everywhere they go. And they are coming down into Sotik now....

There is a prayer conference at Kijabi beginning Jan 20 and Bob has been asked to speak. After that is the K.M.C. at Nairobi and it may be possible we will all get to go, that is our family. I have never been to the conference at Kijabi and would like so much to be there. And we surely do appreciate the honor of his being asked to take a service, as there will be speakers of renown there. The Lord has given us many friends. Bob has a winning disposition and we are grateful to Him for it all, as it has meant much to our Mission. The K.M.C. is the conference of all missions in Kenya and we were admitted to membership last year, as you will remember. They have treated Bob with great kindness and have taken us in as equal with the oldest and largest missions here. That will also mean much toward our being accepted by the North American Council of Missions also. You remember E Stanley Jones gave us a recommendation and even then we were turned down so it is one of the most important things that has happened, our membership in K.M.C. We were strongly recommended by the A.I.M. and upon their recommendation were admitted....

I am sending you under separate cover the first rose that bloomed on the station. It was a beautiful cream one like Dad gets you for your birthday and is one off of the bush I bought for 50 cents. At the same time we are sending Mother Smith the first carnation that bloomed. I grew the carnations from seed and this was a lovely deep red like we wear on Mother's Day. Just yesterday I picked the first rose to bloom from Mr. Hotchkiss' bush that we brought down from his place at Chagaik. It is a lovely pink like a bride's maid's bouquet and was one of Mrs. Hotchkiss' most cherished roses. I am going to send it to him....

Must close for now with much love,   Catharine and All

"I'm sending you under separate cover the first rose that bloomed on the station."

204

"…he was regarded as "Machi (No person).... "

Kitty had found that if she used an eyedropper, the tiny mouth would latch around it, and sometimes he would suck and swallow. She had had him now for weeks. His wizened little face was beginning to fill out. The strain of every two-hour feeding night and day was taking a toll, but how different he now looked from the day that he was first brought to her, vomiting the green poison he had been fed. He was a child who was the product of the native female circumcision rituals; consequently, he was regarded as "*Machi (*No person)," and his mother was required to kill him at birth. He had been found in the bushes by a Christian and brought to Kitty.

"Can you save him?'

Kitty stared at his tiny form and knew that if she didn't try, he would surely die. "I'll try. Please pray to Jehovah that He will help me." And He did.

The children loved to help with his bath. He had grown chubby, and he smiled when they tickled his tummy.

"Children, today is the day Naomi and Johana are coming for the baby."

"He's not going away is he, Mommy?" John's expression changed as did his little sister's.

"Yes, my dears, he is going to have a brand new home." Kitty smiled as she thought of his new parents.

"No, Mommy, please don't give him away," John Boy begged urgently.

"Naomi and Johana will bring him often to see us."

And so the new mother and father came. There was a tearful separation, and the dear little one was gone.

But it had truly been the best of days. Naomi and Johanna were no longer childless. Kitty would never forget the look on Naomi's face when she held him and little Musa was truly hers.

Musa grew older and in the meantime Johana and Naomi adopted other unwanted children. Rev. Johana holding Shadrach and Miriam, Naomi, and Musa

Kitty wrote to her mother:

The Bible school begins tomorrow, the other school has already begun and I have a new baby. Don't get excited. It is a black baby, an abandoned one, one of those I wrote about before that they try to kill. They almost succeeded in this case. The head was banged up, and all over the little body were black and blue marks where it had been pinched. He is now past two weeks old, and I have had him a week. It has been a fight to keep him alive, but I've just pled with the Lord to let him as he is our first one, and much depends upon it. I have a little bed for him in a box and have cared for him night and day, often getting up three times a night to feed him. His capacity is only about 2 oz. as he was so nearly starved, his stomach seems to be shrunk. He was simply skin and bones. When we got him our head evangelist was here and he came around back where I was bathing him for the first time. He is Johanna [sic], a brother of the Petro I wrote about, and has never had any children. Everyone has begged him to get another wife, and that failing has tried to get her to go with another man to see if perhaps Johanna [sic] may be to blame. But they have both stood true. So I asked him if he'd like to have this baby if he lives, and he was simply tickled to death. Well he stood here and watched me bathe him, and the tears rolled down his face as he said, "Oh! That's so good to see the little one in a mother's arms." So I said, "What is he to be called; you name him." and what do you suppose he chose? Musa (Moses)! So little Moses he is....

"So I said, 'What is he to be called?'...and what do you suppose he chose? Musa (Moses)!"

Mercy has converted more souls

than zeal, or eloquence or learning

or all of them together.

S. Kierkegaard 1815-1855

Dear Homefolks all: Feb. 8 1936 Tenwik, Sotik, Kenya B.E.A

We just received the letters telling of your Christmas and New Years.

...We wrote just before going to Kijabe, I believe. Since we got back, we have been so busy the letters have been neglected again, but we've thought so much about you, and it delighted our hearts to hear of Dad's success and that the boss gave the $10,000-man prize to Dad....

I enjoyed the conference at Kijabi. We get so few contacts with Europeans that we get real soul hungry for food and fellowship. There were some very fine speakers there, Mr. Ford, Clara's father, among them. He spoke on Jesus, our High Priest, and it was wonderful. He is truly a great man and a fine speaker. I hope you may meet him sometime. He (Mr. Ford) is considered one of the outstanding missionaries of East Africa and much in demand, yet very humble. Another speaker I so much enjoyed was Cannon Bucher of the C.M.S....

It was nice to be with the other missionaries, but it was also very nice to get home again. We have been busy since picking up loose ends and getting started on these three months work.

Must tell you a bit about the kiddies and then close. Last night John was jumping on the couch and fell off and knocked quite a skinned place on his lip. He was crying and carrying on with it, and Anna Verne stood it as long as she could, and then she said, "We will tell Jesus about it, John, and He'll make it all better." She has a dear little way of holding up one finger when she's very much in earnest, and her eyes are very big and round and gray. So I said, "That is a fine suggestion; let's ask Him to do it, and as we were about to eat, we said something to that affect on the end of the blessing. I had about forgotten the incident when this a.m. at breakfast, John said, "Mother, Jesus came and slept with me last night. He put his hand on my lip like this, and it stopped hurting, and I went to sleep. And you see this morning it has a scab on and is all better." "Except we become as a little child."

Well must close. Lots of love to all. Bob, Kitty and the Kiddies

"I enjoyed the conference at Kijabi."

The Friends Mission had a rule that children of missionaries could not return under their mission. For that reason, Clara Ford had applied to our mission. Her sister Esther married Earl Andersen, the son of Andrew and Vivian Andersen, and worked for years at Litein station under Africa Inland Mission. Clara's brother Arthur and his wife also applied to work with our mission at one time as Mother mentions.

Feb. 28, 1936, Tenwik, Sotik, Kenya, B.E.A

Dearest Mother and All,

At last we are home again after two very strenuous weeks of learning to do book keeping and trying to help Faye and Kirk get off. Bob was to leave for Nairobi for K.M.C. with Mr. Ford on Wednesday. A.m. So we left here on Tuesday and I was to stay at Kirks' and go over books etc. and they were to leave on the following Wed. and take the car to Nairobi with their stuff and Bob was to bring it back. Well, they received word that their boat would be delayed so they decided not to go till Friday, then not till Sat and finally didn't get away until Sunday. It had been raining and the roads were in terrible condition, so they didn't get into Nairobi until nearly midnight. Bob got back Tuesday and after doing some things for Kirk, closing the house etc., we got away Wed. a.m. at about 10:00. We stopped a little while at Litein and then came on. After about half way the roads became terrible and we skidded first into one ditch and then into the other. Then I'd drive and Bob would push. Twice we nearly turned over. But the Lord brought us through and we arrived home about 3:00 p.m. mighty glad to get here. While we were sliding all over the road John said, "Isn't this fun? We do just like a boat!" and Bob answered "I'm afraid John, you and I may be the only one enjoying it. I've an idea your mother isn't." So John looked at me and said. "Aren't you enjoying this Mother?" And I said, "I guess I would have to confess I'm not." And then in his most persuasive tones, he said, "But you must, just think about it and enjoy it."

I made Donald a lovely little tan coat out of that old one of mine and had enough left to make a nice one for Anna Verne with a bit or piecing....

Little Moses has gone to his new black mamma and I surely miss the little tike....

Johanna [sic] and Naomi are as happy as kings with litttle Moses. He made a bed for him and went to the duka and bought Palmolive soap to bathe him. Just ordinary soap wasn't good enough! I gave them an outfit of some baby clothes Faye left and some of my old ones: three shirts, three bands, three outing gowns and some old diapers and two blankets. It is the most complete outfit any baby around here has and they are very happy with it, and I believe will keep it nicely....

Thank you beforehand for the things that are coming with the girls but especially for the big hug and kiss. I shall surely collect them full measure, and try and imagine I'm getting them direct....

Well must close for this time....   Lots of love to all, Kitty

"Thank you...especially for the big hug and kiss."

208

*Hannah with Anna Verne, John, and
Donald Kirkpatrick*

Playmates

CHAPTER 15
TENWEK—MARCH & APRIL 1936

Friends in the Homeland

In a memorial written about Mother, the comment is made that she consistently recognized and acknowledged those who had supported their effort in Africa.

" We can never cease to praise Him also for those of rare vision who, though not much in the public eye, yet carry a burden for lost souls all round the world. If we truly continue to obey the Great Commission, we have a glorious outlook."[*]

In addition to the correspondence with family, according to Dad's letter, there were 800 names on their mailing list. This correspondence was a time-consuming effort but remained consistently attended to throughout all of our childhoods and into their retirement. In this typed letter, she was describing their day.

It did our hearts so much good to be remembered by so many of you dear folk. We know you have been interested in and praying for us, for God has kept us from danger so often. But when you sent us personal gifts, and money to help send the parcels, it made us feel just a little closer to you. And I want to say, too, that we appreciate the quality of the things you sent. Everything was of the best, and all were so useful. There is only one way in which you could fully appreciate our thankfulness for these lovely things, and that would be for you yourselves to be in a far country where it is almost impossible to get things such as you sent, and if it is possible they are so expensive that our pocket books usually do not encompass them. Every time we wear something you sent or put a garment on the children, we say to ourselves, "This is so and so's love gift." And we know also the sacrifice that is behind many of them.

March 3, 1936—Written to "Dear Friends in the Homeland"

---

[*] "Missionary Tidings," May 1988

Up at 6:00 (Bob usually earlier, but not today because he was sick). He then started the men to work, and I did up the early morning work, and dressed and started two small people on their busy day. Breakfast at seven, then family worship. Then I finish the morning work, see about food for dinner, and any baking necessary. After breakfast Bob went out and began taking the truck to pieces to put in new piston rings. Then he built the form for the fireplace we haven't yet had in the garage because we ran out of cement. Then he poured that. Also he supervised the rock cracking for the permanent house foundations, and the building of forms for one of the out buildings.

I taught John for about twenty minutes, as he is beginning to learn his letters, and numbers, and then taught my two native boys who are helping me. The one will enter the school here on Monday, but we as yet have no one as far advanced as the other, so I have to devote at least an hour a day to him. Then I did the dispensary work. Among those who came today was a tiny baby with pneumonia. He is very sick and I am afraid will not live through the night. Then I took a tour of the grounds to see about the transplanting of flowers and the cutting of some others, and grass, and the fruit trees in general. In the meantime we had the mid-morning prayer for the workers, and Bob one or two conferences about out-school work. We call them *shauries*, and there really isn't an English equivalent that exactly expresses it. It means troubles in general, and a solving of problems and leaving everybody concerned happy or contented, and if not at first in good humor, winning them to it. By that time it, was noon, but as the fireplace was not quite finished, Bob worked about 20 minutes overtime. Then we had dinner, and I washed hands and faces and afterwards put two tired little playmates to bed for their afternoon nap. Bob finished up the truck job, and I rested a bit, then started to work on the copying of the Kipsigis Dictionary, which I have been working on for some time. I finished it about teatime, and Bob came in from fitting window sashes into the frames. Since then he has been resting a little, and I have been writing to you. I have just completed arrangements for supper, and the kiddies are amusing themselves by dressing up in whatever they can find of mine, Bob's or each others clothes. They are usually pretty good children and play well together. They come in for their share of naughtiness, however, and also their share of spankings. We haven't reached that advanced stage where we can raise children without it. It may be lack on our part...but anyway it is so.

So there you see a typical day.

Continued from March 3, 1936 letter "...started to work on the copying of the Kipsigis Dictionary...."

Without medically trained people to do so, it fell to Mother to care for people who came to her door with medical or dental problems. Dad's brother Eddie had sent along one of his medical books, and this was referenced frequently. She did not have surgical needles, so she sterilized regular needles and thread and made that do. We heard many stories such as the ones that follow.

"...she uttered not a sound."

The old woman sat looking frail and in pain. Her chin was cradled in her hand, and her face was visibly swollen.

"*Kang'wanit mising kosiir.* (The pain is too great.) *Imuche itoretan-i?* (Can you help me?)"

"*Iseng'eng'eny, Mama, sikobitageer.* (Open you mouth, Mother, so that I can see.) *Gonan ageer orit.* (Let me look inside.)"

The tooth had broken and a sharp edge protruded from the angry looking swollen gum. Her tongue bled where the jagged tooth had torn it.

Old Kalenjin woman

"*Amuche atutun keldet kobaten matinye chebo ng'wonindo, ak ng'wonitu inne mising.* (I can pull the tooth, but I have nothing for the pain, and it will be very painful.)"

"*Kaigai, kaigai itutut keldet.* (Please, please pull the tooth.)"

Kitty found the pointed nose pliers and boiled them in water. When they had cooled, she took them in hand and began to pull the tooth.

Tears slid from the old woman's eyes, but she uttered not a sound. Kitty's hands trembled as she moved the tooth back and forth until finally it gave way and came out. Kitty packed the hole with gauze until the bleeding stopped. She patted the old woman.

"*Kaigai ngunon-i, Mama?* (Is it better now, Mother?)"

"*Ee, ee* (Yes, yes)," she murmured, "*Kongoi, kongoi mising* (Thank you, thank you very much)."

"*Atinyei chaik che belebich.* (I have some hot tea.) *Amache keei twan kotoretin.* (I want us to drink it together to help you.)"

"*Kongoi.* (Thank you.) *Kongoi mising.* (Thank you very much.)"

The old woman was just one of many patients. Kitty had no formal medical training but she used her common sense and sewing skills as they were called upon.

"Kitty, what are you doing?" Bob looked at Kitty on her knees with one of his brother's medical books on the bed in front of her. She was desperately paging through it.

"This baby is breach; there is only one leg out, and I'm not sure what to do. I'm praying that the Lord will help me find the right page, so I will get it right. Oh! here it is—footling breach," she read as quickly as she could. "You know the Africans don't come in for help unless there is something terribly wrong."

She ran back up to the dispensary knowing that were this America, the child would be delivered by C-section. Pushing the leg up, she reached with her finger for the other leg and pulled both legs out. Then turning the baby so that the face was down, and holding both ankles with one hand, she reached up again and found the baby's tiny mouth. She put her finger in the mouth, pulled down delivering the head. The baby gasped, breathed, and then cried heartily.

Picture from "Call to Prayer" article

"*Kongoi! Kongoi!* (Thank you! Thank you!)" the new mother said again and again.

"*Kongoi Jehobah!* (Thank God!)" said Kitty.

"*Memsahib*, someone needs your help."

Kitty stepped out of the back door and looked down the path. Two men supporting a third were walking in her direction. Quickly she brought a wooden chair for the man to sit on and began questioning those who accompanied him.

213

THE DARKEST TIME IS JUST BEFORE THE DAWN

"He's been gored by a bull," the men reported.

Old Kalenjin man
Courtesy of Consolata Fathers

As his loose blanket slipped away from his abdomen, Kitty could hardly believe her eyes.

Three huge safety pins held together a long gash. Cow dung was seeping from the wound and was plastered along the opening. Kitty knew a little of sterile technique. She carefully washed her hands. She was grateful for the water she had recently boiled, and she quickly gathered other instruments and materials she thought she would need.

"Please bring me the water and some cloths, and find *Bwana* Smith," she instructed the men who had gathered around. "Tell him I need his help," she said as she unfastened the safety pins and watched the contents of the patient's abdomen roll out onto his lap. She looked anxiously at the man who seemed little perturbed by what was occurring.

Meticulously she washed away the cow dung and foreign material she could identify, moving the bowel back and forth as necessary. Still the man sat watching in a detached way. Finally, with Bob's help, they lowered the man to a blanket on the ground. Kitty sprinkled sulfa powder, the most recent miracle drug, sent to them by Bob's doctor brother Eddie, into the abdominal cavity. Then with Bob holding the edges of each layer together, Kitty sewed with ordinary cotton thread and then dressed the wound. Then they both knelt and prayed. "We have done all we know to do so now, Lord, please will You touch him." He was housed in the hut that had been their former home. Two weeks later, they watched as he bade them farewell and walked unassisted toward his home.

Executive meeting - Chicago - Mon. September 9, 1935 - an evening service.

The application of Miss Mildred Ferneau for service in Africa was considered, and in view of the fact that her support has been provided, it was decided that we send her to Africa with Miss Day, subject to a proper physical examination. It was further decided that she be requested to raise her passage and outfit money, if possible.

The amount of outfit allowance for outgoing missionaries to Africa was next discussed, and it was the conviction of those present that $250.00 would be a reasonable amount to allow for Misses Day and Ferneau.

The application of Mr. & Mrs. Arthur Ford was next considered, and in view of the fact that a man is urgently needed in Africa, and inasmuch as he has already been there and he and his wife both seem suitable in every way for missionary service, it was felt that they should be invited to our Annual Convention at Evansville, Indiana.

---

* *Kipsigis*, Consolata Fathers—Nairobi, Kenya—Distributor Text Book Centrel—Nairobi, Kenya
Printed by Stamperia Artistica, Nazionale—Italy

In September of 1931, at the same meeting in which the Kirkpatricks had been put under appointment, Alice Day had also been accepted for appointment with the understanding that she would not go to Africa for one more year. In fact, five years had passed by the time the board actually saw their way clear to send her along with Mildred Ferneau to the field. Alice was involved in education and continued to work in Kenya for over thirty years until her sudden death from pancreatitis after abdominal surgery. She is buried on the Tenwek station. The Fords did not come, nor did another couple being mentioned in Kitty's letters named the Rogers. Gertrude Shryock, known as Trudy, arrived in March of 1937, and she was the first fully qualified nurse serving twenty years at Tenwek. Mildred Ferneau also had some nurses training, and her fiancé did come later; they were married soon after he arrived, and he remained for a brief time allowing the Smiths to return to the States in 1937.

> In connection with the opening of the work there has been untold legal red tape to unwind, and we were simply buried with office work until Miss Day came to our rescue. She has been typing steadily and we are beginning to catch up. She is also typing the manuscripts for the publication of the first translation of the Scriptures in Kipsigis. These are being prepared in co-operation with the African Inland Mission. Mr. Anderson of Litein is doing the translating and we the manuscripts. Besides this both young ladies were anxious to begin language study at once and have been making steady progress in it. We plan that Miss Day shall begin her supervision of the children's and girls' day school work after the May holiday.
>
> July 1936 — CALL TO PRAYER

Excerpt from article written later by Kitty

Raining constantly

We are now in the rainy season. It has been raining steadily for many days and the natives say it is not finished by any means. There are many advantages in having lovely rain, as our grass, gardens, trees, flowers, etc are just jumping, but it has hindered us also in transportation. You will have to imagine yourselves again in a place over 50 miles from the nearest market town of any size, and about three times that distance from Nairobi, where most of our buying for the buildings has to be done. That means that all our cement, iron for roofing, glass for windows, nails, putty, hardware etc. etc. has to be brought by truck at least the former distance. That does not seem very far when you think of miles at home, but just imagine driving that truck over plowed fields just after a good thunder shower.

Excerpt from earlier March 3, 1936 letter

We remember Dad coming in mud covered and exhausted with stories of yet another impassable road. If a bridge was washed out, he built a new one. His constant battle with the roads and equipment made every effort more difficult and more time consuming. When the vehicles would not go through, he sent for the oxen, something that happened often during those early years. Eventually, he built another road called the forest road that bypassed some of the trouble spots but was far from trouble free. When there was no other way, cement and sand for some of these buildings was brought in on the backs of donkeys. The house he built for the single ladies was made largely without nails, as they were unavailable in Kenya during the war. Instead he glued pieces of doweling to hold boards together. Resources, availability, and the means of transport for building materials were a constant challenge.

Dear Home Folks: Tenwek, Sotik, Kenya, B.E.A., April 23, 1936

I am sending this airmail as I have rather neglected to write you lately and am afraid you will be anxious about us. It seems we have been so very busy since the girls came that we just haven't had the time for writing we wish we had. Besides, there has been an extra lot of business to take care of in connection with their goods. We have been absolutely marooned here since their arrival. It rained almost constantly every day until the rivers were so high all the bridges were unsafe. In fact, three of the largest have gone out, and the other day when Bob attempted a trip to Kericho after a slight let up of rain, he had to build a bridge before he could go on. Consequently he got to Litein after dark and stayed there all night. He went on to Kericho the next day and got some supplies and saw to a great deal of pressing business and started back. Everyone said he couldn't possibly get through, and now he doesn't know how he did except that the Lord brought him. For two days, our men have been out on the road helping fill in a hole as big as the motor-car. The government officials arrived this a.m. and are surely fed up with trying to get through. I was about like "Old Mother Hubbard" as far as my cupboard was concerned and mighty glad for an additional supply of groceries. We prepared for being marooned again but had two nice days in succession so far.

The girls seem to like it here fine. I told you or Anna how near they came to being without a roof or side-walls on their rooms. But we finished in the nick of time, though we didn't get settled in. They are working on language now. That means an hour a day teaching for me. I have been helping Bob out in Bible School and then my cook got the chicken pox, so I've had the cooking besides. My poor old head does get rattled at times....

We have had word of the coming of Rogers and Miss Gertrude Shryock. We knew her well in Asbury. In fact, she was school nurse when Bob had the mumps there. Perhaps you have met her. Such a sweet girl. The girls tell us the Rogers are lovely. How Bob longs for a man to help share his pressing burdens. We had such a nice letter from Mr. R. sent through the office asking questions about equipment, a car etc. So we each wrote them in this mail. They are to sail in May or June, I believe.

All this rain has held up building. It has been impossible to get supplies in. Now Bob has made arrange-ment to have things transported by ox cart. Also the girls' [Alice Day and Mildred Ferneau] freight is coming in this way. A truck just couldn't get through....

As it looks now, we will be sailing about next March or April. It will take Rogers a year to be ready to take over.

Love to you all, Catharine

"It rained almost constantly.... In fact...he had to build a bridge before he could go on."
Pictures—Courtesy of Richard Adkins

216

This is the house for Alice, Mildred, and Trudy that was first a single story and then completed as a double story building in Bob and Kitty's second term. House under construction—Courtesy of Richard Adkins

John recalls, "When in my development I began to show signs of intellectual curiosity, Mother was quick to note it and just as quick to foster it. Some of my happiest memories center around her deep interest in literature. Bible stories came first in my childhood; then as I was able, Mother introduced me to the classics." As children, we all often enjoyed listening as she quoted poems she knew by heart. She read to us daily, and we enjoyed *Pilgrim's Progress, The Kontiki Expedition, The Last Days of Pompeii,* and many other books. We especially loved the times she quoted "The Village Blacksmith" by Henry Wadsworth Longfellow, mostly because Dad would stand in the background miming while Mother quoted, "Under the spreading chestnut tree, the village smithy stands—she Smith a mighty man was he with strong and powerful hands and the muscles of his brawny arms were as strong as iron bands...." Dad would flex his muscles and beat on his chest while we laughed. Perhaps the most frequently quoted poem, however, was "The First Snow Fall" by James Russell Lowell. Mother was likely to have quoted it on such an occasion as this.

"…burden of great sorrow."

The news had just arrived (see the following letter) and everyone was shaken. Alice Day, the new missionary teacher, had come over from her house to comfort Kitty. She had made some tea. Even though she had just arrived, Alice already understood that tea was an inextricable part of most social exchanges in this country.

"It reminds me of when my baby brother died," Kitty observed. "It was in February. The cold of the winter added to the sadness, and in the ensuing years when the snow fell, I often saw my mother looking out the window, perhaps thinking of her only son under that snow. I suppose that is why I loved and memorized James Russell Lowell's, "The First Snow Fall." I love the imagery in it. Have you ever heard it, Alice?"

"I have, but I'd love to hear you quote it again, Kitty."

And so Kitty, speaking softly began to recite. Alice felt cold chills run up and down her spine as Kitty's expression-filled words painted the incredible picture.

Alice and Kitty sat quietly together for a long moment thinking. Kitty wasn't sure why she had thought of this poem. After all, the new little grave was not in a place where it would ever be covered with snow. She wrote to her mother.

Excerpt. - April 23, 1936

…Besides this we have had the burden of Kirk and Faye's great sorrow. Perhaps you heard, their lovely little Marilyn was left behind in Port Elizabeth beneath a small white stone. We had the word of her condition about two weeks before the cable that she'd slipped away. It is a long story and would seem she had been ailing before they left, but all thought it was her teeth. It turned out to be an infection of her kidney and bladder. She went into convulsions on the boat and they stopped at Port Elizabeth and put her in the hospital. At first she took a turn for the better. But at last was worse again and died a week after her first attack. She was just a year old that day, such a sweet flower and blooming so short a time. I loved her almost as much as if she had been my own and the shock of the loss has been almost more than I could bear. Also I am so concerned for Faye. She was worn out before they left and I am so afraid she will collapse entirely. The Lord surely sees the glory in it and we know he doeth all things well but it is hard to understand indeed. Had she been here or born at home it would not have been so hard to understand but on the way and then to have to go and leave her precious body! I told you about the sweet dresses I made her. Faye tells me she put on the lovely pink organdie, her lovely white shoes her Grandma Craig sent and wrapped her in her lovely rose wool blanket…. I see how good God has been to us to let us keep our kiddies. It makes us realize, however, that they are sacred trusts loaned us for a while perhaps….

"…our kiddies…are sacred trusts loaned us for a while perhaps…."

The First Snow Fall
By James Russell Lowell

The snow had begun in the gloaming. And busily all the night
Had been heaping field and highway with a silence deep and white.
Every pine and fir and hemlock wore ermine too dear for an earl,
And the poorest twig on the elm-tree was ridged inch-deep with pearl.

From sheds new-roofed with Carrara came Chanticleer's muffled crow
The stiff rails softened to swan's down, and still fluttered down the snow.
I stood and watched by the window the noiseless work of the sky,
And the sudden flurries of snowbirds, like brown leaves whirling by.

I thought of a mound in sweet Auburn where a little headstone stood;
Now the flakes were folding it gently, as did robins the babes in the wood.
Up spoke our own little Mabel, saying, "Father, who makes it snow?"
And I told of the good All-Father who cares for us here below.

Again I looked at the snowfall, and thought of the leaden sky
That arched o'er our first great sorrow, when that mound was heaped so high.
I remembered the gradual patience that fell from the cloud like snow,
Flake by flake, healing and hiding the sear of our deep-plunged woe.

And again to the child I whispered, "The snow that husheth all,
Darling, the merciful Father alone can make it fall!"
Then, with eyes that saw not, I kissed her and she, kissing back, could not know
That my kiss was given to her sister folded close under deepening snow.

CHAPTER 16
TENWEK—MAY & JUNE 1936

Tenwek, Sotik, Kenya, B.E.A. June 14th, 1936

Dear Mother & all:

We received your letter written May 6th in yesterday's mail. In the same mail came one from Mother Smith airmail and one from Bro. Hotchkiss air mail. The former gave the details of the operation and the fact that Father Smith's condition was a bit hopeful. The latter told of Bro. H.'s marriage which you perhaps already know about. He also said that Livingston had married. They, he and his wife (Miss Mary Hendrickson) will stay on in Cleveland for the time being as David is making his home with them and going to finish his schooling...[more family news]

How my heart has been torn these days. It is surely hard at a time like this to be so far away. But I had written Mother Smith not long ago that the one prayer of all our hearts was that we all be reunited once more on this earth if Jesus tarries and somehow felt He was going to let it come to pass. She probably has that letter while I am writing now for it has had time to get home I think. [The nature of this illness is unknown to us].

It surely was wonderful the way the Lord answered prayer for that dollar you wanted for the work. I wonder why we don't trust Him more truly for even the small things....

We have been seeing some marvelous answers to prayer here. We spent Friday and Saturday at Kiplelji, an out school where there has been a great deal of trouble and resultant backsliding. We felt that unless the Lord wonderfully undertook we would surely lose the school. We had a good p.m. service, then a service at night for the women and then next a.m. Bob preached. The whole thing broke up, people fell under the power of the Spirit and began to confess, from murder and stealing of 1,500 shillings and 1,100 shillings to other things until people began to cry for mercy and pray through to victory. The trouble was sifted down and everything made right and the people are happy as can be today.

We are trusting the Lord for even greater things. Alice is busy in the school. Mildred has the dispensary & hospital....

We still have no sand, so the houses sit as they have been for several weeks. Last week a few donkeys went to bring it to a place the ox cart can get to, to get at it. So we hope to have some sand by the end of this week.

We had an earthquake last night. It wasn't a heavy shock and lasted only about 30 seconds. There were two lighter tremors after it. But it was peculiar in the fact that it sounded so loud. It was like thunder but was under the ground instead of in the sky. We had another slight shock this a.m. and again the peculiar noise....

...our furlough slips farther and farther away as they put off sending workers....

We haven't had any word from Faye and Kirk since they arrived at home. I suppose they have been just too busy to write. I haven't even had the books yet. I was made treasurer when Faye left and haven't yet had their books, so am quite at sea about finances up to the time I took over.

We are glad for the poem Anna rescued and sent. I must enclose one on John for Dad. I had scolded him and set him on a chair and he said, "Now you are making me mad and you're going to make me cry." So I answer, "Yes, but you didn't mind me." At this he tried hard to frown at me but the effort was too much and he burst out laughing. Then he said so disgustedly, "Oh dear! All I can do is laughing. I don't know how to do bad on my face."   Love to all, Catharine

"...our furlough slips farther and farther away...."

221

"Our people could not understand....".

In Dad's retirement years, Anna Verne arranged for him to tell some of his stories, during one of his visits to the WGM headquarters where she was working at the time. For six hours he was recorded as he told many of these stories you are now reading. "You have to understand the culture of the people." Dad declared, "A missionary can't just go and quickly superimpose his ideas on people who have a different way of thinking. You need to have a call, and a commitment, and **you have to know the people.**" We can all still see Dad talking, sitting and walking with Johana while he patiently explained his people to Dad and counseled him. We suspect cumulative conversations may have had the following content:

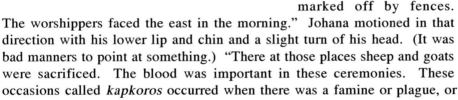

Bob and Johana walked many miles together across the hillsides, going to meetings of one kind or another. Other times they were together simply because they enjoyed each other's company.

"Tell me about your tribe, Johana. Do they worship a god?" Bob asked. "I know that most of the tribes in Kenya are fetish worshippers and animists, believing in magic and that things in nature have spirits that can exist separate from their bodies."

Kipsigis women grinding bek (millet) on stones
The middle woman holds the earthen pot containing
a mixture for preparation of beer.

"Our people worship the sun. Many years ago, members of the tribe would come together in high places that were marked off by fences. The worshippers faced the east in the morning." Johana motioned in that direction with his lower lip and chin and a slight turn of his head. (It was bad manners to point at something.) "There at those places sheep and goats were sacrificed. The blood was important in these ceremonies. These occasions called *kapkoros* occurred when there was a famine or plague, or war or crisis."

"Ah, I have heard that your people migrated down the Nile. These are customs very much like those of the people in the Middle East and even recorded in the Old Testament. This is very interesting."

Kipsigis bride
Courtesy of the Consolata Fathers

---

* Content gleaned in part from unpublished writings of Earl Andersen.

"The people became tired of walking to these places, so pieces of the fences were pulled up and carried home. This clump of sticks, called the *mabwita,* is stuck into the ground on the east side of the hut. Each morning when the man comes from his house, he looks to the east and asks for blessings for the day. There are also celebrations when a child is born that involved this clump of sticks. It is used during initiation rites, sickness and death. A goat is most often sacrificed, the blood sprinkled over the sticks and then one who knew divination would read the entrails and tell whether the goat was acceptable to the spirits or not. If not, then another goat must be slain. By now, though, the influence of the *Laibon* (witch doctors) has replaced some of the old sun worship, and now our people believe in taboos and spells that these witch doctors place upon them. The witch doctors are not from our tribe."

Kipsigis warrior
Courtesy of Richard Adkins

"*Aikwek*! (Expression of surprise!)" Bob shook his head. "There is another thing which I notice is different in this tribe. There are no villages. The huts are scattered all over the hills." Bob waved his long arms across the horizon.

" *Kweli!* (This is true!) But people of a certain geographic area unite to form what is called a *kokwet* that is a cooperative unit. Woman from the same *kokwet* work all the gardens together. These are often all put in the same place so that they can be fenced easily. This system of working together is called *morik.* In the old days, the huts were owned only if they were occupied. The grazing areas and the gardens were common property, and the tribe moved a great deal. Men owned their wives, cattle, sheep, goats, and occasionally beehives."

"How much must a man pay for his wife?"

Kipsigis warrior   "Usually two heifers, two cows with calves, and sixteen sheep and goats."

"And he may have as many as he wishes?"

"*Ee* (Yes)—as long as he can pay."

"But the land can handle only so many cows! Soon the land will be destroyed!"

"These customs make it very hard for our people to accept Christianity. To have only one wife lowers your standing in the tribe."

"Yes, I can see that, but is it not better to give your daughters away and not treat them as chattels? In God's sight they are persons and not property."

"*Kweli!* I know this is true!" Johana looked away into the distance.

"Is a like a clan?"

Young warriors completing initiation with a lion kill—Courtesy of Alice P. Smith

223

"Not really. There are several *kokwets* within the clan and there are four clans within the Kipsigis tribe."

As Johana and Bob walked along, they came upon some children squatting down, and one was gathering stones from a small indentation in the dirt. Bob noticed that there were two rows of such indentations, and now the boy was dropping a stone from his hand into each of the holes.

"What are they doing, Johana?"

Young boy during initiations
Courtesy of Consolata Fathers

Johana laughed, "It is a game of stones. The children play it often."

Bob stood observing the children for a while. "Johana, what was it like in Kipsigis when you were a child?"

"It was different *kabisa* (completely). Men were warriors. They protected their families. But to prove their manhood, they were required to do a brave deed—kill a lion, elephant, rhino or buffalo, kill a person from another tribe, rob some cattle or earn money away from the tribe. Women worked the *shambas*, gathered wood and provided meals. The bad thing was that we did not know how to store food for the famine time. They came year after year for fifty-two years. The maize and beans would run out. Men and women's bones would show through their skin, and children's bellies would swell, and their hair would turn yellow. When the children were listless and old men too weak to move, and everyone was desperate for food, our tribe would sell their girls for food."

" *Aikwek!* This was a bad *shauri*. It must have been very sad and very hard."

"*Ee, Ee.*" Johana looked at the ground.

"To whom were they sold?" Bob tried to imagine selling his sister out of sheer desperation.

"The Kisii, a neighboring tribe, most often. Besides this trouble of starvation, every day in those days, we looked for raiders who might plunder and take our cows. The Maasai did this to us most often. They would steal our cows at night. When we were young, we began to learn the ways of moving through the bush without making noise. We would follow them and steal back our cows."

"What weapons did you use?"

"There were no guns, but we had spears. Some used bows and arrows; also some used *pangas* (machete-like knives). We had shields, too, for protection."

"*Kweli!* (Really!) I see these things even now. Most men still carry spears everywhere and the clubs you call *rungu*."

Warriors gathered for ceremonies
Courtesy of Richard Adkins

"They are still needed for protection from animals and raiders, but now the government protects, and there are fewer raids. In the old days, the men were proud and brave. They would stalk the raiders, trying to get back the animals that had been captured; some of the men would be killed, but if they returned with the animals or others in their place, there would be a time of great celebration. The white men call them chiefs, but our people choose their leader by who was the bravest warrior, and we call him *Kiptaiyat.*"

Bob was surprised and interjected, "That is the word we use when we speak of Jesus, the Lord."

Johana nodded, "That is right. It is the most honored name," he paused and then went on. "When a man became too old to be a warrior, he could stay at home. Then his business was to have jurisdictions over the young men in matters of religion, the setting of the planting season, migrations, and settling of disputes between people. The old men settle things by consensus. No one ever makes a decision alone and, in fact, within a group the decision has to be unanimous. The men sit for many hours discussing things and drinking beer."

"How did the people accept the government and the British rule?"

"Our people could not understand the ways of these strangers. Think of this, *Bwana.* If all a man's wealth is tied up in his animals and someone arrives and says to you, 'All of the fighting is finished between you and the Maasai and between each other in the tribe. I am in charge now; I will bring you peace, but for this you must give me a goat or a calf as a tax.' You see, as yet our tribe knew nothing of money. That was a great mystery. No one could believe that a small piece of metal could be exchanged for an animal or other goods. It took a long to time to believe this was possible. *Pole-pole* (slowly, slowly) they began to understand."

Men drinking beer

"*Aikwek!* (Well, I'll be!) I never thought of that!" Bob shook his head trying to imagine how difficult these concepts must have been to grasp.

"More difficult for our people to understand was the idea of rulers beyond our native council. Very few traveled, so to imagine a ruler in another land across many seas, whom these new rulers here in our country were required to obey, made no sense. I remember when a white stranger, wearing his khaki suit with the many shiny brass buttons, and a large badge, arrived in our village." Johana waved his hands across the front of his chest and sleeves indicating all the places the buttons appeared.

Bob burst out laughing. In their dress uniform, the District Commissioners were resplendent, to say the least.

Johana laughed as well and then continued. "Through an interpreter, he asked for someone who could be a leader. The stranger explained that he would make a pact with this new leader. He was to be made the most powerful man in this area, but for this he must obey the D.C. For his obedience, he would receive protection, and he would receive a salary. If someone killed or stole or injured another in a dispute, the matter would be brought to the D.C. who would send his men to care for it, and the white man's law would settle it. If the leader lied to the D.C., he would take his power away, and the man would be disgraced and dishonored. My brother, Petro, was chosen to be one of those leaders."

"I see! Did the people understand this and accept him?"

Johana looked at the ground and shook his head. "No, it was quite impossible. The leaders they chose were often young men like my brother, but it was the old men in the tribe who were respected. A young person does not give orders to an older person. Nor can a person bring a judgment against his relative. Also, they listened only to the warrior leaders in *shauries* about war. In *shauries* of law, they listen to the elders' council, and in *shauries* of magic to the witch doctors—*laibon.* So there was great confusion.

Because the leaders were paid, they gathered wealth, and their wealth made them more powerful. They were required to count the huts and collect the hut tax. People did not like this. Gradually, though, the people began to understand, and *shauries* were taken to the district ruler to be settled. Still the older rulers did not accept this, and they continued to resist the white rulers."

"Has this system helped the people?"

"In some ways, yes. Now there are fewer raids, and men can do other work instead of being warriors."

"But it seems many men do not want to do other work." Bob thought of how difficult it was to find reliable workers.

*Kipsigis woman
Courtesy Richard
Adkins*

"There was great honor in being a warrior but little honor in doing other work. It is especially demeaning to do the 'work of a woman.' Now the missionaries are teaching God's ways are ways of peace but also of work. These are mysteries to our people. A man cannot be in charge of anyone older than himself, so it is hard for our men to understand a headman in the work place."

They were nearing Johana's house.

"Of one thing I am sure—God meets a person at his place of need. Where your people need help, that is where He will meet them. But there is so much for me to learn. Thank you, *rafiki* (friend)!"

Bob tried again to imagine how difficult the messages and ways of the white man must be for these people to understand. At times, he felt defeated by the African logic which did not follow his own. He appreciated Johana's unswerving commitment to Christ and endless patience in explaining things to him again and again.

Women in the market place

As Bob walked on he considered other factors. In order for churches to be planted and then be sustained with a paid pastor, people would need to learn other trades. The tribe needed to be less nomadic, and the influence of the *laibon* would have to be overcome. Bob knew that the *laibon* were not actually Kipsigis but had infiltrated the tribe from the Maasai. These witch doctors had effectively convinced the Kipsigis to believe and adhere to their systems of charms, medicines and immunities. They had so effectively penetrated the tribe as to become powerful leaders with an efficient secret service. They sought out and persecuted converts to Christianity with great regularity. He remembered vividly the efforts the *liabon* had made to get the Local Native Council to disallow the mission from being set up in this area when he and Kitty had first arrived. He thought of how progress was being made. Mr. Andersen had imported millstones from India and been able to teach many how to use the energy from flowing water, particularly at waterfalls, to power small mills to grind their corn. Now, many such mills were scattered throughout the Kipsigis tribe.

The original gristmill below the Tenwek falls

The stone is now on display below the falls.
Courtesy of the Fishes

227

CHAPTER 17
TENWEK—JULY—SEPTEMBER 1936

Bob is away again today at an outschool. The services at these outschools have been wonderfully blessed of the Lord with many coming to confession and repentance. These have been going from place to place witnessing and with wonderful results...

Excerpt from July 27, 1936 letter

Education/Preaching—hand-in-hand

"Outschools" were locations in which a church and a school had been established for national Christians. There were six in 1935. These were Siwot, Kong'otik, Tulwetab Mosonik, Kipleji, Mengit, and Kimagata. Kimagata was Johana's *kokwet* (community) just across the river from Tenwek.

At each outstation was a mud and wattle building where classes and services were held. Pastors were also schoolteachers. They each had been to the equivalent of grammar school, knew how to read and write, and could teach what they knew.

Typical outschool building in the early days

By 1938, the number of outstations had expanded to sixteen. "Before a new school was opened, usually several visits were made to the community.... When enough interest was shown, there would be a *baraza* (discussion) and a vote taken as to whether the community wanted a school. If the vote turned out affirmative, some of the twelve elders would go to the community along with the missionary in charge of the educational work, and they would choose the location for the building.... The teacher/pastor was paid in part or full from the Native Teacher and Evangelists fund; the portions to be paid by the mission and from local funds would change from time to time as agreed by the mission group and the Native Finance Committee.[*]

The Evanglist-teachers in these past months have grown by leaps and bounds. It is really true that thus far they have faithfully walked in all the light they have received. Few of them have had much educational advantage, and they are very eager to learn more that they may be better ministers to their people. Some of them walk as far as eight miles to their schools every day and back again to the station in order to be in school here. I wonder how many in the home land would be that zealous to grasp their opportunities. Two new schools have been opened; one in the district that the Catholics were trying to force an entrance into. The natives have in each case furnished the materials, and built the buildings themselves. There are others crying for the same privilege, but there are no more available teachers at present.

July 1936   CALL TO PRAYER

Kitty wrote about them in the "Call to Prayer"

At the present, however, the church is completely indigenous. Pastors who have not had the privilege of attending a formal Bible training institution are given on-the-job training through Theological Training by Extension. Qualified teachers conduct structured classes in Bible and church-related ministries for pastors and Christian leaders at the local church level. Those who have had formal

---

[*] Fish, Burnette and Jerry, *The Place of Songs*, Second Printing by Spillman Printing, Sacramento, CA. World Gospel Mission, 1990.

THE DARKEST TIME IS JUST BEFORE THE DAWN

Bible college training can take pastorates on graduation from Kenya Highlands Bible College or step into supportive roles in church administration, Christian education, literature production, broadcasting, and secular teaching. Some graduates have gone on to receive higher degrees, thus preparing themselves for teaching positions at the Bible college or elsewhere.

July 27, 1936

Dear Folks:

I have noted the date of my last letter to you, but having sent it airmail I expect I better send this one likewise or it will be so long between them you'll think something has happened. I find I have one dated June 14th but I think I wrote since then. Anyway here goes again....

The Board is considering Arthur Ford and his wife. If they come it would be possible for us to get away much sooner as Arthur already knows some Swahili and could take over quicker than a brand new man. So we are again sort of looking that way....

The folks sent Bob $50.00 for a suit. It has arrived but he plans to use it here, and send them the price of the suit from our allowance at the office, that is $25.00 plus postage. Then he will save out of this for duty and in that way have an American cut suit. In this country the cuts are so funny he'd rather not get one to come home in. This suit will be the only one he has outside of his dark one, so I'd rather too, it would be something he can get a lot of use out of at home. We will write Mother S. about it. She said she'd have Roy help pick it. That was before they sent the money....

I am planning to send in an order to Montgomery Ward's for some things for John, that is a wool suit and perhaps a topcoat. He is so big and it is just folly to try and sew for him when you can get the tailored things so cheaply. If anyone is coming soon, I'll have them bring it. If not I'll have it mailed as well. So in that way we'll get outfitted nicely....

Well must close. We are about as usual except that Bob has been having some stomach trouble (it may be a form of dysentery) and Anna Verne has been ailing some. She ran a fever for two days but seems to be better today. Everyone is trying to persuade us to go to Mombasa in Sept for a rest. In some ways I'd like it. If we feel we should we'll do it though I do hate the expense right now....

Did Dad get John's letter?   Much love to all, Catharine & all

"If they come it would make it possible for us to get away much sooner...."

Mother's letters are beginning to show her hopes for returning to America. As always, she struggled with wondering what everyone was to wear. Usually by the end of a term of service in Kenya, the choices of clothing had dwindled quite remarkably. Still Mother could usually magically turn something old and bigger into something new and smaller for us children. It was a very rare occasion when she would send in a mail order, but that did happen on occasion.

African Children—"How easy...to love!"

Dad was always clowning around. He was able to make the Africans of all ages laugh, but he particularly enjoyed the children.

Kitty loved to see him. Bob was at it again. The African children were laughing so hard they could hardly stand up. Some of them actually were rolling on the ground.

"John and Anna Verne, come look at your daddy." They ran to her from the other side of the room, and they all watched out of the window. Then the children ran outside to join in on the fun.

It was all a mime. He'd pat his hip, and then he'd take hold of an imaginary crank and begin to crank up his leg. As he cranked, he would elevate his hip until the leg appeared at least two inches shorter. He would then turn his foot inward and take limping steps on his shortened leg. At first the African children would look in awe, mouths open. Then he would pat the hip again, once more taking hold of the imaginary crank. Magically he unwound the leg until it was the right length, and away he would walk with his normal gait.

Anna Verne and John ran to him. "Daddy, be a monkey, be a monkey!"

Batik of African children

African children

"Okay," he said as he put his lower teeth over his upper lip and repeatedly bit on it while at the same time scratched his ribs as was so characteristic of monkeys. The African children again were overcome with laughter. What beautiful smiles and bright happy eyes they had!

Kitty thought, "How precious they are in the sight of the Father. How easy they are to love!"

Dear Folks   *Tenwek, Sotik, Sept. 9 1936*

[Here Mother is discussing for her Mother the various scenarios that might develop to allow them to return to America. She and Dad have come to believe that if the board chose to send Kirk back to Kenya, it would be a choice that excluded them.]

However, Mother, ... we'd rather stay another whole year. If the Board decides that is what they want, though, we'll say OK though it may mean they have chosen between us and chosen him. Nevertheless we don't feel it would be possible for us to work together in perfect harmony. Not anyway unless a miracle took place. However, somehow we have felt there would be a way, and the surprise may be just around the corner.

I had such a sweet letter from Mrs. Bishop. She said she had felt impressed to write me, and her letter was such a blessing.

Well, we are actually going on a vacation. We've decided to make it a real one and just eat and sleep and swim. We were planning to start tomorrow but had a telegram Fords are coming through, so we will wait until Thursday. We'll be able to clear up a few more things hanging over us.

We are glad to hear Dad's business is moving along. Some people predict a time of unprecedented prosperity before Jesus comes. If so it will be nice in one way at least, and that is that the folks can get all their debts paid up before they leave this old world. I'd be happy not to leave a thing outstanding wouldn't you? British Israelites say He is coming the 16th of this month. If so, we'll see each other before you get to read this. However, I don't expect Him according to any date now set....

Did I tell you Bob found a little secondhand bicycle for John in Nairobi? When he went away, John confidently told me he was going to bring one back. I kept telling him no, because absolutely Bob had no such thought. But John persisted, and when he saw it on the top of the truck he said, "There it is, Mother." He has persisted until he rides it well, but he's had some terrible bumps. The other day a donkey ran out ahead of him and he piled up and ran a tooth through his lower lip. I thought of the time I slid down Aunt Emma's haystack; do you remember? But even that didn't daunt John. He is simply wild about that bicycle. I tried to get a snap of him riding it. Hope it is good.

Well must close for now. Much love to all, Catharine

"...the surprise may be just around the corner."

The surprise to which Mother refers turned out to be that the conflict was resolved naturally in the following years simply by separation. (See below)*

---

* The Kirkpatricks returned to Kenya in 1937, and in June of 1939 loaded up their truck and headed for Rwanda-Urundi where they pioneered under WGM. They labored there until 1955, stationed at Kayero, Murore and Mweya. Following this, Kirk worked as a traveling evangelist and undertook pastoral training. He continued in this capacity under his own board until 1978. Faye died at the age of 84 and Kirk at 93, both having been used in a great cause in God's service in Africa. Courtesy of Dr. Charles Kirkpatirk.

"…jolly good butter you're eating."

Bob loved to talk, and it was that characteristic that made him a friend to many. Mr. J.R. Woods became Bob's friend after a chance meeting at an Asian shop where he had brought some equipment from his ranch to be repaired. Mr. Woods appeared to like him, and Bob by nature was inclined to like everyone at first, so the two of them got on royally. The Smiths would become frequent visitors to this Englishman's ranch.

"Well, I'll be jiggered! That's you, isn't it, Mr. Woods? How are you? It is so good to see you." Bob set down his teacup and stood up. "Won't you join me?"

"I'd rather like that. I was just coming to tea myself. Jolly good to see you, old chap." Mr. Woods drew up a chair and sat down.

"What brings you to town?" Bob thought about the settler's ranch at Njoro, one of Lord Delamare's first places to settle in Kenya.

"It's meetings again. I've never wanted to have a thing to do with politics, but sometimes there is no choice."

"How's that?" Bob enjoyed his friend's get-to-the-point attitude.

"When we first came to Kenya, there was nothing to be done but try to have one's voice heard. The parliamentarians didn't have a bloody idea what was going on here and yet regulated everything in the country. It has not changed much. If a man wants land, land laws regulate what amount he can have, the rent, and the conditions under which he holds it. His application has to be approved by land officers, forest officers, and provincial officers to see whether any native rights are involved."

"Worrying about the natives' rights is commendable," Bob interjected.

"Right you are, but those involved sometimes have no idea what is right. All the government surveys are at our expense. If I need labor, government regulations lay down conditions under which I employ my men. If I want to sell a piece of land, government permission is necessary. If I want to cut timber, destroy vermin or draw water running through the land, government must give me leave. If I produce something for export, government fixes the amount I must pay to have it transported to the coast. Whatever I try to do in my daily life, I come up against government policy. At first there was no channel through which to convey our complaints, so we settlers had to get involved. In other countries, such continual contact between government does not usually occur, but here it does out of necessity."

Bob reflected on the months and years of not knowing who was preventing the approval for the mission sites. "I can certainly relate to the issue of getting the land. From the time that we arrived in Africa, it has taken us years to be granted the mission plot on which we now work. I have found this system very complex. It is difficult to know to whom to appeal. Then everything takes interminably long to come through."

His friend nodded, "The British colonial system is the most advanced working form of state ownership and control in the world. The state is supreme and its servants, like the Communist party, are absolute dictators of the country's economic life. All sources of wealth—land, minerals, forests, rivers, and lakes—belong to the state. All forms of transport—railways, roads, lake steamers and accessories such as wharfs and harbors—are state built and state owned. The only important commodity in the country, land, is prohibited except by government consent. Laws are made and amended by simple proclamation of the director (the Governor and behind him the Minister of State) without ever consulting those of us who obey them. It was a bloody dictatorship, so we have had to make our voices heard." He was getting aggravated remembering the frustration of those earlier days.

"In the mission, we also answer to a board in the United States who, many times, have no concept of what we are up against. By the time a message reaches them and a direction is given, we have already had to solve the problem and move on to the next. God helps us along those lines."

Mr. Woods regarded Bob's words. There was another dimension to Bob's purpose here in Africa, and the settler respected that. "Won't you and your wife come on out to Njoro and visit us sometime?"

"We would truly enjoy that. Thank you for your invitation. Let me extend to you the same if you are ever up our way." Bob appreciated the wealth of information this gentleman had and thoroughly enjoyed his company.

"The last time we were together you mentioned Lord Delamere. Did you know him well?" (Lord Delamere was an early settler who was very influential in setting the patterns by which British East Africa was settled.*)

"My first meeting with him was when I hauled my first crop of oats to his place in Njoro. He had stock that required oats. I had grown it on my land grant. I didn't know that he would buy it, but he did. He supported the idea of self-reliance and had promoted settlers coming to Africa. We became friends, and eventually he recruited me to manage his ranch at Njoro at the time he moved to Elementaita." Mr. Woods looked up from where he was sitting on the veranda of the New Stanley hotel at the statue of Lord Delamare that he could see in the middle of the roundabout just outside of the hotel. "The old bloke was quite a man. He did his part to make this country a livable place. He saw the need for adaptation, not only of humans but of animals, plants and even insects and micro-organisms to climates foreign to them."

"It seems there was no end to what the man tried, was there?"

Mr. Woods nodded, "There were many times when his enterprises failed. Livestock brought in from England often died after a year or two. But he was a believer in science, so he got experts from overseas and discovered the East Coast Fever."

"That affected the cattle, didn't it?"

"Yes, it is a parasitic disease that is transmitted by brown ticks. For some reason, the tick avoids volcanic soil and black cotton soil but abounds in the brown soil throughout Kikuyu, around Lake Victoria and the Mau. After the cattle were dipped regularly and fenced away from the brown tick areas, the dying stopped."

"I've noticed the big dipping operations going on even up in our part of the country. Is that Lord Delamare's doing?"

"Right you are!"

"What about wheat? I hear that was a challenge."

---

*"When Delamare set foot in the highlands of Kenya in 1897, Queen Victoria was on her throne and Britain at the height of her imperial glory…The land to which Delamare came was, by European standards, wholly primitive. Its scattered peoples, grouped into separate and mutually hostile tribes, were pagan, frequently nomadic, ignorant of the outside world and of such simple devices as the plough, the wheel, the pump, the loom, the coin; they had evolved no alphabet, built not cities, made not roads; their tool was the digging stick, their dress the skin, their weapon the spear. Only twenty-six years had passed since the meeting between Stanley and Livingstone, and large regions of the continent were still unknown to Europeans." Preface, *White Man's Country* Lord Delamere and the Making of Kenya, Elspeth Huxley

"At first he lost one crop after another, but then he learned about the rust viruses that destroyed the wheat and developed varieties that were resistant.   He undertook one venture after another, often failing, but eventually he prevailed. He developed one of the first creameries in Kenya. Hence that jolly good butter you're eating."

"This is jolly good butter!" Bob paused. "My stars! Here I am sounding like 'a Britisher.' That will never do!" He winked at his friend as the African server approached to pick up the cups and teapot.

Mr. Woods chuckled and then checked his watch, "Oh my! I must be going. Cheerio, then, Smith! It's been jolly good seeing you."

"Good to see you, Mr. Woods. God bless!" Bob stood and shook his hand.

Among the many settlers Dad and Mother knew were Cannon and Mrs. Leaky—parents of Dr. Leaky, the anthropologist; Dr. Burkitt, whose son, also a physician, was known for naming Burkitt's lymphoma; Baroness Karen von Blixen, famous for her book, *Out of Africa*; Galton Fenzi who drove the first car up from Mombasa six years before Dad and Kirk's experience. Also, Dr. J.W. Arthur, successor to Henry Scott of the Kikuyu Mission, was one of the first missionaries Dad met in Kenya along with Carey Francis, an educator, and eventually the head of Alliance High School—"a most remarkable man," Dad said.

I need not journey far this distant Friend to see,
Companionship is always mine, He makes His home with me.

I envy not the twelve, nearer to me is He,
The life he once lived here on earth, He lives again in me.

Maltbie Babcock

CHAPTER 18—TENWEK
OCTOBER 1936 THROUGH JANUARY 1937

…Bob…was completely speechless.

It was much too wet for Bob to be working on his building projects. It seemed as if it had been raining forever. The hills were wonderfully green, and all the flowers and trees that Kitty had planted were faring well. The little station was taking shape. Kitty was realizing her dream of a lovely haven, but there were volumes of plans and dreams yet to come.

Confined by a rain, Bob was glad for a rare opportunity to catch up on some of his correspondence.

Kitty thought if she could just lie down for a little while, perhaps she could get rid of her headache. That morning, her neck had felt stiff, and standing up had made her head throb, but she tried to continue her daily routine. The children were active and full of joy. She loved to see how they were developing. Everyone had been so happy lately.

"Bob, I'd like to take a little nap. Would you mind tending the children?'

"Not at all, Kitty."

She had fallen quickly to sleep, but when she awakened, the pressure in her head was unbearable. "Bob, something is wrong. I can't seem to get any relief from this headache. Do we have some aspirin?"

The aspirin wasn't helping, and the pain was increasing. Kitty was strong and not one to give in. She tried once more to get up, but it was as if a knife were tearing at her neck and back.

"I'll send for Dr. Dixon. I'll send a runner right away." Bob saw her nod in agreement as he stepped outside. It would take even the fastest runner more than a day to reach Kericho. Still, there were no alternatives. She could not stand a ride in the car. The roads were nearly impassable from the relentless rain anyway, and he could not leave her and the children.

"Please, Lord, give him strength and speed," Bob prayed as he watched the Kipsigis runner disappear over the hill.

Two days had passed since the time the runner should have arrived. Kitty's fever had risen on occasion to 104^0. She was becoming rigid, and her jaws were clenched shut, making it almost impossible for her to speak. Bob sponged her frequently with a cool cloth. Her hair was soaked with perspiration, and when he combed or brushed it, large bunches of it came from her head. In places, she had lost most of her hair. The children didn't understand what was happening. They wanted to be close to her and hug her, but the least movement of the bed made her wince, and Bob watched as the tears ran from her eyes. Tears sprang to his. He felt helpless.

"Bob, I can't make it another night. I just can't," Kitty said as she closed her eyes, wincing as she did.

The roads were now impassable for cars, but Dr. Dixon had finally arrived by ox cart, exhausted and muddy. He had become a close friend, and there had been many times of sharing while they lived in Kericho. Besides being a devoted Christian, he was a good doctor.

"You have meningitis, Kitty. It is an infection around your brain and spinal cord. We don't know of any cures, but I do have pain medicine that will help the pain," Dr. Dixon said as he looked tenderly at Kitty. "That is the best I can do."

He stepped outside with Bob.

"What can we do? I have to do something." Bob pled desperately.

"Bob, realistically there isn't anything that you can do. If you have to do something, then the only constructive thing I can think of is for you to build a box. I think you will have to bury her. I am so sorry, Bob. Kitty's life is truly in God's hands."

Dr. Dixon left, and Bob gathered the children up on his lap. "We need to be quiet for Mommy. She is very, very sick." He tried to imagine what it would be like without her. Just the care of the children would consume his time. How could he begin to try to do God's work without her?

"I love you, Kitty," he said, choking on the words. Is there anything I can do to make you more comfortable?"

It had been three more days. She seemed to be drifting in and out of awareness. He felt helpless. His heart was crying out, "Don't leave me, Kitty! Don't leave me!"

Hours passed as he read to the children and tried to entertain them.

"Come on, kiddies, let's go have some supper." Kitty had baked bread before her illness, but Bob and the children were getting down to the last few pieces. There was also stew that she had canned. That would do just fine, but he wondered what he would do after this day.

"It's good, Daddy!" John Boy said.

Suddenly Bob felt the hair stand up on the nape of his neck. It was as if he were in a dream.

"Oh, Bob, you're doing such a good job, but let me help finish feeding the children."

He couldn't believe his eyes. Kitty was standing there before them looking completely well. She was terribly thin, and her hair was almost entirely gone. It was one of those rare times when he was completely speechless.

"Did you see Him, Bob? ... Jesus came into the room. He came to my bed, and He touched me on my forehead. I could feel the fever move from my head, down through my body, and out my feet. It is gone, and I feel completely well. Someone must have been praying."

"You were healed, Kitty. There is no question about it." He could only stare at her in disbelief. How good God was to them.

"Muddie! Muddie! Look, little girl, Muddie is better!" Little smiling eyes looked up at their mother.

"Finish your supper, children. Then Mommy will read you a bedtime story." How she adored these little ones.

"Kitty, I'll finish up. You get back to bed. I don't want you doing too much too soon."

"What I really want to do is write a letter to Mother." She sat down at the table. "Dear folks at home, I want to tell you about the most amazing thing that happened today."

David remembers the rest of the story being told this way:

It was a normal Sunday morning as Mother and Father Biesecker arose to prepare themselves for church. Mother B. cooked the breakfast, poured the coffee, and they both sat down to eat followed by morning devotions. Next she started the pot roast, which always included an extra potato, a few extra carrots, onions and mushrooms for the guest who might show up unexpectedly. When preparations were ended and the pot roast was in the oven, she put on her black hat and pushed the hatpin through her topknot. One final check in the mirror and they went out to the curb where the 1932 Chrysler was parked. Father B. opened the passenger side door and took Mother B.'s hand to help her into the seat. He walked around the front of the car, slid in behind the steering wheel, put the key into the ignition, and turned it on. Before he pressed the starter he glanced at his wife and thought to himself how beautiful she was, "Sarah, you surely do look lovely today."

"Oh, pshaw," she responded with a smile, and a flush of red blushed her cheeks.

He pressed the starter button and the engine roared to life. He pulled the shift lever into gear, let out the clutch, and they were on their way to Noble Street where the little clapboard church stood on the corner. They had attended this church for years. The pastor's name was Thomas Hermiz, the father of a lad by the same name. This young boy would grow up to eventually become president of the World Gospel Mission.

Grandfather ushered his wife to their seat on the second row at the right side of the aisle.

Pastor Hermiz stepped to the pulpit and placed his hands on both sides of the lectern. "Dear Ones, I came prepared to preach a message, but as I was praying this morning, the Lord placed a burden on my heart for Catharine Smith over in Africa. I don't know what is wrong, but I do know that she is in serious trouble. I would like for as many as would to gather around the altar and pray as long as it takes to lift the burden.

The Bieseckers knelt at their seat in the second row as almost everyone else came to the front and knelt on both sides of the altar and front row seats. As intercession was being made, the thought of possible danger, illness, misfortune, even animal attacks were racing through the minds of two concerned parents.

In a short time, the burden was lifted.

Back at home after lunch, Mother B. sat down in her rocking chair, located by a large window that looked out on a cherry tree and the bird feeder her husband had made. She watched as a cardinal landed, cracked and started eating the sunflower seeds. She smiled as she thought: "His eye is on the sparrow…."

She reached into the bag, which rested on the floor next to her rocker, and pulled out a writing pad and pen. "Dear Catharine, I must write to tell you about a most amazing thing that happened at church today…."

Of course Kitty would not receive her letter for another six weeks—just about the time Mother B. would be getting hers.

Tenwek, Sotik - Nov. 29th 1936

Dear Folks:

It seems I have two letters since I last wrote you. The first was sent Oct. 12th, the second Oct 26th. I think I sent you an airmail after I was sick, but there has been so much since that I haven't had time to do much letter writing.

We went to Nairobi as Mildred had to have her teeth fixed and wanted me for "Chaperon." While we were there, the rear end went bad in the car, and we were held up for 4 days. But one thing about it was good, that is that I got a real good rest. We stayed at Miss Slater's, and she insisted that I take my breakfast in bed every morning. Wasn't that a luxury? Miss Steiner, the nurse from Litein, came down and stayed with Alice and took care of the children....

We had a letter on the last mail from Mary Eva saying they had mailed us a Christmas box. We have always had lovely ones from you all. I only wish we could have done something for you all this time. We are going to try and bring each one something nice when we come....

Mary's baby is adorable. I can hardly wait to get hold of her. And the song music is lovely. Thank Mary for me, and I'll write her later. Love to Anna when you write and pass on the news.

Much love to all,
Catharine

"I think I sent you an airmail after I was sick...."

Kitty continued to feel the impact of her illness. Her hair was beginning to grow back. The little curls framed her face. Bob thought she looked beautiful and told her so often. Still her strength was not complete, and so Bob insisted that Dr. Dixon check her out. In addition to being extremely tired, she felt confused at times—and not surprisingly—as it turned out that she had had a form of bacterial meningitis that had caused inflammation at the base of her brain which resulted, unrealized by her at the time, in the permanent loss of central vision in one eye.

Kitty was grateful for Mildred and Alice who had come to help, and now Trudy Shryock was about to arrive. The Miss Harris to whom she refers in the next letter ran a guest home for missionaries in Nairobi.

Tenwek, Sotik, Jan 24th

Dear Folks:

I can't remember just when I wrote you the last letter but think it was while I was at Dr. Dixon's. I sent Anna the $5.00 in it and I think told you about my goings and doings at that time.

Well since then we have had the arrival of "Trudie" and it has been a happy time. But to go back. When Bob had to leave for Mombasa to meet Gertrude, I took the children and went to Miss Harris where I kept them until Mildred came back from the wedding. That was (not the wedding) from Tuesday till Friday p.m. The wedding was Friday. Then I went back to Dr. Dixon's and Mildred kept the children until the following Fri. when Bob came for us and we came back here. I had to promise to be good and take breakfast in bed and not work. It is now 9:20 and I am still in bed tho' I've been up and around a bit this morning. But I think I am doing fine. Besides the iron tonic I am taking shots every other day to build up my blood. I am still quite exhausted, however. I think I came near having a nervous breakdown. My head gets so confused, and I can't control my thoughts like I'm used to doing. It seems such an effort to think or to try and remember things.

" I'm still quite exhausted...."

Your letter was here when I got home. The one in which you told of Father Smith's fall. I do hope he is better now. I wonder if he became dazed and fell or the daze was the result of the fall. If the former it looks like a slight stroke. I do so hope nothing happens to him before we get home. It will be such a disappointment to Bob if he doesn't get to see his father again.

Bob has seemed very tired since he got back. There is so much to do. But he is taking a course of injections like he had before and we're hoping they will buck him up again. I think the biggest encouragement he'll get will be when Mr. Leonard arrives. He will feel he's got a man to help shoulder the load instead of a bunch of women to add to it. But he's not complaining about it. I just said that. However, he'll be glad for some help.

You spoke of Dad enjoying to hear of John's antics. Here's another one. He was riding his bicycle yesterday and suddenly we heard a spill. Bob went out to see if it were serious and arrived in time to see John standing very vindictively in front of Anna Verne, pointing a finger at her and saying, "Now see. That's just what I told you, you ran out in front of the bicycle and I had to make an accident." Then at noon Bob told John to do something and he wasn't quite ready, so to gain some time said to Bob. "Please say that again, Daddy. I didn't quite hear."

Gertrude brought the things you sent and the children have been enjoying the books. I haven't let them have the scrapbooks yet. I'd rather save them for rainy weather or for the boat. Gertrude also brought us some nice presents too. John got a streamline train, Anna Verne a tea set, I a lovely piece of silk for slips and Bob a pair of pajamas. It was so thoughtful of her, and I do need some good slips so badly. and the only thing Bob didn't get for Christmas was pajamas. It seems so nice to have Gertrude here. Already she is taking hold and pitching right into work. I am sorry you couldn't get to know her better, as she is such a wonderful girl....

I'm enclosing a dollar. I've wanted to send you one for a long time and it just came to hand. Now it isn't for a missionary offering, but for something you need....

Must close with lots of love, Catharine

"...you told of Father Smith's fall. I do hope he is better now."

"...the question that haunted them."

Kitty and Bob looked at each other in silence, each knowing the question that haunted them. Mother Smith's letter described in great detail the accident. Father Smith had been driving his horses pulling the wagon full of hay around a bend in the road. He was sitting on top of the load, and as they rounded the corner, the load shifted, a pitchfork fell to the ground with the tines pointing up, and Father Smith fell right on top of the pitchfork. The tines had pierced his lungs, his left hip and elbow had been fractured, and now he had pneumonia. The seriousness of the situation was obvious, but they had no choice except to wait for word.

Things were progressing well on the new plot. No sooner was one building completed than a new building was needed. Bob's years on the farm had equipped him for the hard work that was involved. He took the demands in stride and continued to find life entertaining and agreeable. Always cheerful and friendly, one could often hear him coming by the wake of spirited laughter that followed him. Then when he arrived, atmospheres often changed from quiet and somber to lively, excited and enthusiastic. He delighted in the Africans' sense of humor, and he took every opportunity to take advantage of it.

In the African world, nothing was straight. If one looked across a hillside at a footpath or tried to traverse one, it became readily apparent that no attempt was made to create a straight and direct line. No obstacle was ever moved but would simply be walked around, and even when no obstacle was in the path, it would take a tortuous course. Corners were known to be places where evil spirits lurked. Accordingly, the African hut was built in the round.

Bob was finding any available materials for building. Rock was abundant in the hillsides and with chisel and hammer could be chipped into blocks that were then laid for walls and foundations. To assist with the concept of a straight line, string guidelines were set up, and over and over Bob explained that the blocks must line up along the string in a straight line.

"*Nimstari kama meno ya kuku*? (Is it a line like the teeth of a hen?)" he asked as he gazed down the string. The workmen doubled over with laughter.

As Bob came in for dinner, he was laughing.

"What are you laughing at?" Kitty asked.

"I think the workmen, in some convoluted way, finally understand what I mean by a straight line," he said, as he explained what had just occurred.

The letters from the first term that Grandmother Biesecker kept ended with the January 24th letter. It is unclear why. We guess that Grandmother Smith, with whom she always shared letters, distressed by Grandfather's death, perhaps had failed to return them to Grandmother B. It is unthinkable that Mother stopped writing.

"…he'd never again be able to speak with this man whom he had so admired…."

Bob stood stunned by the realization that it had been six weeks from the time of his father's death and only now was he hearing the news. His father was buried and lay cold in the ground, and his youngest son hadn't known. He felt sadness, mixed with guilt, and some remorse over not being there for his mother and brothers. But mostly, the realization that he'd never again be able to speak with this man whom he had so admired, turned his stomach into a hard aching knot.

Dad truly admired his father, and he told us often about him—what a tireless farmer he was—he never skimped when it came to doing his part, and he always added an extra portion to anything he sold. "His dairy farm was meticulous," and Dad would go into elaborate detail to describe the pains to which our grand father went so that his milk was unblemished. Born on 9/15/1861, John Elsworth Smith had died 4/7/1937. At the time of his fall, his hip and elbow were both fractured, but the pneumonia that ensued from his punctured lung claimed his life.

When he got the news, Bob wept briefly and then, knowing it would not lighten the pain to cease from working, and bound by his own stern moral code to do both as he had promised his supporters and what he had set out himself to do, he slipped on his helmet and said, "Kitty, I need to get back to work."

"I think you're right, my dear. You go ahead and get busy."

As Kitty watched him trudging back up the hill, she thought over the past years, remembering the haunting fear that somehow there was no place for them here in Africa, that all their efforts would be wasted. At last, though, everything had changed; all around them God's plan was being revealed. They had not missed these precious opportunities by being too shortsighted. She thought of the transforming moments that had shaped them and expanded the dimensions of their understanding. She thought about the baffling interpersonal relationships that threatened them at so many turns; of how they had had to come to terms with the human failings of those they loved and love them still. She thought of the wonderful friends they now had from many different missions and persuasions, all with the same goal they held dear. She thought of how they had had to restructure their vision, address its inequities and do away with its distortions. She thought of the faithfulness of God upon which they had come to rely with certainty, and of all the emotions—wonder, awe, tenderness, grief, joy and compassion—they had experienced in these years. She thought of all the natives who had cared for and supported them in their efforts. She thought of the thriving churches and schools and the many converts who would be sustained and taught in these institutions. She thought of the fellow workers who had come to help and how meaningful their relationships had become as they shared fully and communicated freely. And even in the midst of the bitter sadness they now experienced in the death of Father Smith, it was worth it all.

In October of that year (1937), they would be sailing for America for their first furlough, but Kitty knew with certainty that this would be only the beginning of their African experience.

Dad and Mother served another three terms in Africa and were joined by a large number of other extraordinarily talented missionaries. The mission grew from its two fields of service, Kenya and China, to 15 countries served by over 350 missionaries.

Dad was injured severely in an automobile accident, fracturing his neck and paralyzing his right arm. He and Mother returned to America in 1958 for Dad to have corrective surgery and remained in this country thereafter. Mother taught school into her seventies and lived to be 85. She read her Bible daily, and on the last day of her life, Dad found her Bible opened to the passage—"I have fought the good fight, I have finished the course."

He continued to live out his Christian adventure, delighting in each bend in the road, fully engaged, ever questioning, but completely confident in his God's faithfulness. Over and over he said, "This story is not about us. It is about a plan that God had all along. Everywhere we went, we saw that He had been there before us working out His plan. We just got to have a small part in it."

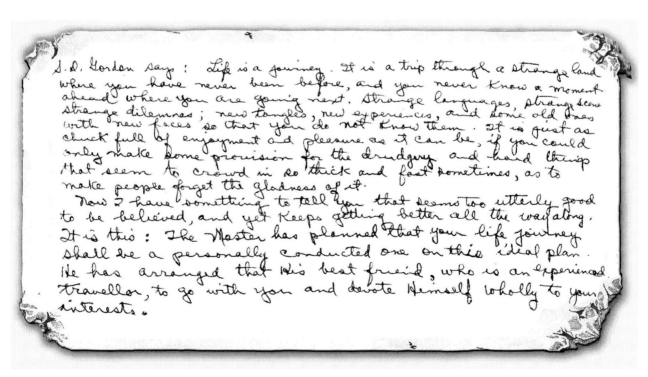

From Bob's collection of writings in his own hand

OUR HERITAGE

IN SAWDUST ATTICS BENEATH COBWEB TRELLISES—
IN TRUNKS LATCHED WITH RUSTED HINGES AND LOCKS,
SOME FIND THEIR HERITAGE.
WAR MEDALS, PICTURES, RELICS AND HEIRLOOMS
MARK ALL THAT'S LEFT OF THOSE THEY LOVE.

BUT WE HAVE MORE—
A LEGACY THAT SPANS CONTINENTS AND SEAS.
ITS BLOOD RUNS RED THROUGH GROUND AS DEEP AND DARK AS THE NIGHT.
ITS VOICE IS HEARD IN PLACES WHERE LIONS HAVE ROAMED.

ITS ARMS STRETCH AS WIDE AS NAIVASHA'S DAWN-TINTED HORIZON,
SIMMERING AND RIPPLING IN THE SCORCHING AIR.
ITS BREATH IS THE WIND ON THE SERENGETI—
DANCING THROUGH AND EMBRACING A RESTLESS LAND.

WE HAVE PIERCED OUR BODIES ON HER THORN TREES
AND SEEN SOVEREIGN ANGELS GUARDING HER PROGENY THERE.
AND WE HAVE KNOWN A MAN WHOSE NOBLEST POSTURE
WAS ON BENDED KNEE BEFORE GOD.

HE WAS OUR HERITAGE-MAKER AND SHAPED OUR LEGACY
WITH WONDER, ADVENTURE, AND MARVELOUS CONSEQUENCE.
HE WAS A WITNESS TO GOD'S FURIOUS RESCUE—
AN IMMUTABLE REDEMPTION OF A FAR AWAY PEOPLE.

HIS MOST ANGUISHED TEARS WERE RESERVED FOR SOLITUDE—
WHEN HE SEARCHED FOR AND COMMUNED WITH GOD.
IT HONORED US TO KNOW HIM AND TO CALL HIM
FATHER, GRANDFATHER, MENTOR, FRIEND.

AND AS THE LINES IN HIS FACE MARKED A JOURNEY OF WEARINESS AND JOY,
THE SKIES AND DISTANT STARS MARK HIS GOING NOW.
WHEN ONCE HE JOINED TWO WORLDS IN OUR TIME
HE NOW JOINS BEYOND THEM OUR HERITAGE BETWEEN HEAVEN AND EARTH.

WRITTEN BY
LORI SMITH CAMERON

FOR HER GRANDFATHER'S
FUNERAL

World Gospel Mission now has 350 missionaries and support staff serving on six continents and in more than 15 countries.

WGM's main ministries in Kenya, in cooperation with Africa Gospel Church, are church planting, evangelism, discipleship, theological training at Kenya Highlands Bible College and Kaboson Pastors' School, Theological Education by Extension, medical work and training at Tenwek Hospital, community health and development through Tenwek Hospital and among the Maasai and West Pokot tribes, children's work through the Africa Gospel Church Baby Center, and mass media. WGM missionaries in Nairobi are also involved in evangelism, medical work, and orphanage ministries to children in the capital city.

Africa Gospel Church: Africa Gospel Church, headquartered in Kericho, Kenya, is the outgrowth of WGM's work in Kenya. AGC is administered by a moderator, assistant moderator, and church administrator and operates seven departments—Media, Christian Education, Radio, Publications, Youth, Women, and Evangelism. AGC has more than 1,300 congregations throughout Kenya with an average weekly attendance of 300,000.

Tenwek Hospital: Tenwek Hospital, one of the largest Protestant mission hospitals in Kenya, began as a humble clinic in 1935. Tenwek, working under the motto "We treat, Jesus heals," is located in rural Kenya, 140 miles west of Nairobi, in the fertile highlands of the Bomet district. In addition to being the primary hospital for the area's one million people, it is also a referral hospital that receives patients from other parts of the country. Each year, Tenwek's staff treats more than 10,000 inpatients and 70,000 outpatients. In addition to the hospital, Tenwek's programs include Tenwek School of Nursing; the L. Nelson Bell Chaplaincy School; the medical intern training program; the Community Health and Development Department of Tenwek; and INFAMED, the hospital's family practice residency program.

Kenya Highlands Bible College: Kenya Highlands Bible College, a post-secondary level school near Kericho, was started in 1953 by WGM missionaries. The school seeks to train young people to emulate Christ as church leaders by providing Bible, theology, and Christian education training for students from a number of African countries and tribes. Approximately 80 students attend KHBC each year, and most graduates go on to serve with Africa Gospel Church.

Kaboson Pastors' School: WGM and Africa Gospel Church joined forces in 1993 to open Kaboson Pastors' School in southwest Kenya, approximately 20 miles south of Tenwek Hospital. The school was opened to meet the vital need for national pastors to get the formal education and theological training they were lacking. After graduation, more than 90 percent of Kaboson graduates go into full-time ministry as evangelists, missionaries, or pastors.

Africa Gospel Church Baby Center: This home for orphaned and abandoned babies is being built near Nakuru and will serve as an outreach of Africa Gospel Church. The center will house approximately 50 orphaned or abandoned babies, ranging from newborns to three year olds. Every effort will be made to place the children for adoption into Christian homes whereby they can grow to reach their God-given potential and become productive members of the community. Those children not adopted by three years of age will be referred to other facilities geared toward that age group.

www.wgm.org

APPENDIX

Original Hotchkiss Memorial built by Bob Smith now replaced by a much larger capacity building with balcony (below)

School of Nursing

Composite of a small portion of the Tenwek Hospital

IN THIS PLACE FIND RESPITE
IN HONOR OF THE PIONEERING
VISION AND LOVING SERVICE OF
ROBERT AND CATHARINE SMITH

"COME WITH ME...TO A QUIET PLACE
AND REST," MARK 6:31
"THEY THAT WAIT UPON THE LORD SHALL
RENEW THEIR STRENGTH," IS. 40:31

DEDICATETED ON 2nd JULY 1989
BY
HIS EXCELLENCY HON. DANIEL T. ARAP MOI, C.G.H., M.P.
PRESIDENT OF THE REPUBLIC OF KENYA
AND COMMANDER-IN-CHIEF OF THE ARMED FORCES
TO THE GLORY OF GOD AND IN HONOR OF THOSE EARLY PIONEERS WHO BROUGHT THE LI
OF THE GOSPEL TO THIS AREA
DR. WILLIS HOTCHKISS   REV. JOHANNA NGETICH
REV. ROBERT K. SMITH   OTHERS
JESUS SAID IN JOHN 12:35, "I AM THE LIGHT OF THE WORLD, HE THAT FOLLOWETH ME
NOT WALK IN DARKNESS, BUT SHALL HAVE THE LIGHT OF LIFE"
THIS HYDROELECTRIC PROJECT WAS MADE POSSIBLE BY THE GENEROUS CONTRIBUTI
THE FOLLOWING ORGANIZATIONS:

AFRICA GOSPEL CHURCH   MISSIONARY WORLD SERVICE & EVANGELISM
ANONYMOUS   RAINBOW FUND
BILLY GRAHAM ASSOCIATION   SAMARITANS PURSE
EZE   WORLD GOSPEL MISSION
HOPE INTERNATIONAL   WORLD VISION-KENYA
MAINTENANCE FOR MISSIONS   IRVIN L. YOUNG FOUNDATION

SPECIAL APPRECIATION IS EXPRESSED TO WORLD RADIO MISSIONARY FELLOWSHI
INVALUABLE TECHNICAL ASSISTANCE AND TO THOSE INVOLVED IN THE PROJECT

REV. JONAH CHESNG'ENY - CHAIRMAN OF THE BOARD   MR. BILLY FULLER - CONSTRUCTION SUPERIN
TENWEK HOSPITAL BOARD OF GOVERNORS   MR. BRUCE RYDBECK - CIVIL ENGINEER
DR. ERNEST STEURY - MEDICAL SUPERINTENDENT   MR. BILL WRIGHT - ELECTRICAL ENGINEER
MR. EZEKIEL KERICH - ADMINISTRATOR   MR. JERRY CALLICUT - SURVEYOR
DR. DAVID STEVENS - PROJECT COORDINATOR   MR. ROSS CHATFIELD, MR. EARL HARTWIG
DR. ERIC MOORE - PROJECT DIRECTOR   MR. STEVE BYRON, MR. HAROLD HAYDEN
MR. HUGH MCKAY - PROJECT CONSULTANT   MR. CHARLIE SNYDER, MR. STAN SNYER

Composite of Tenwek's hydroelectric project and nearby park dedicated to the Smiths

250

Composite of a part of the campus of the Kenya Highlands Bible College